Also by Alexandra Chauran

© Sarah O'Brien

ABOUT THE AUTHOR

Alexandra Chauran is a second-generation fortuneteller, a third degree elder High Priestess of British Traditional Wicca, and the Queen of a coven. As a professional psychic intuitive for over a decade, she serves thousands of clients in the Seattle area and globally through her website. She is certified in tarot and has been interviewed on National Public Radio and other major media outlets. Alexandra is currently pursuing a doctoral degree, lives in Issaquah, Washington, and can be found online at EarthShod.com.

Alexandra Chauran

365 Ways

✻

to STRENGTHEN *Your*

✻

SPIRITUALITY

SIMPLE WAYS TO CONNECT WITH THE DIVINE

Llewellyn Publications
Woodbury, Minnesota

First Edition
First Printing, 2015

Book design by Bob Gaul
Cover design by Ellen Lawson
Cover and part page art by iStockphoto.com/15537382/©jeja
Editing by Rhiannon Nelson

Llewellyn Publications is a registered trademark of Llewellyn Worldwide Ltd.

Library of Congress Cataloging-in-Publication Data
Chauran, Alexandra, 1981–
  365 ways to strengthen your spirituality: simple ways to connect with
the divine/Alexandra Chauran.—First Edition.
      pages cm
  Includes bibliographical references.
  ISBN 978-0-7387-4012-6
1. Spiritual life. I. Title. II. Title: Three hundred sixty five ways
to strengthen your spirituality.
  BL624.C4485 2015
  204'.4—dc23
                          2015026999

Llewellyn Publications, a Division of Llewellyn Worldwide Ltd.
2143 Wooddale Drive
Woodbury, MN 55125-2989
www.llewellyn.com
Printed in the United States of America

Contents

Introduction

Perhaps you've always been a seeker, asking probing questions of anyone who seemed to have their religious life all put together. Or maybe you're just starting to wonder about a higher power or higher powers in the universe that might offer you confidence, comfort, success, or other blessings. No matter what you pursue in life, be it financial stability or wealth, true love with a soul mate, family harmony, or physical bliss, something will always be missing if you don't also search for a way to get in touch with Spirit. Conversely, even if you live a simple life in solitude, you can feel fulfilled with a richness of Spirit.

What Is Spirit?

Spirit, in the context of this book, represents a source of spiritual inspiration, a well of energy and love from which you can draw and inform your life. Spirit is available and accessible to people of all faith traditions and can be conceptualized in many different ways. It is okay if you don't know what you believe or understand about Spirit at this point in time. Throughout the course of this book, you will grow to feel more comfortable and at home with your idea of Spirit the way you might feel in a worn pair of jeans that feels just right. For now, be aware that there are many ways that people conceptualize Spirit. For the purposes of this book, Spirit can include the following contexts:

God or gods—The idea of god encompasses many religions. God can be immanent, right here on earth, or transcendent, existing on another higher plane. God can be a single source or there might be many gods. God can be unknowable or an intimate friend.

Goddess or goddesses—The divine feminine can also be a single diamond with many facets or there could be many goddesses that populate the human experience. She could be creation itself or the mighty essence of love and fertile new beginnings. She can work with a consort or alone.

Universe—For those who steer entirely away from the anthropomorphism of deity, Spirit can be that abundance out there in the universe just waiting to be poured out as blessings. The universe is filled with life and death, mystery, energy, and untold wonder, which can form the concept of Spirit.

Higher Self—For many, the concept of Spirit is a human construct and resides entirely within an individual's heart, mind, or soul. Spirit can be the best and wisest part of yourself, and Spirit can be that spark we see in the eyes of others we meet that encourages us to feel compassion.

My Case in Point

Of course, though Spirit is for everyone, my concept of Spirit is my own. It is my hope that I can guide you to discover your own personal connection with Spirit, whatever that might mean to you. I've always been a spiritual seeker myself, drawn to reach out to Spirit and to understand how others explore Spirit. As a child I was highly spiritual, and as a young adult I was given to gentle debate about Spirit. I never shy away from participating in the faith traditions of others, trying to understand how the eyes of others see each path. I've participated in varied local religious services from *Salah* with Muslims to a Vodou ceremony. I'm the person who always invites the witnessing Mormon, Jehovah's Witness, and Bahá'í missionaries to come in for tea, making my home a center for spiritual discussion.

I went back to school at the University of Washington to study Clinical Pastoral Education to act as an interfaith chaplain at Harborview Medical Center and the University of Washington Medical Center, helping people of all faith traditions confront jarring tragedies and end-of-life issues. I like to help others tackle issues with Spirit intellectually, emotionally, and on the front lines, in the trenches of real-life experience, which inspired me to write this book as a guide to all the perpetual seekers out there. I was particularly inspired by good friends of mine who envy those who do have a close connection with Spirit. I wanted to find a key to the door of belief for those who are doubtful but willing.

How to Use this Book

This book is organized so that each day should be read in succession, and with exercises also practiced in order. Some skills build upon each other, so skipping some exercises could make future ones more difficult to perform.

In some cases, I have organized parts of this book so that your beliefs and understandings inform your practice, and in other cases I've purposely switched the order so that you must first gain experience in order to populate your belief system with new ideas.

Though you shouldn't skip around until you've worked through the entire book in order, it is okay to slow down and spread the days out over a week or more. Just please try not to rush through several days' work in one day. This isn't a school assignment, and reading this book isn't like cramming for a test. You'll need time to digest the material inwardly, even though it is simple, so that you can integrate it into your life. Finally, remember that this entire book can be repeated over again. Your relationship with Spirit will change over time as you move through the phases of your life and your adopted roles in our culture. The key word here is "relationship." As you move through this book, remember that you are getting to know Spirit rather than turning on a lightbulb. Give yourself some slack and some serious kudos for your efforts.

Part One

———✳———

Environment

The first section of this book begins outside of you, where so many of us begin our search for Spirit. Of course, you may already have an inkling that there may be plenty of Spirit inside of you. However, many aids or barriers to Spirit exist all around us. You may occasionally find yourself lacking the time, energy, or concentration for Spirit. Ideally, your life should serve as an inspiration to consult Spirit, and your relationship with Spirit should inform the way you interact with the world around you. From the creation of sacred spaces to the joy of finding Spirit in service to others, this section of the book is dedicated to the Spirit that surrounds you.

Day 1: Keeping a Spirit Journal

Your first step in this journey with Spirit is to procure a journal in which record your innermost feelings, thoughts, and experiences as you go. You don't have to worry about your journal being attractive or well-written. You never have to share your Spirit journal with anyone else. In fact, you can get started right now with any scrap of paper that can later be inserted into a binder with a simple hole punch.

There are several reasons for keeping a journal. Our memories are faulty, and you may not be able to see that you are progressing with your endeavors to get in touch with Spirit unless you can refer back to your earliest attempts. Interacting with Spirit can be some of the most fulfilling moments of your life, and you should record them with reverence in the same way that you might photograph weddings or new babies.

Finally, the act of writing can help solidify your beliefs and understandings. While your thoughts about Spirit exist as a jumble in your head, they can change before you can act upon them to see if they are true. If you pause to write down your thoughts like a scientist writes down a hypothesis, you can then test yourself and progress forward alongside Spirit instead of simply spinning your wheels.

> * *In your Spirit journal, write down three goals for the year. One goal should be physical or material, one goal should be intellectual or emotional, and one goal should be spiritual.*

Day 2: Getting in Touch with Nature
··

Throughout history, many religious leaders and followers alike have found nature to be an inspiration to get in touch with Spirit. There are those who believe that Spirit created everything that exists in nature personally and with great care. There are others who believe that nature is Spirit itself in tangible form. Time spent in nature can result in other benefits as well, such as reduced stress, lowered blood pressure, and a greater attention span.

The importance of the connection between nature and Spirit cannot be overstated, so during this section of the book you will be led through several exercises that have to do with nature. However, I recognize that not everyone is comfortable interacting with the natural world. There are some people who would rather be in a climate-controlled shopping mall filled with shiny and entertaining products than in a cold and damp forest that is dimly lit and littered with bugs.

Your mission today is to set a goal for beginning to get in touch with the beauty of nature that is appropriate for yourself. For some of you, that may mean going outside your work building for ten minutes each day. For others, it could mean getting up at dawn to watch the sunrise from your porch. Nature buffs might set an ambitious hiking goal after work each day. Make sure that your goal is realistic and sustainable. The simpler, the better, when it comes to just getting started with any activity that reconnects you with Spirit.

* *Prescribe yourself a daily dose of nature.*

Day 3: Noticing the Beauty Around You

Our mental filters help us live life in a flexible way. Sometimes they help us tune out the annoyances in our environment. For example, I used to pile my mail up in the middle of a table every time I came in the door. Pretty soon, I tuned out the big ugly pile of mail and didn't notice it. I didn't even notice reaching around it to grab other things on the table. However, other people who walked into my home could immediately see it for the messy eyesore that it was. Similarly, you can actually tune out beauty in your life rather than fully appreciating it, in the same way that a loving partner can be taken for granted.

Noticing beauty around you can be tricky if you see it every day. In fact, you might get into a sullen mood in which you don't think anything in your life could be described as beautiful. However, if you begin looking for beauty and cultivate your search as a skill, you will begin to notice it everywhere. Beauty is one way that Spirit communicates with us and blesses us. Noticing your blessings is the first step toward expressing gratitude.

Keep in mind that beauty doesn't need to mean physical beauty in this context. I think that my first cup of tea in the morning is a beautiful moment. I think beauty is in the way my husband phrases his questions when he consults me about things in order to make sure that I know he values my input. I even think that the way my three-year-old daughter plays the harmonica is beautiful, however odd the tune may turn out to be.

* List the beautiful moments, sounds, sights,
  attitudes, and other things you notice today.

Day 4: Living in the Moment

In our modern Western culture, we spend a lot of our time either obsessing about and regretting the past or thinking forward to the future. I'll admit that I've spent long hours awake at night either ruminating over mistakes I made during the day or going over plans and duties in store for the next day. It is extremely hard to slow down and live within the moment, so this is another activity that will come up again and again in this book.

Certain practices such as physical exercise and meditation will help you develop the mental fortitude that it takes to push your thoughts back into the present moment. However, once you notice the benefits, you'll find that it becomes easier to accomplish. In the "now" is when you will meet Spirit. If you keep hurrying through the present to get away from the past or toward your goals, you just might miss a very special moment with Spirit.

For today, your mission will be to try to draw your attention back to the moment. If you are miserable due to something that has happened to you or due to something that is coming up that is stressing you out, focus on the positives in the present moment. For example, you might be in a sheltered place that has a nice temperature, you might have a belly full of food, and you might feel a sense of safety in the moment. If you feel too busy to spend time with a loved one or to give somebody your full attention, be mindful of your commitment to live in the moment and see if you can't find some time.

* *Bring your attention to the present moment when you become aware of stress over the past or future creeping into your mind.*

Day 5: Noticing How Your Environment Affects You

In our earlier exercise about noticing beauty, I explained how our mental filters tend to tune out many aspects of our everyday environments. However, some of those environmental factors can still affect you even if you don't make careful note of them. For example, a dark and dreary living room or a messy desk at your office may drain your energy, depress your mood, and make you less likely to connect with Spirit in day-to-day life.

As you go through your day today, make some notes about how you feel in different surroundings. Is the way you feel at work different than at home? How about at the grocery store, in a car, or on public transportation? List all of the settings that you pass through on a given day and start thinking about how they influence your mood, energy level, and attitude. Sometimes it is not what is present in an environment that is the problem, but what is missing. A little thing like cleaning up clutter, letting in some fresh air, adding live plants, or placing decorative rocks can sometimes spruce up a place and make it feel more sacred.

Once you've noticed how various surroundings affect you, try doing one thing to change your most unpleasant environment to make it a little more spiritual. Try adding something beautiful, something from nature, or something that triggers joy such as pictures of your family or pet. Later in this book we'll further develop the idea of sacred spaces, but for now try to focus on making all of your spaces just a tiny bit more sacred.

* *Observe how the environments you pass through during your day affect you and do one thing to spiritually improve your most negative environment.*

Day 6: Attuning to the Present Season

The world is a magnificent place, and connecting with its seasons and cycles is one way to feel more in tune with the universe at large. Attuning your life to the seasons is also a wonderful way to experience a metaphor for life's ups and downs. For every barren winter, there is sure to be a colorful springtime to follow. For every season of long, dark nights, a season of bright and early sunrises warming the land is sure to follow. Humanity evolved connected to the earth's cycles through hunting and gathering and then agriculture and farming. Nowadays, however, we're all sort of sliding through life without that intimate connection with creation. With well-lit, temperature-controlled homes and workspaces, it can be hard to notice exactly what's going on outside.

Over the next few days, I'd like to get you started thinking about the seasons. They're more than just holidays. Try to experience the season that it is today where you are as if you were a prehistoric human. Imagine the amount of faith it would take to know that weather extremes were transient and seasonal. Feel the excitement that you would feel about the upcoming season and what it might mean to your family and community. Make time today to notice something seasonal going on outside near your home.

* *Observe a sign of the season today. How does this make you feel? How do you feel about the current season and the one to come?*

Day 7: Winter
....

If it's winter where you are, you're in luck today. If not, mark the winter solstice on your calendar as time to start observing the signs of the season of winter. The winter solstice is the longest night of the year, and it occurs around December 21 in the Northern Hemisphere, but in June in the Southern Hemisphere. Wintertime is a dark time of the year. It is a time for rest and renewal. In ancient times, many people had to subsist off of stored foodstuffs that they had carefully preserved. Winter is a wonderful time for baked goods filling the home with smells of spices. You can see how some signs of the seasons creep from the out of doors to indoors, especially at home. This is how it should be, and can help you connect with Spirit since Spirit dwells within the soul of humanity.

On the solstice, the long and cold night must have been a hair-raising experience for primitive peoples. Even in modern times, some people choose to hold a vigil through the night, experiencing the relief and joy of the sunrise heralding longer days to come. My family has a tradition in which we crack open a geode to reveal the sparking crystals within as a metaphor for the revelation of the sun. Even though our culture is fairly insulated from the harshness of winter, lean into the experience of winter and be grateful for the good friends and good food you have during that time. Notice how your mood changes during the winter. Note when you start to feel the lengthening of days.

* *Mark your calendar for the winter solstice so that you can observe the season during that time. Consider planning a vigil, entertaining family guests with lively conversation, or preparing good-smelling food to bring the season into your home.*

Day 8: Spring

Spring is a time for new beginnings. New beginnings often require clearing space in your life, both physically and emotionally, for new blessings. This is why spring cleaning is a custom followed all over the world. Think of spring cleaning as tilling the soil and preparing the garden beds for seeds to be planted. Spring cleaning can happen in your home, your workplace, your car, and even on the list of people that you include in your life. Then, think about what good seeds you wish to plant in your life. What will help them grow? What do you want to have in your life three to six months in the future?

Connecting with springtime in nature is enjoyable in many climates. One of my favorite activities is to go outside and sketch a flower bud each day as it blooms. Listen for the sounds of springtime. I live in a pretty rainy area in the Pacific Northwest, but I love the smell after the rain comes in the springtime. It reminds me of renewal, and the earthy scent seems heavy with the promise of abundance. Things change quickly in the spring, which tells you how quickly your own life can change for the better. Special spring holidays include the spring equinox, usually around March 21 in the Northern Hemisphere and September 21 in the Southern Hemisphere. The first of May is also a lovely spring holiday in many Northern Hemisphere climates, especially if hawthorn trees bloom around that time where you live.

> * *Mark your calendar with the spring equinox and the first of May, if appropriate. Spend time on those days spring cleaning, observing nature, and pondering which new seeds you'd like to plant in your life.*

Day 9: Summer

....

Summer represents the zenith of joy. The promise held in each tiny seed during the spring is revealed and matured. The summer solstice is the longest day of the year, and is around June 21 in the Northern Hemisphere and December 21 in the Southern Hemisphere. The heat of the sun may be represented by bonfires. Notice which fruits and vegetables may be getting ready to harvest in the summertime.

Metaphorically, the solstices represent peak experiences and the equinoxes represent those precious brief moments of balance in our lives. Think of a pendulum swinging. It seems to pause at each end of the movement and swing quickly through its arc. Each pause is the extreme, like the solstices, in which it can be hard to see that things will change to their opposite. In the middle of summer, the coldness of winter may be difficult to imagine. This is how it is in our own lives. When we're extremely happy or extremely sad, perspective can be hard to see. Conversely, those moments when everything is in balance are so fleeting and rare.

Find ways to enjoy the heat of summer in your climate. Whether a community barbeque or camping is more your style, make time to celebrate while you can. Remember that the coldness of winter is not far behind. Likewise, when you see successes and cause for celebration in your own life, don't wait to make an excuse to party.

* *Mark the summer solstice on your calendar
  and find a means to celebrate!*

Day 10: Fall

·····················

Autumn is a beautiful season where I live. The leaves change color, but there is still a vibrant green from the frequent seasonal rains. Autumn is a time for harvesting and for metaphorically reaping what you have sown all year long. Autumn equinox is around September 21 in the Northern Hemisphere and March 21 in the Southern Hemisphere. There's a reason we have no tradition of fall cleaning, for it is the counterbalance to spring. Fall is the time for stockpiling your blessings to last through the winter ahead.

There are various harvest festivals celebrated by cultures throughout the world in the fall. Autumn is a time for celebrating grain harvests and baking bread, if you're so inclined. In some regions it is a time for berry harvests. I love to make cobbler in the autumn. Fall is the time to recognize the sacrifices that are made in nature so that people can eat. It's a time to be thankful for the farmers who helped to bring food to your table, and to be thankful for the living things that are food sources for you.

Seeing signs of hibernation and even death in nature can sometimes be saddening, but it's important to celebrate the dark half of the year. There must be death and the clearing away of old things in order to make room in the world for the blessings of the coming spring. So, observe nature for the beauty you can see in bare tree branches and in the preparations animals make for the winter.

> * *Mark the autumn equinox on your calendar. Look in nature*
> *for signs that the world is preparing for the winter ahead.*
> *Bake things in your home.*

Day 11: Dark Moon

The moon phases affect our lives, moods, and spiritual practice just as the seasons do. It's easy to see how more sunshine and less cold might lift your spirits. Since the dawn of time, people have also observed how the full moon draws the eye and causes the spirit to soar. The different moon phases create different effects within the mind. Over the next few days, we'll go over the moon phases as symbols, and how they can help you look at various aspects of your life spiritually. Check a lunar calendar, look online, or download an app to find out when the moon phases occur. The peak of the phase may even be listed as a time. Mark out the full moon for each month on your calendar. For the next month at least, mark out the other phases as well so that you can observe how they affect you.

Sometimes the effects of the universe on your body and mind can best be observed by their absence. The dark moon represents the absence of the moon's power. The dark moon is a time for resting and contemplation. During the dark moon, you should not be pushing forward with your life's goals, but rather taking a rest. Rest in between ambitions is important. It is during this spiritual time of rest that you can feel a sense of rejuvenation and take the time to gain proper perspective.

> * *Mark out the moon phases on your calendar. Try not to make any important life decisions during the dark moon.*

Day 12: Waxing Crescent Moon

....

The waxing crescent moon is when the moon looks like a thin crescent, shaped sort of like a letter D. This represents a time of beginning. Just as springtime is the time for you to plant seeds in the earth and in your life, the waxing crescent moon is a time for you to begin things that you'd like to see played out within the coming month. Think of it like making a wish, but instead of a passive wish on the first star you see, you can put your work behind this wish and have it come true.

Seeing the crescent moon has been inspiring to people of many cultures, and it is still used in some modern religious practices. When your calendar marks the crescent moon, go outside at night to try to catch a glimpse. If you don't see the crescent moon due to cloud cover, try again the next day. When you finally see the moon, speak aloud about your wishes and kiss your hand to the moon.

* On the day of the waxing crescent moon, make a note
  to go outside and try to catch a glimpse to make a wish.

Day 13: Waxing Half-Moon

The waxing half-moon is when the moon is a perfect half-circle in the sky. Everything between the dark moon and the half-moon is the crescent, while everything between the half-moon and the full moon is called the waxing gibbous. During and after the half-moon is a good time to check in with yourself on what you've been doing to work toward your goals this month. If you've been applying for jobs, for example, and you've seen no response, it's time to increase your efforts. If you have seen some good results, however, it's time to hit the ground running.

Remember that you are always in control of your own destiny. You can change the course of your life through small choices in the same way that you gently steer a car while driving. The waxing half-moon is a good time to make small corrections and to boost the aspects of your life that you see going well for you. Consider the upcoming fruits of your labor, and when will be the most auspicious time to harvest them. This moon phase is the time for strategic planning.

> * During the waxing half-moon and waxing gibbous moon, take stock of where you are in your goals this month. Make changes accordingly or boost your efforts where they are working.

Day 14: Full Moon
....

The full moon is the epitome of abundance. Its image has been likened to that of a full-bellied pregnant woman. Primarily, the full moon is a time to celebrate your blessings. Recognize the fruits of your own labor and enjoy them. Secondarily, the full moon is a time to ask for what you need. This time, you don't have to pay careful attention to whether it will happen within the month, or whether it is just starting or on a roll. The full moon's power can be harnessed for whatever need you may have.

Abundance can mean physical fertility, financial wealth, or any number of things. The full moon represents the very opposite of lack. If you have any high hopes or dreams that you can't envision slowly coming to fruition, ignore the why and the how in order to wish for them during the full moon. The energies of the full moon tend to surround the actual day by three days before and after. So, if you forget to make your wishes on the exact date, it's not too late for you.

> * *On the full moon, make special time to celebrate what you have. By giving thanks, you ask for more of the same. Make your wishes for the highest and best things to come in your life during this time.*

Day 15: Waning Half-Moon

The waning half-moon is that perfect half-circle between the full moon and the crescent. The waxing half-moon is between the full moon and the waxing half. Waning energies represent a decline in the spiritual abundance from the full moon. During the waning gibbous, this effect is subtle, hence the reason why some people delay celebration of the full moon until within three days of the full moon event. The waning gibbous moon may represent a steady decline in energy, but the decline isn't that bad. Just as the waxing half-moon was a time to make small adjustments in your life, the waning half should be a time to only take small steps as well. The difference is that the small steps you take should begin to focus more on getting rid of bad habits or decreasing negativity rather than asking for increased blessings.

During the waning half-moon, think about things that you've already started to eliminate from your life. For example, you might be working on losing weight, reducing frivolous spending, or ridding your house of clutter. Gently assess where you are and how far you've come. If your goals no longer suit your life, consider giving them up entirely. If you've met with some success, redouble your efforts.

> * *During the waning half-moon, think about things*
> *that you've been working to eliminate from your*
> *life, and reassess where you are in those goals.*

Day 16: Waning Crescent Moon

As the moon wanes to a tiny sliver, you have the powerful opportunity to use that moon energy metaphorically in your own life. This powerful energy can really boost your efforts to clear up the negativity in your life. Your wish can be something that you've been working on for a while, such as getting rid of a lack of confidence in your career path, or it can be something that you've just decided to start, like a vow to stop swearing.

Changing your life and working with the universe during the waning moon, particularly the waning crescent, can be challenging. We tend to think about what we want rather than what we don't want. However, you can reword your wishes. For example, instead of working on getting more money in your life during the waning crescent moon, you can work on ridding yourself of money worries. Then, wait until the waxing or full moon before working more on creating abundance in your life. You'll find that if you go with the flow of the universe, rather than fighting it, your timing will always be perfect.

* *During the next waning moon, prepare to get rid of some negativity in your life. Small or large, pick something on which you can make large strides.*

Day 17: Stargazing and Moon Gazing

....

Gazing up at the heavens has long been a practice that provided union between people and the Divine. You've gotten a little taste of how the moon's phases can have a big effect on your psychology. Those who worshipped the sun in the past got a burst of inspiration from going out into the sunshine, and there are still those today who believe they gain spiritual nourishment from the sun. There's something very sacred about the fact that the living things that sustain us get their nourishment from the cosmos.

Stars have always had spiritual meaning as well. From constellations that tell great mythic tales to astrology that tells the personal story of each one of us, the stars dance up above to reflect our lives down below. The next time the sky clears, find a peaceful moment to stare up at the stars and reflect on your own small place in the vast universe. Consider searching the Internet for information on when the next meteor shower will be visible in your area. Perhaps you've already had the pleasure of making a wish on a star. Connect that excitement from your childhood to your adult faith and your hopes regarding the universe.

* *Make a wish upon a star.*

Day 18: Camping
....

Spending time out in nature in an extended way can be one way to remove yourself from your everyday life and go on a simple spiritual journey. Even if you're not the type to rough it in the wilderness, going on a brief cabin camping trip and finding a home away from home can be your version of a spirit journey. It can also be a wonderful excuse to unplug from electronics and daily distractions for a weekend or more. Opportunities for stargazing should abound, if the weather holds up. And, you may even have some close encounters with wildlife.

Plan a camping trip that is within your comfort level. Decide which sort of spiritual retreat you need most. Do you want to go solo, and spend time by yourself? Would you rather join in spiritual fellowship with your family or with some close friends whom you consider spiritual peers or mentors? Plan a short or a long retreat and decide just what things will feed your spirit. What should you bring along, and what should you leave behind? Consider bringing books to inspire you and leave all the distracting trappings of work behind.

* *Plan a camping spiritual retreat to get in touch with nature.*

Day 19: Tree-hugging

The phrase "tree-hugger" isn't always a positive one, as it implies that the person is such an environmental activist that he or she goes so far as sharing an intimate embrace with an inanimate object. But why don't we hug trees? Trees are an easy interaction point with nature because they are plentiful and easy to touch and appreciate. Anyone can feel sheltered in the shade of a tree and can enjoy the beauty of the blossoms of a tree in the springtime. Consider asking a tree's permission before you next take a fruit or cut a branch. Ancient lore includes stories of trees housing the spirits of nature.

What do nature spirits have to do with Spirit in general? For many cultures, it isn't enough to think of Spirit as being something detached and amorphous. Personifications of nature are a way to make the ineffable more approachable. You may not be able to understand how a tree got here from the formation of the universe billions of years ago, but you can certainly think about it as having its own sort of consciousness or character. Today, find a tree to get to know. Interact with your tree in a way that is appropriate for the season. Perhaps ask for a bit of fruit, take shelter under the tree, or lean against it and enjoy the beauty of the spreading branches above.

* *Hug a tree.*

Day 20: Altars
....

In most religions, there is a special table or set space called an altar. An altar is set with symbolic tools to commune with Spirit. Even a small studio apartment or dorm room can have a tiny space set aside as an altar. You may even have seen small altars asking Spirit for prosperity in Asian restaurants.

Altars can have beautiful and meaningful things arrayed on them. You can have tools and supplies, such as a pen and paper for journaling. You can have statues or works of art that you find pleasing and hope will please Spirit as well.

Later in this book you will learn more about symbols that you can place on the altar to represent the elements of this universe or to give offerings of thanks to Spirit. For now, you can think about the objects that make you think of Spirit in your own life. Things that make you joyful, thankful, worried, or faithful. Gather those objects within your home and prepare a space where you can reflect on them and connect with them.

* *Build a little altar at home so that you have a*
  tiny space in which you can connect with Spirit.

Day 21: Shrines

....

A shrine can be very much like an altar. Shrines can be outdoors or indoors, built on a little table or in an alcove. A shrine is usually built for a specific spirit, deity, or purpose. If you already have a spiritual relationship with a divine persona, you can build a shrine to your higher power. If not, you can consider building a shrine to your ancestors. Getting in touch with your ancestors is one way of connecting with Spirit, since Spirit has played a part in the relationships that have existed since humanity began, in order to bring about the person you are today.

To build an ancestor shrine, dig up any photographs of deceased ancestors that you can find. These photos should not have living people pictured in them. If you have any artifacts from your ancestors, such as jewelry, place those on the altar in a decorative way. If you didn't know your ancestors, you can place items that represent your ancestors' nationality on the altar. A glass of water is a traditional offering to ancestors, as is incense or joss sticks. Joss sticks are a special sort of incense used in some Asian countries for purposes such as these. Place the altar somewhere prominent so that you can see it every day. The more you show an appreciation for your ancestors, on whose shoulders you stand, the more you will be connected with Spirit through time immemorial.

* Set up an ancestral shrine, or include
  ancestral elements on your altar.

Day 22: Sacred Spaces

....

Some sacred spaces are much bigger than a tiny bookshelf altar. Nearly every spiritual tradition has a structure or some sort of sacred place designated for spiritual activities. Those that do not have ways of making any place special for a temporary point in time. I am lucky enough to have space in my home to devote a room as a permanent sacred space. In this room I have an altar table, plenty of imagery that is sacred to me, and a writing desk. There's enough space for me to dance if I desire, and the space is mine alone in which to burn incense, no matter how cloying it may be to others. Before I had this room of my own, I had a small shed in a yard that I used for the same purpose. And before I had even a shed to call my own, I was able to make temporary sacred space.

Temporary sacred space can be done in many ways. Sometimes all one needs to do to make a sacred space is to recognize it as sacred. Finding a beautiful spot in nature, for example. Or removing shoes before entering the home of a respected elder. You might want to mark the boundaries of your sacred space. If you're out in nature, gather a few rocks to make a circle, or mark a circle using white flour. Indoors, try marking the boundaries by hanging scarves or tapestries, or putting up a privacy screen in a strategic location.

* *Create a permanent or temporary sacred*
  space, or go out in nature to find one.

Day 23: Grounding

Have you ever felt exhausted for no reason? Or wound up and jittery when you'd rather be calm and relaxed? We refer to these experiences as changes in our "energy level." You can think of this energy as the force that permeates the universe, especially all living things. There are practices that you can undergo in order to stabilize your energy. This process is called *grounding*. Grounding is important for connecting with Spirit because if your energy is all wonky and wild, it will be nigh impossible to concentrate on the subtle energies of Spirit. Furthermore, you may find that when your energies are not grounded, you have a hard time finding perspective in life. Little things going wrong in your life might feel like everything is going wrong. And it can be hard to remember the importance of Spirit when you're fighting with life's daily minutiae.

To ground yourself, first take stock of your present energy level. Would you say you have too much energy, making you anxious or angry? Or would you say you have too little energy, making you feel blue and tired? Regardless of the direction of any energy imbalance, first try pushing out negative energy through your feet. You can visualize a flow of light or a system of roots if you choose. After you've flushed out the negative energy, draw in fresh energy from the earth. Again, you can visualize light or colors, or simply focus on the sensation, if you wish.

* *Practice grounding daily.*

Day 24: Centering

....

Centering is a practice that is done directly after grounding. Centering helps you anchor your attention in the here and now, rather than letting your mind run wild thinking of past regrets or future obligations. Centering is also a way to spiritually become at peace with your place in the universe. Hence the word *centering*, as if you were to find yourself at the center of your particular universe.

There are many different techniques for achieving a centered state of mind. Different methods work for different people. For some, a visualization such as a pillar of light coming down over the body may do the trick. For others, clearing the mind of distractions and taking a moment to forgive any wrongs or release external obligations may be in order. It can take some practice to feel centered, and at first it may seem to last only for an instant. These are the spiritual moments that people seek, so celebrate any instant that you feel centered. Feeling chronically uncentered may be a problem you can tackle a piece at a time, by figuring out what in your life creates a barrier to being present in a spiritual moment.

* *Ground and center yourself daily.*

Day 25: Shielding
....

Shielding is a practice of spiritual protection. Think of a force field or a bubble of protection surrounding you in order to ward off negative interactions and intentions from others around you. This may seem like a science fiction plot device, but shielding is something that everybody does naturally on a daily basis. We do this to avoid taking in unnecessary stimuli or unwanted conversation from others. Think of your personal space that you cherish around yourself. The boundaries of your personal space bubble are your shield, and when you feel threatened, those boundaries may expand or strengthen accordingly.

Again, different people find that different shielding techniques work best. Try visualizations first. Picture a bubble of protection, a protective case, a ring of fire, or a circle of guard dogs around you. If you find it helps, imagine yourself in a stressful situation, such as navigating a city that you've never visited. In those cases your natural shields may become more bold and noticeable in your mind. Practice taking down these shields as well. Imagine yourself in a relaxing and loving space in which everyone in the room accepts you. It's helpful to know how to take down your spiritual shields so that you can let people in.

* *Practice shielding and letting down your spiritual shields when appropriate.*

Day 26: The Energy of People Around You

You've worked with the energy inside your body while grounding, and with energy that extends outside your body when shielding. You may have already begun to notice the energy that extends outside the bodies of people around you. If not, that's okay. Noticing the energy of people around you is another one of those natural functions you have, so it may have become a subconscious process for you. Today, take the time to be aware of the energy of others, and to try to sense it in whatever way works for you. Taking notice of this energy can help you realize the spiritual similarities between other people and yourself.

What is the energy of other people like? Some people may see the energy around others as a light or color or even a slight blurriness. Others may sense the energy of others in a more tactile way. The energy radiating off other people may feel like a heat that extends outside their bodies or a fuzziness or prickliness. You might discover that occasionally you have an emotional reaction to the energy of others. Have you ever known someone who leaves you exhausted after interacting with him or her, no matter what the context? You may be feeling that way because of the person's energy or because of how their energy interacts with your own.

* *Take note of the energies of others around you today.*

Day 27: Connecting with the Earth

You've already learned to connect with the earth through grounding. Grounding is something that is typically done a session at a time. People might ground once a day, twice a day, or multiple times a day according to need. However, connecting with the earth in a simpler way can be done with much more frequency. There are those who believe that the earth is an expression of divinity, or even a divine entity itself. Your connection with the earth can not only bring you the benefits of grounding, but can help you to forge a sort of relationship with divinity through the idea of the creation, or creator, that earth may be.

Another way to get in touch with the earth is to do so literally, by taking off your shoes. Going barefoot in your home while you practice your grounding is one great start. When you feel ready, try taking your bare feet outside and stepping on some soft grass. Take the time to feel the sensations from the earth while you also work on your visualization for grounding. The two combined will give your brain more information about your own energy level, and about how you feel in relation to this great earth that we all share.

* *Go barefoot outside and practice your grounding.*

Day 28: Ways of Sensing Energy
....

There are many different ways to sense energy, both your own and the energy of others. You may find that there's a pattern in the way you sense the spiritual energy of the universe, and this pattern can help you expand your ability. For example, if you sense your own energy level as a sort of glow about you or a light in your eyes when you look in the mirror, you might tend to sense all energy visually. You could see the energy of others as a light or another visual feature as well if you look carefully enough with intention. Likewise, you might sense energy visually in the world around you at large.

Some people may sense energy as a tactile feeling of fuzziness, warmth, or prickliness. Some people may even have energy tickle their other senses, coming in as a sweet smell or the sound of a hum or even a taste. And some people don't sense energy through one of the ordinary five senses. Instead, these people have a perception, a feeling of knowing that the energy is there without a doubt. This isn't a lesser way of sensing energy. In fact, it may come as a combination with other perceptions. Practice sensing your own energy and the energy of others and see if you can expand your sensory perceptions.

* *Practice sensing energy in different ways.*

Day 29: Sensing the Energy of Plants, Animals, and Inanimate Objects

···

Humans aren't the only things infused with Spirit. The energy of plants, animals, and even inanimate objects may be more subtle to sense. However, now that you have a good idea of how you tend to sense energy, you can stretch and reach to perceive things you may never have noticed before. If you have a pet, your pet may be the easiest place to start. Approach your pet while he or she is resting. If possible, you can touch your pet to observe whether you feel energy as a sensation in your hand. If possible, you can synchronize your breathing with that of your pet to observe whether you feel a connection as a sense of knowing or as another perception.

To sense a plant's energy, find a plant you are familiar with and that you enjoy. Perhaps the tree you found during the tree-hugging activity. Familiarize yourself with the plant in question by observing it from all angles, touching it, and, if it is safe, even tasting it. Close your eyes and try to recreate the plant in your mind. This practices your visualization skills and allows you to look for perceptions in your mind's eye that you may not have noticed with your eyes open. You can also try this technique to try to sense the energy of inanimate objects, such as stones or crystals.

* Try to sense the energy of an animal, plant, or object.

Day 30: Connecting with
Global Energy of Other People

There are a lot of common wishes for the world. A lot of people wish for world peace. Many hope for a day when no people on earth go hungry. Perhaps you have high hopes for the global education of children. These kinds of hopes and dreams often seem impractical. How can one person affect the life outcomes of millions of unnamed people, some of them perhaps very far away? Hopefully, we all do the best we can in our everyday lives to minimize our impact on global issues and to contribute what relief we're able to give. Beyond that, the sense of helplessness we all feel is one reason why people turn to Spirit for help.

One first step may be to simply try to connect with the energy of people all over the world in the way that you naturally interact with the energy of others every day. Try closing your eyes to meditate. Now imagine yourself connected to others in the world. Picture yourself holding hands in a line with all humanity. Or imagine somebody in need having his or her needs fulfilled, like a starving child receiving a free meal and loving medical care. See in your mind's eye the solutions already in place to promote healthy and happy people. You can also practice spreading peaceful energy by first stilling any conflict in your own heart and then visualizing that peace radiating outward to everyone on the planet who wishes to accept such positive energy.

* *Share the energy of a bigger cause.*

Day 31: Connecting with the
Energy of a Shared Ideal or Concept
....

You've practiced working with a goal that is bigger than yourself that can affect the entire world. There are plenty of concepts that live as a larger ideal. For example, the idea of love. We can think of love expressed in many forms. The love of a mother for her child. Romantic love between two people. And many other beautiful relationships that make up the people on this earth. Love can also be expressed symbolically in many ways. You can visualize the word *love* spelled out. You can picture a giant heart, the symbol for love. Some people believe that Spirit is both the source and the ultimate expression of love.

Today, brainstorm some other big concepts that you'd like to invite into your life, and perhaps the lives of others. Think about all the symbols that express those things. You might even come up with songs and colors and other things that spring to mind when you think of that concept. When you meditate upon spreading those ideals within yourself and around yourself, strongly visualize the symbols that came to your mind.

* *Come up with some ideals and their
   symbols to meditate upon and share.*

Day 32: Elven Chess
....

Today's activity is a good way to get in touch with nature as well as your intuition with Spirit at the same time. Go outdoors to a natural space full of rocks, twigs, branches, leaves, or other natural things. Take time to sit and meditate as you survey the scene around you. Then, slowly and mindfully pick up a rock, a twig, or a branch and place it somewhere that feels right to you. You might place it somewhere aesthetically pleasing or just someplace to which you feel drawn. Pick up another stick, rock, or something else and place it nearby. Continue this activity. You may find yourself forming a pattern that looks like a spiral, a mandala, or some other shape. You might not be able to see any pattern at all.

As you work on this "elven chessboard" of satisfying movement of nature's pieces, stay in tune with your intuition. At some point, you will feel like you are done. Sit back and survey your work. Take time to meditate on the scene before you. Some people use this as a way to create beautiful works of art. Others practice this as a way to be thankful for what Spirit has given in nature.

* *Play a game of elven chess with yourself.*

Day 33: Counting Your Blessings

There's something to be said for counting your blessings and making a grand attempt to be thankful for each and every one. Instead of feeling pulled down by life's challenges, if you focus upon blessings you'll find yourself noticing more good things in your life. When I read *One Thousand Gifts: A Dare to Live Fully Right Where You Are* by Ann Voskamp, I learned that one can literally count blessings. The idea that Voskamp espouses is this:

Get a notebook and write down a blessing from today. It could be the way that your breakfast smelled in the morning or the light that glistened off the frost on the sidewalk path on a winter day. Then write another blessing and another, until you can't think of any more. As new blessings arise, write them down as well. You'll soon find yourself on the hunt for blessings, like a scavenger for joy in your own life. I took part in this challenge and found it very beneficial in my own life. The act of writing down the blessings also aided as a meditative and calming practice when I felt stressed out. I still keep my ongoing list of blessings to this day.

* *Begin counting your blessings.*

Day 34: Charity

....

In some faith traditions, money is a symbol of desire and is anathema, but in others money is a metaphor for spiritual energy. Money changes hands frequently, and giving money or resources to those who have less is one way to spread the love and caring associated with Spirit. You can do this directly by giving away things that you no longer need to those in need. You can also work with charities so that you can join forces with those who have already identified needy populations and their needs.

Some religions advocate tithing, which often means giving a proportion of income, say ten percent, to the religious organization. Even if you're not affiliated with a religion, you can still set up a tithe for yourself and instead donate that money toward a charity or group of charities of your choice. If you don't have enough money to spare, try giving in-kind donations—for example, donating old clothes. Another option is to raise funds for charity by asking friends and family for their support. Signing up for a charity walk or run is one way to gather donations associated with an event. It can feel very spiritually fulfilling to complete your walk or run after raising money and awareness for a cause.

* *Find a way to donate money or other material*
  support to a charity or church of your choice.

Day 35: Volunteering

....

The word *namaste* is a South Asian expression that means "the divinity in me greets the divinity in you." Recognizing that Spirit is in each and every person is one spiritual belief that crosses the boundaries of many religions and cultures. Service is thus one of the highest forms of spiritual practice. Volunteering in service can also be an excellent way to donate your time to charity if you are low on money to give. It can also be the key to unlocking compassion and that spiritual recognition of the Divine in others, even if you have not yet experienced such a thing.

You don't have to stretch too far beyond your comfort zone if you don't want to. Think of the sorts of people who already bend your heart. If you have a heart for children, for example, consider volunteering to read to kids at a children's hospital. If you have a heart for the elderly, sign up to visit a nursing home and make friends with some residents who don't see very many visitors. Think about how each person you serve reminds you of yourself or of somebody you love, or of love and compassion in general.

* *Get yourself a volunteer job.*

Day 36: Social Justice

When you get involved with human issues as a whole, some may begin to jump out at you as important to you. Social justice is the idea that certain rights should be afforded to all people, and that action can be taken to ensure parity and equality, or even just to assure necessities where none are present. Some people are taken with feminist ideals, while others may focus on race or other social justice issues. There are those who believe that Spirit guides people toward ethical decisions regarding social justice.

Think of a social justice issue about which you are passionate. It could be one that you've been raised to consider important, or one about which you've only recently become aware. Brainstorm some ways you can become more involved in solving the issue of your choice, and spend some time in meditation thinking of positive symbols about the issue. For example, if education is important to you, you might choose to meditate on the symbol of an apple and to write your political representatives about increasing funding to schools near you.

* *Become involved with social justice spiritually and practically.*

Day 37: Service

....

Service doesn't have to mean volunteering with nonprofit organizations. You can serve Spirit without ever leaving your home. Performing random acts of kindness for your significant other, your family members, and even your pets can be acts of service that bring spiritual joy. Even if you live alone, the actions of cleaning your home and taking care of the environment around your household can bless you with positive emotions and a sense of purpose. When you leave your home, acts as simple as opening a door for a stranger or offering to help a neighbor with yard work can be spiritual service.

Today, seek and find a random act of kindness that you can rationalize as spiritual service. It can be something that makes you feel good inside, or something that makes a difference close to your home. To me, the most remarkable acts of service are those that would otherwise be mundane drudgery, but when done with a song in the heart can be transformed into work for Spirit. For example, sweeping the house can be done while rolling your eyes, feeling annoyed that it will just get messy again. Or it can be done with a song and a prayer, happy that a beautiful house can bring joy to your family or even just to yourself.

* *Perform a random act of kindness as spiritual service.*

Part Two

*

Body

Day 38: Nutrition and Listening to Your Body

Do you believe in a wise creator or an inner guidance? Spirit gave each healthy person an inner wisdom about which foods to eat, when to start eating, and when to stop eating. The problem is that many people are just as detached from their own bodies as they are from the cycles of the seasons. Getting back in tune with your own body may be a tricky business. Of course, inner wisdom can be supplemented with external knowledge. If you've got a craving for chocolate, you don't have to eat all chocolate all the time. However, it is a wonderful spiritual practice to listen to when your body is hungry, to eat gratefully what you need, and to stop when you are full.

To practice listening to your body, allow yourself to get hungry. Then pause and really assess what type of food your body craves. Sit down to a mindful meal and give thanks. Take your time and savor your meal. If you are used to eating quickly, it may help to take smaller bites and to take a sip of water between each bite. Stop as soon as you feel a sensation of fullness. You can always eat more later if you feel hungry again.

* *Eat a meal slowly and mindfully.*

Day 39: Food Preparation

Preparing food is a way to connect with Spirit in many ways. Food preparation helps you become more connected with the source of your food, and to be thankful for the provision of Spirit. Imbuing your food with love as you prepare food allows you to share those spiritual values with family or simply to be mindful of them yourself. Creating traditions of food preparation in alignment with holidays can help bring sense and rhythm to your year. The scents of your favorite foods are like extra decorations for your house during special seasons.

Try mindfully preparing food today with the purpose of bringing positive things to you and to your family, if applicable. For example, when I bake bread for my family, as I knead the dough I think about how it will nourish my body and my family. When my kids help me, I tell them to put their own love into the bread. My three-year-old daughter signs "I love you" at the dough in sign language. Keeping food preparation a special act makes it more fun for all of us, and it helps us connect with Spirit at every single mealtime.

* *Put some Spirit into your food preparation today.*

Day 40: The Dining Table

The dining room table is like an altar. It's a space that we devote to fellowship with friends and family and for nourishing our sacred bodies. We often decorate the dining room table with candles or centerpieces that showcase the seasons. For this reason, you should have a special space in your home set aside for dining. Don't pile papers or other things on the table. Treat it as yet another sacred space in your house, but this one is for nourishing your body and catching up with loved ones over a good meal.

There are many ways to honor your dining room area as another sacred space. Keeping it clear and clean and decorating it is one way. Saying a prayer before meals in order to establish gratitude and a sacred time in the space is another. Some people keep an offering plate at the table for Spirit. We even have special rules of etiquette and decorum for the dinner table to establish a special sort of attitude when sitting down for meals. When all of these embellishments are used mindfully, they can be a way to connect with Spirit at every meal and snack time.

* Respect your meal table like an altar; decorate it accordingly and observe etiquette.

Day 41: Exercise
....

Your body was meant to move every day. Anyone can exercise the body as a way to be grateful for being alive while connecting with Spirit. Choose an exercise that is within your own personal ability, and talk with your doctor if you have any doubts. Get your blood moving and your endorphins flowing; this heightened state has been associated with spiritual ecstasy in many cultures. Exercise enthusiastically. After all, the word *enthused* comes from the Greek word *entheos,* which means "possessed by a god."

Over the next few days we'll go over some exercises that have been associated with Spirit. However, any exercise you choose can be devoted to your spirituality. This is why many sports teams pray together before games or competitions. If you already have an exercise or activity that you love, try performing it mindfully with a moment of silence before and some words of gratitude after. Make a commitment to connect your body with Spirit by moving it actively in some way every day. Try a number of your favorite exercises and ask yourself if one of them seems to be more spiritually meaningful to you than another.

* *Exercise your body mindfully every day.*

Day 42: Sacred Dance
....

Dance can be used in many ways to connect with Spirit. Dance can be used to tell stories and secrets with your body. You can perform a playful dance that expresses meaning that cannot be shared with words. Dance can be used as an exercise to induce a trance in order to commune directly with Spirit. Dance can also be used to raise energy in your body that can then be used by Spirit or by yourself. You don't have to be good at dance in order to practice sacred dancing. Indeed, unless you want to dance with others to forge fellowship, nobody need ever see your dancing at all.

If you are new to dance or just want to try out a little bit of ecstatic dance, you can follow these simple instructions to the best of your ability. Begin grounding yourself by shaking out your body. Shake your hands and your arms, wobble your head, shake all throughout your upper body and your lower. It may feel silly, but it can loosen up your joints and allow you to ground stuck energy that might otherwise be difficult to push out through your feet into the earth. Turn on some music and allow yourself to move freely to it in order to express yourself, or to lull yourself into a trance.

* *Try sacred dance.*

Day 43: Martial Arts

·····································

When you think of martial arts, you may think of fighting techniques passed down from masters to students. One thing that all martial arts have in common, however, is that they work with spiritual energy. Some fighting martial arts involve moving your own energy or manipulating the energy of others. Note that martial arts are most often practiced barefoot, to facilitate grounding of energy. In slower-moving martial arts, like Tai Chi, energy is moved very consciously through and around the body, sometimes in order to facilitate health and wellness.

You might consider training in martial arts if you're lucky enough to have a teacher near you. However, you can manipulate energy around your body on your own. First ground yourself, and then sit down to try this experiment. Rub your hands together until you can feel the tingling of the blood coursing through your veins. Hold your palms apart and feel the heat between them. Visualize a ball of energy between your palms. Try moving this ball around using your mind's eye and the movements of your hands. See if you can make your perception of the heat and tingly feeling of that energy move to other parts of your body or even other parts of the room. When you are finished, ground yourself again.

* Practice moving energy around your body.
  Consider a martial arts practice.

Day 44: Walking Meditation

Going for a twenty-minute walk can lower your blood pressure, calm your mood, and even put off hunger pangs. There's something magical about unplugging to take a walk during a busy day. When you combine walking with meditation, or use walking as meditation, the act gains a sense of holiness. Holy spaces will sometimes have gardens on the ground in which to walk, or even a labyrinth. If you want to trace out a labyrinth in your driveway with chalk and walk it or find a beautiful park near you, either can be effective to evoke a sense of Spirit.

Think of a topic to ponder before going on your walk or meditation. Your topic could be related to the seasons, life, death, the Divine, or anything else under the sun. Ground yourself and then begin your walk. Choose a focus, such as your breathing or the chirping of birds or your own footfalls. Keep that focus for the duration of your walk, allowing your meditation to lull you into a trance or to bring you other sensations and perceptions. When you get back from your walk, ground yourself and perhaps write down your thoughts about the experience.

* *Go for a meditative walk.*

Day 45: Loving Your Body

In myths the world over, humans are created by Spirit, and oftentimes they are created to look just like the Divine. Yet so many people have low self-esteem that is derived from body-image issues. Loving your body is one way to be grateful to the creative spirit and to honor what Spirit has given you in this life. Learning to love the body you have can also be a way to connect with Spirit through that feeling of love for the self, for Spirit always dwells within you.

Loving yourself can be a long process in life, so don't feel bad if you can't manage it right away. That would defeat the purpose. Examine yourself in the mirror without comparing yourself to any other person. Sit or stand with good posture, allowing your stance to become large and confident. Consider that you are a perfect expression of Spirit even with any flaws. Meditate upon your mirror image, allowing yourself to see the beauty in your body as if it were a landscape, and the depth in your own eyes as windows to your soul. If any judgmental thoughts come up, allow them to gently float away.

* *Meditate on loving your own body.*

Day 46: Where Does Sexuality Fit into Spirituality?

Sex and spirituality are perceived as polarized, and therefore seen as a dichotomy, in some faith traditions. The union of male and female is seen as sacred in many of them, and the creation of new life that sex can bring is revered in all of them. Sex also has a power, and can be viewed as a sacred and special act. For this reason, it is important for a spiritual person to be mindful about his or her own choices regarding sex. Even abstinence from sex for a period of time can be viewed as powerful, as it builds up a sense of purity and a focus on the intangible. Sex is a symbol of the union between the sacred and the profane, and thus it can easily be seen as one or the other.

Meditate upon how sexuality fits into your spirituality. Is sex something special that one should save for a specific person or avoid at certain sacred times? Or is sex something that can be used as a form of worship because of the natural joy it produces? Think about how you can invite sacred sexual experiences into your own life, and avoid any sexual encounters that may be less than what your Spirit would guide you to have.

* Meditate upon how sex fits in with your spirituality.

Day 47: Start a Dream Journal

Sleep is an important part of self-care, and one that is so easy to let slip aside. However, the time taken for sleep is a sacred time. This is why so many cultures have prayers upon going to bed and upon waking. In the time before lighting was available all through the night, sleep time may have been broken into two shorter periods of sleep with a wakeful period of prayer in between them. Another important part of sleeping is dreaming. Dreams are often thought to be one way that Spirit communicates with you.

To make sleep a sacred time to connect with Spirit, commit to getting a good night's sleep as often as possible. Turn off electronics a few hours before bed and make sure you aren't staring at any screens. Consider making yourself some herbal tea or drawing a bath. When you go to bed, keep a dream journal by your bedside with a light and a writing implement. Commit to writing down any dreams as soon as you wake up before they fly from your mind. This is easier said than done. This practice will help you remember more of your dreams.

* Start a dream journal.

Day 48: Fasting
....

So many religions value fasting as a spiritual practice. Fasting is the practice of temporarily denying the body food, drink, or both. Fasting can be performed in order to remind oneself of a commitment to Spirit in order to enhance the power of prayer, meditation, or ritual; to show gratitude to Spirit for the body; or simply for health. A fast should not be done for a long period of time, and you can fast by simply cutting out chosen foods from your diet for a day. The most common type of spiritual fast is to fast during the daylight hours for one day, from sunrise to sunset.

Decide what sort of fast you would like to try. If you get the okay from your doctor and are in good health, you can try fasting without food or water for the day, until sunset. If you are pregnant, elderly, young, ill, or an athlete, a pure fast like this may not be practical. Instead, you can try consuming only liquids for the day, or consuming a vegetarian diet for the day, if that is out of the ordinary for you. During your fasting time, pray and meditate periodically.

* *Try a spiritual fast for a day.*

Day 49: Storytelling with Dance and Gestures
....

When you were first introduced to dance as a spiritual practice, you practiced a little grounding technique that can help you lose self-consciousness and notice some of the energetic benefits of dance. Dance can also tell a story or a great myth. There are some feelings, especially about Spirit, that cannot be expressed in words. Those feelings can be expressed through ecstatic movement or by taking on the character of the concept you're pondering.

Today, try saying a prayer with your body. If you're new to prayer, or feeling a bit rusty, don't worry. You'll dive deeper into prayer in the next section of this book. For now, think of a feeling that you'd like to express to Spirit, such as joy, curiosity, or even sadness. You can even add to this story by thinking of other concepts, such as an upcoming holiday. After doing the grounding dance you've already learned, move your body in space to express some of your ideas about Spirit. You don't have to merely pantomime. Notice how you feel when your body is standing tall or stooping low and go by your emotions rather than what you look like.

* *Try expressing yourself through spiritual dance.*

Day 50: Palmistry

Palmistry, also called palm reading or chiromancy, is the art of looking at your own personal characteristics and destiny by looking at your own hands. The palms of your hands are like an ever-changing map of your potential. It's a map to help guide you to your spiritual potential. Palmistry is a complex art that can take time to learn, but today you can explore your hands if you're unfamiliar with this art. It may help to sketch the palm of your hands first, so that the things you notice most about your hands quickly spring to mind. Try drawing the palm of your active, or dominant, hand first.

Take a look at how deep the lines are in your palm. The depth of these lines represents your spiritual energy. The deeper the lines, the more spiritual energy you have in reserve for when you have desires and goals in your life, or even for when you get physically ill. Don't fret if you have naturally shallow lines, though. Some people "run cool" on less energy than others, and that can be its own strength. You can look up the meanings of each individual line on the Internet.

* *Observe the lines in your palms.*

Day 51: Mudras

....

Mudras are the positions that your hands can take during worship, dance, meditation, and other spiritual activities. For example, the classic "prayer hands," two hands placed palms-together, is a mudra. Think of the palms of your hand as vortexes of spiritual energy and your fingers as the conduits for specific types of energy. You can see how the different shapes the hands make can form different meanings to others and yourself. In palmistry, the thumb is often equated to your will, your forefingers to your sense of leadership and direction. Your middle finger is your sense of duty and your ring finger is your artistic and ostentatious streak. Your pinky finger is your business cunning and your health.

Try meditating with your hands on your knees while seated. Connect your thumb and forefinger first on one hand, and then the other. How does your energy feel? Meditate for a few minutes and then check in with yourself again. Next, try touching the middle finger and thumb of each hand. Spend a few moments with this mudra and notice how the energy changes. Repeat this exercise with your ring finger and your pinky finger.

* *Notice how mudras affect your spiritual energy.*

Day 52: Your Aura

....

An *aura* is a word for the field of spiritual energy that surrounds people, other living things, and even inanimate objects. Some people can see auras as halos of color around people's heads or bodies. Other people can feel auras as a warmth or as a fuzzy or prickly sensation several inches away from the skin. Some people believe that the color of a visible aura has meaning. However, the aura changes colors depending on mood, health, proximity to others, and spiritual events. So, your own aura, and the meaning associated with it, can change over your lifetime and even over the course of a few minutes.

To attempt to see your own aura, place yourself in front of a mirror with a neutral background behind you. Take care not to wear bright colors. A bright background or brightly colored shirt can cause the optical illusion of an aura that can confuse your actual sightings. Sit in front of a mirror and relax your gaze. Look at your reflection as if you are looking at something behind your reflection, far beyond the back of the mirror. Look around the edges of your body, moving your eyes at least once a minute to gaze at another section of where your aura may be. Write down notes or sketch what you see.

* *Try to see your own aura.*

Day 53: Feeling Energy
....

You've already felt energy in several forms. You've practiced rubbing your hands together and then pulling them apart to feel your own energy. You also know how the energy of people around you and your environment affect you. Energy can make you feel tired or alert. Energy affects your mood throughout the day. Learning to physically feel energy with a tactile sensation can allow you to better direct the flow of energy for spiritual purposes.

Try sitting in front of the mirror and viewing your aura again. Imagine yourself giving a passionate speech to people you love about a topic you care about. This should help you puff up your aura so that it is larger and more vibrant. Hold your hand against your skin and then slowly move it away from you. You should be able to feel a point at which your aura seems to end. Since your hand also has an aura, this exercise may be more easily performed with a partner whose aura feels different from yours. Notice any change in temperature, texture, or other sensation. If you are successful, try sensing an aura around an animal, a plant, or even an inanimate object.

* *Try feeling energy as a tactile sensation.*

Day 54: Breath

....

Controlling your breathing is one way to induce a spiritual trance. Slow and rhythmic breathing can lead you toward a liminal, or transitional, headspace between sleep and wakefulness. Quick breathing can flush your face and make you see stars. During your meditation, you can pay attention to your breathing and exclude all other things in order to allow yourself to release your chattering mind. In myths the world over, breath is equated to life. Deities breathe life into humans and other creatures. Your spirit may be represented as a breath that can be exhaled from your body at the end of life.

Today, try square breathing. Breathe in through your nose for four counts, hold your breath for four counts, breathe out through your mouth for four counts, and then hold your breath again for four counts. You'll find this challenging at first, especially holding your lungs empty. Set your own pace so that you can do it. You can always slow down your breaths later when you get the hang of the cadence and when you begin to relax into the process. You may find square breathing distracting at first. This is a good thing. Focus only on your breathing and keep doing it for twenty minutes. By the end, you will find that your breathing naturally slows and that the process becomes easier for you to sustain.

* *Practice square breathing during meditation.*

Day 55: Heart Math
·····································

The heart is a special spiritual place. Many ancient cultures believed the heart to be the seat of the soul, rather than the head or the brain. The location of your heart in your body can be perceived to give off emotions or warm feelings, even if its true physical function is merely to pump blood. You can meditate while listening to your heartbeat. You can notice when your heart races due to excitement and elation or slows when you enter a trance or get ready to sleep. Today's exercise will help you listen to your heartbeat and feel the answers that your heart gives to you.

Think about an issue or a problem in your life. Focus on this issue as you begin to meditate. Now, turn your attention to your heartbeat. You can try square breathing using your heart as a metronome. Breathe in for four heartbeats, hold for four heartbeats, breathe out for four heartbeats, and hold your breath again for four heartbeats. Think again about the problem or issue in your life. How does your heart feel about the matter? Pay attention to any sensations in your chest or emotional reactions as they arise.

* *Practice listening to your heart.*

Day 56: Physical Connection with Others

In many cultures, spiritual healing involves the "laying of hands"—one person placing hands on the body of another in order to transfer energy or provide other spiritual consolation. Physical touch between two people can be comforting, sexual, energizing, or sacred. Some people tend to touch others frequently by placing a hand on an arm or offering a hug. Others may be more standoffish due to cultural standards or personal preference. However, allowing yourself to have more contact with people can change your spiritual outlook.

Today, try to find a way to connect with your loved ones through touch. Cuddle a baby, tickle a child, hug a friend, kiss an elder on the cheek, and find excuses to run your hand across your lover's shoulders lovingly when you walk by. Notice how your energy feels when you touch others. Do you feel a zing like electricity? Does it feel relaxing? How does your energy feel at the end of the day after making sure to get your physical connection with others? A bonus extra credit exercise would be to use your sense of touch to give comfort to someone. Hug a crying child or give a back rub to a loved one who isn't feeling well.

* *Physically connect with others today.*

Day 57: Stimulation-Induced Trance

Physical sensations on your body can be one way to induce a spiritual trance in order to better connect with Spirit. Imagine smacking yourself with eucalyptus branches in a spa. The gentle but invigorating sensation of the branches on the skin changes your state of mind. It can simultaneously excite and relax you, sending you into a sort of trance. In some spiritual traditions, this sort of ritual flogging was taken to a degree of penance. Don't worry, I won't ask you to whip yourself senseless for this one.

This relaxing exercise can be done before meditation in order to get in touch with your body. Sit down and start by giving yourself a massage from toe to head. Rub your feet, your legs, your hips, your belly, and your back, all the way up to your shoulders, neck, and scalp. As you do so, consciously relax each muscle that you rub. Next, repeat the action of waking your body with light tapping. Start at the bottoms of your feet and continue tapping all the way up your body until you reach your face and the top of your head. Again, remind each muscle to relax as it is tapped. You can try other sensations as well, such as brushing your body with quick motions of your hand, from toes to head again.

* *Meditate while applying different sensations to your body—
  for example, first massage, then tapping.*

Day 58: Ecstatic Dance

You've used sacred dance as a way to ground yourself and to express your emotions. Another form of sacred dance is ecstatic movement. Ecstatic dance is a combination of expressive dance and grounding dance. The purpose is to release energy with wild abandon and to reach a headspace that feels positive and spiritual. I suggest you get music for this one. Pick some music that really moves your spirit, preferably starting with a long song that is slow at the beginning and fast and frantic toward the end.

Start out by grounding yourself using the body shake-out you've practiced earlier. Turn on your music and start thinking of moving your body. Ecstatic movement doesn't need choreography, but if you're new to dancing, here's a suggestion: Move your body in circles in every way that you can. Move your feet in circles, turn your body, roll your head. How many ways can you make a circle with any part of your body or with your body as a whole? Focus only on that movement until you run out of ideas and then start over again. When you are finished, ground yourself and check in with your energy level to see how you feel.

* *Try dancing ecstatically to music that moves your spirit.*

Day 59: Energy Raising with the Body

Spiritual energy is raised from within the body and can be released to Spirit in worship, to other people, or to the world around you. We've already been over one of the ways to raise energy within the body, which is through ecstatic or expressive dance. You've also used meditative tapping on the skin to raise energy within the body, and these sensations can be made more or less intense depending on the energy raising desired. Another way to raise energy is by singing or drumming or playing some other musical instrument. To feel the energy raised, it's important to ground yourself before the energy raising. Ground again afterward if you're not directing that energy anywhere else in particular. You should feel a notable difference in your level of excitement and in sensations within your body.

Today, ground yourself, and then try to raise energy through dance, song, or both. If you have no musical instruments, clap your hands and stomp your feet. If you have a drum or a rattle, play these carefully as you move. Perhaps take a step with each shake of the rattle or beat of the drum. Move slowly at first, and if you feel comfortable, you can pick up the pace. When you are finished, place your hands on the ground and release the energy to Spirit to be used for whatever positive things in the world need such energy.

* *Try raising energy within your body and directing it to Spirit.*

Day 60: Energy Transmission with the Body

In yesterday's exercise, you used the body as a sort of battery. You charged your body battery and then used it to light up Spirit in the world. The body can also be used as an energy conduit. In this way, Spirit is the wall outlet, and your body is the wire that sends the energy out into the world to be used by others. Think of it as another way of volunteering. You can meditate and use that time to connect with Spirit and then let Spirit shine into the world through you. This can motivate you to help others and generally make the world a better place with your very presence.

To use your body as a conduit for Spirit, seat yourself in meditation and focus on a spot right in between your eyebrows on your forehead. This is your third eye. Opening it allows for spiritual energy to enter your body. As you sit in meditation, clear your mind of any other thoughts other than your focus on your third eye. You may feel a tickling or buzzing sensation on your forehead or a sense of pressure. This is normal. Try to maintain your concentration for at least twenty minutes. After you're done, ground yourself and go about your day knowing that Spirit works through you.

* *Try using your body as a conduit for Spirit.*

Day 61: Elements and the Body

There are four spiritual elements that are seen in several cultures' spiritual disciplines and magical practices: earth, air, fire, and water. Spiritually, these four essential building blocks of the universe are said to make up all physical things. Some people add a fifth element, that of Spirit, to the mix. Within your physical body, however, the four elements are represented through body processes and systems. By meditating on each of the four elements, or the four elements together, you can connect with the creation of Spirit. Some people feel an affinity to one element over the others, but others believe that to have a balance is ideal. Over the next few days you'll get acquainted with each of the four elements. For today, consider this meditation.

Close your eyes and seat yourself for meditation. Think about the points at which your body contacts the ground or chair in which you're seated. Meditate upon the fact that your body is a solid physical manifestation of Spirit. Your body is thus the earth element in action. Next, turn your attention to your breathing. Your breath is the element of air. Feel your heartbeat and meditate on the blood flowing through your veins. Your blood is the water element. Finally, feel the heat rising from your body through your metabolic processes, and note that this, as well as the desire in your heart, represents the element of fire.

* Meditate on the four elements as represented in your own body.

Day 62: Earth

....

The element of earth represents physical manifestation. The earth is solid under your feet. Everyone you've ever known and loved has lived out their lives on this planet. The earth represents jewels and everything of tangible value. The earth also represents the silence of motionless mountains and the coldness of their snowy peaks in winter in the Northern Hemisphere. In sacred spaces, the earth is often represented by salt. Salt represents crystalline, pure, clean earth. It is added to holy water, sprinkled around sacred places, or simply kept on hand as a symbol.

Today, meditate on the element of earth. Place a dish of salt on your altar or in your sacred space. Connect your feet to the ground and think about your connection to the planet that can never truly be broken as you live throughout your life. Ground yourself. Give thanks for all of the tangible gifts of the earth that you've received in this lifetime, and that you have yet to receive. After meditating, consider taking a walk in nature to continue connecting with the earth element. Search for green things, as green is the color of the element of earth.

* Meditate on the element of earth.

Day 63: Air

....

The element of air includes the breath in your body and the wind through the tips of the trees. The element of air also represents the feeling of inspiration and intuition. Imagine exhaling after an idea that seems to take your breath away. No wonder so many spiritual traditions honor the element of air by burning incense or using sweet-smelling herbs and flowers. The element of air represents new beginnings, like the sun rising in the east. It is associated with studying and the color yellow.

Today, meditate on the element of air. First, find a representation for the element of air to place on your altar or in your sacred space. You could use a bird feather, anything that smells sweet, or some incense. As you meditate, if you used something that smells nice, focus on that scent and allow inspiration and intuition to come to you from the element of air. Turn your attention to your breathing and concentrate. When you are finished meditating, write down any ideas that came to you. Immediately afterward, take the time to engage in an intellectual pursuit such as reading a book. Let the element of air be your guide today.

* *Meditate on the element of air.*

Day 64: Water

·······················

They say that more than half your body is made up of water, though the exact percentage depends upon many factors. The element of water is represented by the blood rushing in your veins and the life waters of the womb in which you floated before birth. The element of water is the swirling cauldron of your emotions. In many cultures, a body of water waits in the mythic afterlife, representing the unknown mysteries of death. Water is represented by the direction west and by the deep-blue color of the sea.

Today, meditate on the element of water. Get a symbol of water for your altar or sacred space. This is easily done by procuring a bowl of water. If you have a dark-colored bowl, you can gaze into the water during your meditation, which may bring you some messages from Spirit. Place the bowl of water in front of you and let the focus of your eyes go soft, just like when you attempted to see auras. You can let your eyes linger on the water if you like. Relax. You may see images in the light playing on the water. Since water is the element of emotions, you may simply feel feelings. Take note of the emotions as they come and go.

* Meditate on the element of water.

Day 65: Fire

....

The element of fire represents the desire that wells up in each of our hearts. Passion for what we do in life. Love for the people in our lives. The strange impetus that calls us to adventure. Fire is associated with the bright red in its flames, and with the heat of the south. The element of fire is at times like energy itself, bidding us to dance or to move. Fire can be destructive, so it represents transformation. Imagine a phoenix rising from the ashes of a great bonfire. Think of the heat in your body that represents the spark of life within you.

The best representation of fire is a candle placed on your altar or in your sacred space. If you're in a place where you cannot burn anything, a light will have to do. However, if you use a candle you can try gazing into the flame for messages from Spirit. Seat yourself in front of the candle and look at the flame. Drive other thoughts from your mind and focus only on the gentle movement and flickering of the candle. Notice any flashes of shapes that you perceive in the tongue of the flame. If you're lucky enough to have a fireplace, you can build a fire and then rake the wood away to gaze at the hot bed of coals.

* Meditate on the element of fire.

Day 66: Energy Healing

When you think of energy healing, you might think of the laying of hands on a person to heal him or her. Energy healing is an energy exchange or adjustment within the body of a person in order to encourage well-being and healing. Energy healing can be done by one person to another, or it can be done alone. Today's exercise will be all about healing yourself through energy. Energy healing is not a replacement for medical treatment. However, it can be a fulfilling spiritual practice that augments and enhances other treatments as advised by a doctor.

Energy healing is best done in the sunlight, but it can be done anywhere by simply imagining sunlight. To perform energy healing on yourself, begin by grounding yourself. Draw healing energy up through the earth. To take advantage of the healing energy of the hands, cross your hands or wrists at your chest so you're giving your heart or yourself a hug. Breathe slowly, telling yourself that you are breathing in all of the medicine you need for healing as energy from the air. Breathe out slowly, visualizing any negativity or illness leaving your body and disintegrating in the cleansing light of the sun. Visualize yourself as healthy and well.

* *Try energy healing on yourself to prevent or heal illness or injury.*

Day 67: Herbs and the Body

Herbs have numerous effects on the body. So great, in fact, that many cultures believe that some herbs are a representation of Spirit. For example, in India, a type of basil called the tulsi plant is recognized as the Divine. All over the world herbs are taken into the body through food; through smoke in the air; through poultices on the skin; and through potions, tinctures, and teas. The act of drinking a cup of tea can be spiritual, as it gives you time to commune with the Divine and share a special moment. Here is a tea leaf reading exercise that you can do using loose leaves of your favorite black, green, or herbal tea.

Procure a teacup with a rounded bottom and a saucer. Prepare the loose leaf tea in the cup and allow the leaves to float freely. Sip carefully, or use a strainer straw to drink your tea while contemplating Spirit or a question in your life that you would like answered by Spirit. When almost all of the tea is gone and only the leaves remain with a bit of liquid in the bottom of the cup, swirl the cup around three times clockwise and then overturn it upon the saucer. The clumps of leaves in the bottom of the cup can be imagined into shapes, in the same way you might see shapes in clouds in the sky. The ones at the bottom of the cup are personality traits and the past, while those farther toward the rim represent the future.

* Share a cup of tea with Spirit.

Day 68: Running

······························

There's something primal about going for a run as a source of exercise. Children run naturally and carefree on the playground, or even to get from one place to another. Adults run to bring the athleticism of a sport to new levels, or as a means to meditate and get away from it all. It may be that running down prey was the original biological imperative of humans who were gifted with the ability to sweat and run long distances in packs. Today, running can be a way to escape the cage of modernity. Get out there and sweat, and find if it connects you with the source of Spirit as it does for me.

If you're new to running, run as slowly as you possibly can while still calling it running. That is, both feet should be off the ground between strides. The point of this exercise is to get in the zone and connect with Spirit, not to wear yourself out. Run for thirty seconds and then walk for thirty seconds. Continue this for about twenty minutes. If you're an experienced runner, let yourself loose on a local trail. Imagine that every footfall is a prayer.

* *Connect with Spirit through the act of going for a run.*

Day 69: Yoga

....

Yoga is a spiritual discipline that aims to transform the body and the mind. Like martial arts, yoga is such a large field that there is too much in the world of yoga to be written here. In the Western world, yoga is often used as a series of poses aligned with breathing in order to connect with Spirit. To learn more about yoga, you can get a book from your local library or search for online videos. However, today I want to give you a taste of what posing with your body can do for your connection with Spirit. Earlier I wrote about how mudras are used as "prayer hands" across the world. Kneeling is another pose that is used by many spiritual disciplines.

In yoga, a salutation to the sun is performed at sunrise. There are many versions of the sun salutation that have a dozen steps or more. However, for an idea of what this practice is like, try pausing to pose and have a moment with Spirit after you roll out of bed instead of heading directly to the shower or hitting the snooze button. Stand with your hands together as prayer hands over your heart, facing the sun if possible, and exhale deeply. Stretch your hands over your head, still pressed together, and inhale. Bend down to touch your toes, if you can, while inhaling, and then carefully sink to your knees while you exhale. After this brief moment of stretching and honoring the sun, go about your day as normal.

* Salute the sun with spiritual poses. Consider learning more about yoga if you are drawn to do so.

Day 70: Chakras
....

Chakras are centers of spiritual energy within your body. You've already worked with several such energy vortexes. For example, you built energy with the vortexes that are in the palms of each hand by rubbing them together. Another more centralized chakra you've worked with so far is the third eye, located on the forehead between the eyebrows. There are chakras or energy vortexes throughout your body. For simplicity, in the beginning it is easier to focus on a single line of chakras that run along your spine. Some people see them as a colorful rainbow, starting with a red ball of light at the bottom and ascending to a violet ball of light at the top. However, the following exercise is meant to allow you to explore your own feeling about chakras, so it's okay if they don't match others' preconceived notions.

Seat yourself and meditate. First think about your root chakra, at the very base of your spine. This is the seat of energy that Spirit gave you for self-preservation. Next, turn your attention to the second chakra, located at your genitals, the splenic chakra. This is the gift from Spirit of creativity and re-generation. The third is the solar plexus chakra, in your midsection, and is the location of psychic energy that you exchange with others. Your heart chakra is another chakra, the source of love. Your throat chakra is the gift of self-expression. You're already familiar with the third eye chakra, which is one of these seven basic chakras. The final one is the crown chakra, sitting at the top of your head, which represents your own divinity and connection with Spirit.

* *Get in touch with a few of your chakras.*

Day 71: Clothing and Jewelry

There have been many approaches to honoring Spirit with clothing and jewelry. Some spiritual people wear nothing at all during worship, while others wear elaborate robes. Necklaces can be worn to represent eternal life and feminine divinity. Wearing gold honors the sun, while wearing silver honors the moon. Wearing the jewelry of a deceased loved one can be a way to invite that ancestral spirit into your life for communication.

The color of your clothes can also be important. Many spiritual traditions choose white as the color of spiritual garb. I tend to wear white, since a spiritual teacher from the Vodou and Ifa traditions encouraged me to do so for Spirit. However, red can symbolize spiritual passion and fire. Orange can symbolize spiritual energy and masculinity. Yellow is spiritual intelligence and the element of air. Green is the element of earth and abundance from Spirit. Blue is healing and the element of water. Purple is feminine energy and can also be seen as a spiritual color.

You don't have to run out and buy a monk's wardrobe. Take a look at what you already own and think about how you can dress yourself to be mindful of Spirit. Which colors do you choose to wear, and how do they affect your spiritual energy? Do you have any jewelry that is special or meaningful to you?

* *Dress yourself in a meaningful way in order to connect with Spirit. When dressing yourself, do so mindfully and with gratitude to Spirit for the protection your clothes provide.*

Day 72: Ritual Bathing and Ablution

One should be clean and purified before coming into the presence of Spirit. So go the instructions of multiple religions. What is the purpose of this purity? The answers are many and varied, but there are two common grounds for this. Firstly, it is a sign of respect to the Divine to come before Spirit with a clean body, and a symbolically clean mind and heart. Secondly, think of it as preparing yourself as a blank slate upon which Spirit can paint whatever creation is needed for you and your life. When should ritual bathing or ablution (cleansing) be done? Before any official forms of worship in which you approach Spirit. You can also perform these acts anytime you feel a need to reboot or to start over.

If you have plenty of time, an herbal bath is a perfect way to cleanse yourself. Add salt or herbs like rosemary, hyssop, or lavender. If white flowers bloom near your home, consider adding some floating blossoms to the bathwater for a beautiful symbol of purification. If you don't have time to take a full bath before saying prayers or meditating, simply wash your hands, feet, and face. Pure water is all that is needed, but you can also prepare a small bowl of herbed water and splash yourself with the mixture as needed.

* *Cleanse yourself before spiritual activities today.*

Day 73: Sage Smudging

Sage smudging, or burning a bundle of white sage, is another way to cleanse the body. This is best used when you feel that some negativity is affecting your connection with Spirit. However, you can use sage smudging anytime, even on a daily basis if you like. You can smudge your spouse or kids at the door as they enter while they talk about their day. You can smudge yourself before worship as a symbolic cleansing. Or, you can simply leave a burning bundle of sage in your sacred space while you meditate or perform other spiritual activities.

To perform sage smudging, procure a bundle of dried white sage. Sage bundles are sold online or in metaphysical bookstores. Conversely, you can tie your own using all-natural string such as cotton. Light the bundle with the flame of a lighter or match and allow it to burn brightly for a few seconds, then blow it out and let it smolder. There should be no more flame but plenty of smoke. You can smudge yourself by waving the smoke over your body with a hand or feather. You can smudge another in this way, or by simply passing the whole bundle of sage over his or her body. If you'd like to keep the bundle burning, use a charcoal incense burner to keep the sage lit, as it will usually go out if left to its own devices.

* *Procure a bundle of sage to try sage smudging.*

Day 74: Seeing the Divine in Your Body

For those of us with self-esteem issues, it can be difficult to see the Divine in our own bodies. When you look in the mirror, it may be easy to see imperfections instead of the perfect creation of Spirit, or even somebody who looks like the Divine's own image. However, embarrassment is no excuse to ignore or reject the divinity in your own body. In fact, refusing to love your body and to use it to connect with Spirit can seriously damage your relationship with Spirit in the long run. If you find that you hate yourself or feel hopeless, you should reach out for help from a professional counselor or therapist to work through your self-esteem or body issues. However, if you just need a little help remembering your divine self, try this exercise.

Prepare yourself for this act of worship with a ritual bath or ablution. This is a perfect opportunity to be clean and appealing to yourself and to Spirit. Prepare an offering to your body such as a cup of herbal tea or a healthy snack that you enjoy, like fresh berries. I'll let you cheat and consider chocolate healthy, if you want. Seat yourself in front of a mirror to gaze upon your visage. You can choose the details, whether you want to be naked by candlelight or wearing your finest clothing. Look at your eyes, your aura, and any parts of your body that have shown growth, change, or scars. Try to see yourself as a child of Spirit.

* Meditate in front of a mirror, seeing yourself
  as divine in your own current body.

Part Three

*

Mind

Day 75: Quiet, Receptive Meditation

Thus far you've been given several opportunities for meditation while performing an activity, thinking about a specific topic, or contemplating a particular image. But the most challenging form of meditation is also the simplest. During quiet and receptive meditation, the goal is to think of nothing at all, not even your breathing or your heartbeat. It's difficult for beginners, but it is very valuable for connecting with Spirit. The quiet and receptive mind is the true blank slate, the purified mind to go with a purified body, upon which Spirit can paint any creation.

Start by choosing a time to meditate. If you're new at this type of meditation, start with a very short time span, such as five or ten minutes. If you're unsuccessful, don't be afraid to shorten it. I think my first successful session was thirty seconds. Clear the room of any distractions and prevent any disruptions. Seat yourself and clear your mind. As any thoughts intrude into your head, observe them as if somebody else were thinking those things and let them float away from your consciousness without taking hold of them. Try practicing this form of meditation daily, gradually lengthening the amount of time until you can manage about twenty minutes or more.

* *Practice clearing your mind.*

Day 76: Attitude of Gratitude
....

The more you give thanks, the more you get. Imagine an ungrateful child. His or her parents will be unlikely to reward spiteful behavior when receiving gifts. Spirit may act similarly toward those who do not show regular gratitude. An alternative explanation is that those who are more thankful for the small things in life truly expand their capacity for joy. Treasuring the small things in life makes each small moment a treasure. Developing your attitude of gratitude depends on how you tend to go through life right now. Be honest with yourself. Do you have a pragmatic or pessimistic temperament? Are you generally upbeat and an optimist?

If you find yourself feeling openly ungrateful for things that happen to you, start by cutting down on the negative phrases you think. Everybody gets grouchy when they miss the bus, for example, but you can strive to find the good in every situation, such as good conversation, good weather, or good health. Add positive statements of thanks to Spirit in your life. When something lucky happens to you, say a quick thank-you to Spirit. If you get the opportunity to eat some wonderful food, meet a terrific new friend, or find a penny on the ground, don't forget to say thanks.

* *Find reasons to be thankful today and
  write down these blessings from Spirit.*

Day 77: The Search for Meaning

One use for spirituality is to aid in the search for meaning in life. This search looks different for different people. Some people may be satisfied with simply finding a purpose for their own lives, a drive and a passion that gets them out of bed each morning. Other people, not satisfied with this, may wish to know greater mysteries about the purpose for humanity or society or the universe in general. There are many ways to search for meaning, and we'll explore some of them in the following days. But for now, as the author Douglas Adams would have it, you must know your question before you begin seeking your answers.

Today, think about the search for meaning you yearn for in your own life. Are you a simple person seeking happiness and a way to serve Spirit? Do you feel that humanity in general has a huge role to play in universal events? Do you feel that Spirit has a plan, and that you are a part of that plan? Do you believe in destiny? Do you believe in free will? Write down your answers to these questions and freely write your own thoughts about the meaning of your life. How will you discover this meaning? Do you think the process is more about the journey than the destination?

* *What sort of grand design or purpose do you think the universe holds? What is your place in it? Is anyone meant to know the real answers? Why or why not?*

Day 78: Finding Meaning through Reading Scriptures

Many spiritual traditions have holy books in which they find keys to life. These scriptures may come in the form of parables and stories about life or history. They may come in the form of proverbs or sayings that seem to ring true. Myths that are not strictly scriptures may also be observed to hold truths that can only be told in story form. You may already know of scriptures that you hold dear. You can also search your local library for scriptures and myths from many different faiths. It can be heartening to see how similar the messages are in different cultures.

How does one find meaning through reading scriptures? Choosing one source of scripture, read it front to back, trying to read for comprehension. Take notes and highlight if you wish. Look up any historical references or words that you don't know. Try to gain context not only from other parts of the scripture but also in your own life. Write down meaningful quotes and look back on them later. When you are finished, you can search for more scripture or scriptural analysis from the same culture, or move on to different myths or scriptures if you are drawn to them.

* *Explore scripture from one of the world's many religions.*

Day 79: Intuition

....

Intuition is another way of knowing things. Your intuitive sense is often the first sense that you have about something. For example, an intuitive flash might tell you whether a person you meet is a good person or a bad person. This intuition is attributed to Spirit. Another form of intuition is a sense of being sure about something. For example, knowing that a person you love is somebody you want to marry and be with for the rest of your life is a form of intuition. This is also often attributed to Spirit. Getting to know your intuition can be an exciting way to connect with Spirit. Not only can it lend a psychic sense to your life decisions, but intuition can be a way to open communication pathways between you and Spirit that are not necessarily verbal, but nonetheless practical.

Several of the techniques you've learned so far can be used to enhance your intuition. Sitting in quiet and receptive meditation is one way to receive intuitive flashes or a sense of knowing. You can add other practices such as gazing into a bowl of water or looking into a candle flame, similarly to how you explored each of the elements. Whenever you receive a sense of intuition, write down your perceptions so you can look back on them later.

* *Encourage your own intuition and write down your perceptions.*

Day 80: Astral Travel

....

Astral travel is the name given to the concept of traveling with your mind to the astral plane. The astral plane is a world entirely of Spirit that you can access in your mind. If you've ever daydreamed about a work of art you were about to make or something you were hoping to build, you were hard at work on the astral plane. It can be a heavenly place or a surreal world of dreams. It can be your own personal paradise or "happy place." On the astral plane, you can build those castles in the sky that can become reality on the earthly plane. For example, if you want to buy a new house or car, first visualize it on the astral plane. Then, work with Spirit to make it a reality.

To travel to the astral plane, try sitting down to meditate and work hard to visualize the very room in which you live. Imagine that there is a door in the floor. Go to the door and walk through it into your own astral headquarters. It can be an indoor place or an outdoor space. Furnish it with whatever you like that makes you feel comfortable and safe. If you see any creatures in your astral space, feel free to tell them to leave if you want. There can be numerous paths or doors out of your astral headquarters. Explore them during meditation to see more of the astral world.

* Practice visualization and astral travel. Create a space all
   your own on the astral plane.

Day 81: Remote Viewing

Remote viewing, also sometimes called ethereal travel, is the name for meditative virtual "travel" that takes place in the terrestrial world. It's not quite as exciting as walking through walls and spying on people. However, remote viewing has been used by spiritual people throughout time to try to become closer to a person or sacred space who is out of physical reach. For today's exercise, find a partner who is far away from you who is willing to try remote viewing. It could be a friend in another city or a family member in another state. The following exercise makes use of remote viewing and dreaming to create a spiritual connection between the two of you.

As you lie down in bed, visualize your spirit body floating out of your physical body. Don't worry, there's an unbreakable umbilical cord tying your spirit to your body so that you can always get back. It expands as you float through the roof. Travel to your partner, flying over roads and street signs. If you fall asleep during the journey, don't worry. That's part of the plan. When you wake up, write down anything you remember about the dream. Call your partner and find out if your dreams had any similarities or if your partner sensed your presence.

* Practice visualization and remote viewing. Meet up with a friend.

Day 82: Who Are You?

....

Spirituality and identity go hand in hand. Many people find a deep sense of personal identity through the traditions and culture of a chosen spiritual practice. In turn, personality weaves back into spirituality. Not every personality fits a particular religion, and that's okay. In fact, you need not even identify with any particular religion in order to have a spiritual identity. Nevertheless, you will have to explore who you are, what you believe, and what you value in order to dig deeper into your connection with Spirit.

In several activities in the coming days, we'll take a look at some of the ways to explore spiritual identity. But for today, think about your identity so far. Write down some labels or roles that describe you. In many spiritual traditions, it is thought that the body and all tangible and temporal concerns are separate from the soul. If this were true, what parts of your identity do you think remain in your soul? What are the deepest and most spiritual aspects of your identity? Do you think that your identity will change after your death? Is this comforting or frightening to you? Is this something that spirituality can help you understand on some level?

* Ponder your roles and labels in life. What is your true identity?

Day 83: Exploring Your Roots

Your life made you the person you are today, and your past can dictate your future relationship with Spirit. Looking back to your roots can be one way to understand your identity. Exploring your roots can mean looking back for generations. But today, I'd like you to think about your childhood and where you've come from in this lifetime. At every point in your life you've made choices that made you feel either more or less connected to Spirit. Some of those choices were irreversible, but others can be re-evaluated today.

What was the religious or spiritual background of your family? Did generations prior to your birth influence religious or spiritual identity in your family? Are there any still-living family members you can call in order to hear more about your personal history? Which traditions from your childhood bring you memories of connecting with Spirit? Do you still do these things, or would you like to begin doing them again in your life? For example, I sang as a child and it made me feel closer to Spirit. As an adult, I have to search for excuses to make music.

> * Which traditions from your childhood roots can
>   you revive in your life to fill it with Spirit? Are
>   there any family members you can reconnect with
>   to learn more about your family's spiritual history?

Day 84: Your Ancestry

....

To some, ancestry is vital to spirituality. Culture, family heritage, and a shared community can bring people of like mind and backgrounds together. Honoring ancestors is an important part of spirituality to many, since their love and support brought us all to life as we live it today. To other people, ancestry may not matter as much in the everyday practice of spirituality. There are no racial borders that prevent people from connecting with new faiths or with the source of Spirit. Nevertheless, exploring your own ancestry can help you appreciate your ancestors and perhaps even lead you to a fresh exploration of an old spiritual path.

Write down as many ancestors' names as you can remember. If you have access to more, look them up and read them aloud to honor your ancestors. Find out if there's any evidence that your ancestors practiced a particular faith. How do you feel about that particular faith tradition now? Are there any traditions that were celebrated or foods that were eaten by your ancestors that might make you feel more connected to Spirit today? Are there any particular racial or cultural connections with kindred people that draw you toward fellowship?

* Explore your ancestral roots and discover the names and
  traditions that form your past.

Day 85: Your Nationality
....

Nationality can also be a deep source of spiritual culture. Even the idea of where spirituality fits into life varies by country or even regions within a country. If you identify with a nationality, this can be a jumping-off point to explore spirituality from a specific cultural perspective. It can also be inspiration for you to travel and visit sacred spaces to get closer to the nationalities of your ancestors. Some friends of mine find themselves inexplicably drawn to ancient cultures in countries like Ireland or Scotland, even though they are unaware of any historical tie to them. If you find yourself called to research a place, go ahead and do it.

List a few nations that may be significant to you within your lifetime or to your ancestors. Are there any cultural practices that you feel comfortable drawing into your spirituality? For example, there could be clothing you could wear or foods you can eat associated with those nationalities and their cultural spiritual traditions. Are there any sacred spaces in your nations of origin? Which ones might you like to visit someday and why? Are there any cultural attitudes associated with those nationalities that might enhance your spiritual experience?

* *Research nationalities in your ancestral past, in your past in this lifetime, or even a distant land to which you feel drawn. Which national spiritual ideas or traditions might enhance your practice?*

Day 86: Numerology

....

Numerology is the study of numbers to discover truths and tell fortunes. Your expression number, for example, is the total of the numbers in your full name assigned through Pythagorean Numerology. Your Life Path number is determined from your birth date. Let's figure out your Life Path number to see your spiritual destiny. Start with the numbers that make up your birth date. Mine are June (6) 4, 1981. Now, add up each of the digits. For me, this master number is 29. Then, keep adding the digits in the sum until you get down to one digit. I have to add twice to get first 11 and then 2. Here are the Life Path descriptions for each final number.

1. You're an individual, likely to blaze your own spiritual trail.

2. For you, spirituality is about connection and relationships. Seek those in your future.

3. Spirituality is about the creative abundant force for you. Find ways to create.

4. Stability and tradition are important in your spirituality, so seek out a strong foundation.

5. You like things to change and be exciting. Seek out novel approaches.

6. Growth and progress are important. Seek spiritual leadership, even if just in your family.

7. The mysterious draws you. Seek spiritual mysteries.

8. You will grow in your own spiritual power, but you will find a need to seek sacrifices.

9. This is a lucky spiritual number, and represents a joy and ecstasy found in faith.

* *Calculate your Life Path number.*

Day 87: Creative Expression

Creative expression is thought to come from Spirit and also to be the most sincere form of offering and obedience to Spirit. When you allow your mind to get into the creative flow of things, you will be able to experience and express spiritual concepts. You don't have to be an amazing artist or a naturally creative mind. The process of creating is more important than the results. Just as a mother appreciates a gift made for her by a child, the Divine will flourish in your life from your creative pursuits.

If you already do creative things, think about how you can integrate your spirituality into your work. For example, if you like to knit, look into making prayer shawls or intarsia designs (using colors to create the pattern) of spiritual symbols. Over the next few days, you'll have a chance to try some creative activities. For now, however, brainstorm some creative outlets in your life. If you don't have any, think back to your childhood and rekindle a love of creativity that you may have had then. For many people, this may be an instrument you used to play. Try to carve out time for creative pursuits in your life. This time can be a relaxing meditation for you.

* *Make time for a creative outlet in your life.*

Day 88: Simile Poetry

Much about Spirit is difficult to comprehend or communicate. By using similes with the words "as" or "like," we can express Spirit in forms that we recognize in everyday life. I'm going to teach you a form of poetry that you can use every day as a meditative exercise. First, think of an object. Then, try it out in a poem. This exercise often works best for me when I pick the first object that comes to mind and try to relate it to myself in a personal way. However, if you like, you can strive to pick something that relates more closely to your spirituality. Either way, practicing this poetry form every day can help you express the inexpressible just a little bit better.

Use this form poem given below. There's an example that follows with a random object. Again, feel free to pick your own, and to use a new one each day.

I am as a _____.
(Descriptors) _____, _____, _____.
My greatest hope is _____.
My greatest fear is _____.

Example:
I am as a house.
Strong, confined, familiar.
My greatest hope is to provide shelter to my family.
My greatest fear is that I will never feel at home.

* *Write a poem using similes and a random object.*

Day 89: Song
....

Music is one way to express the inexpressible. I once had a marvelous experience in a synagogue. I was visiting for a service and was quite unfamiliar with the tradition. There were many customs I didn't understand, but I attempted to respectfully follow along. Then, the cantor (who directs the music for the Shabbat ceremony) began to sing a soulful song. It was a sad tune, filled with minor chords, and tears streamed down his face. The audience swayed gently to his beautiful singing voice, and I found myself overcome with joy and sadness all at once. Though I didn't know the language of the lyrics, I was emotionally and spiritually moved by the experience.

Listening to moving music may be one way that you can connect with Spirit. Swapping out your usual playlist with something that has moved you in the past in a deeper way can change your attitude over time. You can also create your own music. Think about some inexpressible joy in your life that made you feel close to Spirit. Perhaps the birth of a child or a first kiss shared with a new love. Hum, play an instrument, or sing to express that same feeling through song. You can even drum on a table to express yourself.

* *Express an intimate spiritual moment through song.*

Day 90: Drawing

....

Drawing can be used to capture a moment. What makes it more appropriate than a photograph, in a spiritual context, is that the drawing also contains a part of yourself. In addition, a drawing helps capture what you saw that was most important about the image. In this way, even a quick sketch can help you capture spiritual moments. Consider using drawing in place of journaling when appropriate, especially when recording something visual like an aura or a dream.

Here's my favorite drawing exercise. Go out in nature and find something that is going to change over time, like the bud of a plant that will soon burst into a flower. Draw the plant as it is, making sure to enjoy the present moment. Then, over the following weeks, draw that same thing again, noticing its changes. Another exercise is to practice drawing your aura. For this I like to use colored pencils. Keep a sketchbook handy so that you can use it when you want to turn to it for spiritual purposes. Consider keeping your sketchbook at your bedside, along with your colored pencils or other tools, in order to capture the landscapes and symbols of your dreams as soon as you awake.

* *Practice drawing as a tool to capture spiritual moments.*

Day 91: Painting

....

The act of painting can be meditative. Mixing colors until you find the one that makes your heart sing can be exciting. You don't have to be an expert painter or to have plenty of supplies to bring painting into your spiritual life. For today's exercise, you can pick up a simple watercolor paint set from a craft store or the children's section of a department store. Choose a poem or a bit of prose that is spiritually meaningful to you. Then, grab a piece of paper for each line of the poem. Write down the poem line by line, one for each sheet of paper.

Now is your chance to paint. For each line of the poem or bit of prose, sit for a bit and think about what it spiritually means to you. Mix water and colors and let yourself paint freely. You may find yourself seeing visions in your mind's eye of what to paint. You may find that symbols and images appear, or that you are simply painting abstractions that represent your feelings. Either way is fine. When you are finished, you can bind your paintings in a book to share with someone, or you can keep it to yourself for inspiration when you feel that you need it.

* Procure watercolor paints for a simple painting,
  or use other paints if you already have them.

Day 92: Gardening

....

Gardening can be a spiritual act, because you are helping to nurture the creation of Spirit. You can create a garden in your yard, in a shared community garden, or in a windowsill. If you tend to have a black thumb like me, you may wish to try making a rock garden. Building a rock garden can be sort of like playing a game of elven chess, as you've done before. When creating any garden, think about how the space will be when you are done so that you can use it for meditation. Also, think about how the process of creating the garden is like painting or any other form of self-expression. The garden is both an offering to Spirit and a tool for furthering your spiritual connection.

Decide what sort of garden is right for your practical lifestyle and climate. You may wish to sketch out your plan for a garden beforehand. Then, you can create a shopping list if needed. Even if you are going to wing it with a rock garden, the act of sketching out your garden can transform this into a devotional act. Think before you create. In this way, you are essentially creating your garden on the astral plane before you manifest it on the physical plane. Just as you carefully build your garden and help it grow, you can bring forth greater spiritual joys in your own life.

* *Plan and execute a spiritual garden.*

Day 93: Storytelling

....

The way that spiritual lessons are passed down through generations is often by good old-fashioned storytelling. I've encouraged you to be the recipient of storytelling by suggesting you ask your relatives about your ancestors. Hearing those stories used to be an important part of daily entertainment for people before electronics took over our evenings. Now, there may not be very many opportunities for such stories unless you ask for them. Don't let those memories forever be lost to the sands of time. Stories can also hold spiritual truths in the form of myths or parables. Think of your favorite stories from childhood. What lessons did they hold? Are any of them surprising? Are some of them truer than others now that you have grown and understand more about life?

Today's mission is to become the storyteller. Ideally, you would find a young person in your life and share a story that seems to have a true message hidden within it. If you don't have a young person at the ready, consider writing your story. If you're brave, you can post it online and share it with the world. If you prefer, you can save it in a memory box for some young person yet to come into your life.

* *Tell a story that holds a spiritual truth.*

Day 94: Haiku

....

A haiku is a poem form that originated in Japan. The first line of a haiku is five syllables. The second like of a haiku is seven syllables. The third line is five syllables. This makes the haiku a straightforward guide to poetry. Another simple trick about haikus is that they are usually basic observations and not filled with metaphor and complex themes the way other prose can be. The words within a haiku can still be meaningful. A haiku can be quickly written each day based on observations in nature or in your own life. Think of the poem's limitations as helping you prune and form your thoughts to the most basic shape.

Here is an example of a haiku:

Meditation time.
Small child snoring in my lap.
Sunlight in windows.

Try writing a daily haiku capturing your spiritual moments in time. As the seasons change, you may find that the topics in your poems change as well, and that's perfect. The tool of the haiku can hone both your observation skills and your ability to express yourself with small spiritual nuances. It only takes a few minutes out of your day, but can add interest and art to your life.

* *Write a haiku.*

Day 95: Exploring Mythology Themes

Myths are marvelous stories. They teach us lessons about spirituality in a way that is engaging and illustrative. Most interesting of all, some myths have similarities across time and cultures. If you want to explore mythology, you can essentially benefit by choosing whatever mythology you wish. You might choose myths associated with your ancestral culture or your current nationality. You might simply choose myths that are familiar, such as Greek and Roman mythology. Mix up the myths if you like and search for interesting similarities and differences.

Visit your local library or search online to find mythology that appeals to you. Read through the myths, making note when you have an emotional reaction, or are nodding your head acknowledging a spiritual lesson. In mythology, the characters can interact in a way that make us feel good, such as when somebody making bad choices gets his or her comeuppance. Seeing justice in mythology can help us find justice in the world. The same goes for compassion and other values. Make mythology a regular topic on your reading list, and you'll enrich your spiritual world. Mythology also gives you a spiritual language with a cast of characters that can show up in your dreams and meditations.

* Pick a culture's mythology and begin to read it.

Day 96: Listening to Music

You've appreciated music so far by dancing and by making your own music. However, listening to music can also be a way to get in touch with Spirit. In some cultures, listening to drumming is used as a way to drift into a trance or to go on a spirit journey on the astral plane. A steady, fast drumbeat—for example, 250 beats per minute—can bring the listener to an altered state. A slower drumbeat, closer to your heartbeat, can help the listener meditate or even fall asleep.

Meditate today using some of your favorite music. Even though relaxing soft tones are often used for meditation, consider experimenting with music that has a heavy and steady drumbeat. Whatever music you choose, sit and close your eyes to focus only on the music for the duration of your meditation. Some people may see lights and colors in the mind's eye while listening to music. Be observant and allow your mind to register what you see and feel. When you are finished meditating, write down any visions or emotions that came to you while listening to the music.

* *Meditate while listening to music.*

Day 97: Appreciating Art

Some myth tellers didn't do so with the written word. Instead, they told their stories and shared their emotions via painting, dancing, sculpting, or other spiritual activities. Different people are inspired by different forms of art, and that's okay. I tend to be wowed by watching skilled dancers tell stories with their bodies, but am often underwhelmed by trips to art museums. However, if I didn't make an excuse to go and appreciate art by paying to see a dance show, I would feel bereft.

Today, make an effort to appreciate good art made in your favorite medium. You might choose to buy tickets to see a play, a dance, or a concert. You might choose to go to a local art museum. Or, you might choose to go and appreciate public art in your own local area. As you do, imagine that each piece of art was made as an offering to Spirit. What is the lesson in the work of art? Are there any symbols or characters that you can add to your mental dictionary when connecting with Spirit in dreams or meditations? Pay attention to your dreams, too, after appreciating good art.

* *Carve out time and resources in your life to appreciate good art.*

Day 98: Ways of Knowing

Spirit gave us several ways of knowing things in this world. The first way of knowing is through observation and experience. Through this avenue, science has sprung into the modern world and helped us in many ways. There's no reason that spiritual people cannot get along with science. However, experimental observations and conclusions aren't the only way to get to know the world around you. Intuition is another way of knowing. Your intuitive sense comes through in dreams, during meditation, or any time that your alpha brain waves are switched on. Intuition can tell you when a phone call that is coming through is important, or when a person in your life can lead to a deeper relationship.

Allow yourself to use all forms of knowing when exploring the world of Spirit. As you come across new spiritual ideas in your reading, continuously consult your critical mind. Is this something that you can know through evidence by following a specific process? Or, is this something you can only know in your heart, like whether or not you're in love? Today, be observant as you go through your day, noticing how you come to understand things. Accept all ways of knowing, but consciously decide which one you are choosing to use.

* *Watch how you gather and use information in your life. Are you
  an intuitive person, or of a mind to search for facts? Consciously
  choose to try different ways of knowing.*

Day 99: Things That Can't Be Put into Words

So, those strange emotions that you might feel while listening to music or enjoying a beautiful form of art…what do they mean? Many spiritual truths cannot be put into words, even in stories and myths. Instead, these are the feelings that people seek when they go to religious services and raise energy, choose to convert to a new religion, or carry out religious observances. We call these spiritual moments or truths, mysteries. They are universal mysteries that are never meant to be solved, but can be known in an experiential sense.

Many spiritual traditions teach the mysteries as a process of conversion, baptism, or initiation. These ceremonies are like divine plays, theatrics that have worked for many people to send them on an inner spiritual journey to discover the mysteries. Others choose to work out the mysteries on their own, through study of scripture or sincere worship. You don't have to choose a method now, and even if you do, your methods may change over your lifetime. However, what you should do is write about those moments that draw you to spirituality, toward the mysteries.

* *Write in your journal about moments in time when you felt close to spiritual mysteries that couldn't be put into words. How can you seek more of those?*

Day 100: Peak Experiences

Peak experiences are another thing that seekers are often trying to find. A peak spiritual experience might be ecstasy reached when in communion with Spirit. Some people regularly find these peak experiences by worshipping in a way that includes dancing, singing, and other energy-raising techniques. Others have a rare but life-changing peak experience, such as a religious conversion or initiation, which serves as a guidepost for the rest of the days in this lifetime. Seeking peak experiences can be tough and can turn people into religious tourists. Seekers might find themselves trying many spiritual practices and thinking "Nah, that's not it," and quitting before putting in the inner work necessary to have the spiritual experience.

Today, meditate upon and write about your peak experiences in life. These could have included a marriage day, the birth of a child, or a near-death experience. As you meditate, think about what it was that brought you to those experiences. Think of how Spirit may have been involved with bringing those experiences into being. How can you encourage Spirit to bring more of those experiences into your life? What sort of information, relationships, or places can you seek out to try to bring this about?

* *Meditate upon the peak experiences in your life and think about how more could be brought to you by Spirit.*

Day 101: Thinking about Your Life's Purpose

....

Finding purpose in the universe is one thing, but finding purpose in one's own life is quite another. Both could be necessary for your connection with Spirit. Without feeling a sense of purpose in your life, your motivation for seeking Spirit may dwindle over the years. Worse still, you might feel as though you don't deserve Spirit, or that Spirit has abandoned you. If you find yourself feeling completely hopeless, it's important that you reach out for counseling. It could be that you are suffering from depression, from which a therapist and a doctor's treatment might provide respite. That said, a little mid-life crisis every now and again is pretty normal.

When you think about your life's purpose today, go ahead and think about it in layers. Your life's purpose could be as simple as getting out of bed to feed your dog and take her for a walk. Your life's purpose could be as complex as playing a huge role in a celestial dance that Spirit has dreamed up for you. Your life may have many purposes, big and small, that you have to unwrap slowly throughout your entire life. Write down a few of the reasons that you get out of bed in the morning. Think of a few more while you're at it.

* *Write down some of your life's purposes.*

Day 102: Looking for Patterns

....

Finding patterns in life is often thought to be the product of divine intervention. Intuition coming from Spirit may guide the moment when you link two unrelated events and give them meaning. As one of my spiritual teachers always told me, "There ain't no coincidences!" If you think of coincidences as being messages from Spirit, your whole life will suddenly fill with magic and mystery. Following those coincidences to discover what the message might be is part of the fun and the fulfillment.

For example, angel numbers are one coincidence that many people see. When you keep seeing a number over and over again, this number is said to be an "angel number." It may happen, for example, if you look at the clock and it says 3:33 p.m. and then you visit a business with the street number "33," and later are third in line to get your coffee at the café. Today, keep track of the coincidences in your life, whether they are numerical or of some other kind. To what related happenings might those coincidences be drawing your attention? Is there a message inside the coincidences themselves, or do these seem to just be a heads-up from Spirit?

* Look for patterns and coincidences in your life.

Day 103: Astrology
....

In astrology, the dance of the stars above is said to be a pattern that mimics the dance of life here on earth. In some ancient cultures, an astrologer was present at some births. Today, one can still enjoy getting a natal chart drawn up online or by a local astrologer. Natal charts are a snapshot of the sky at the time of one's birth. For daily spiritual guidance, some people choose to use horoscopes or an astrological calendar in order to plan their days. Astrological calendars can be found online if you search for the current month or by purchasing an astrological datebook to guide yourself through the year.

For a simple way to use astrology, you can either read prewritten horoscopes, or you can look in an astrological datebook for good signs. For beginners, it can be helpful to look at the aspects. The more triangles (trines) and asterisks (sextiles) you see, the more harmonious the planets are on that particular day. This can be helpful to all your spiritual pursuits. The more squares you see, which are simply called "squares," the more trouble and strife may occur. The other symbols can be a mixed bag, so start out with just the extremes for now. See if planets can be blamed for bad days in your life.

* *Observe an astrological calendar for aspects, or read your*
  horoscope today.

Day 104: Pendulum Dowsing

Pendulum dowsing is a simple intuitive tool that is used to enhance your own intuition. The idea is that you can use a small plumb bob, which is held like a pendulum beneath your hand, to exaggerate your hand movement. You can ask your pendulum a question and it will answer with swinging movements. Of course, it is your hand moving the pendulum. Spirit is unlikely to throw it around and make it move on its own. But it will help you get at your own subconscious cues.

To make a pendulum, grab a length of string or yarn and a ring. It can be a ring that you wear, or one that is lying around in a jewelry box, or even one borrowed from a friend. Hold the other end of the string between your thumb and forefinger, then catch the string with your pinkie finger so that the ring swings freely under your pinkie finger. Ask your pendulum "show me yes" and watch the movement. Ask it "show me no" and then watch for a different movement. It may swing back and forth, circle clockwise or counterclockwise, or stand completely still. Then, you can try asking it a yes-or-no question and waiting for the answer.

* *Make and use a simple pendulum.*

Day 105: Following Rules

....

One big criticism of several world religions is that there seem to be a whole lot of rules. This attitude can turn people away from religion, toward other spiritual pursuits. However, following rules does serve a human purpose. So, why do people like to follow all those rules? For several reasons. Sometimes, it is to grow closer to Spirit. Each time a chance to follow or not follow a rule comes up, it is an opportunity to remember Spirit and to show faith in the form of obedience. Another reason is that people may think that some of the rules are a good idea.

We all have some general rules in life that we know we should be following, but typically don't. We should eat healthy. We should avoid drinking too much alcohol. We should be regularly exercising. But these can be hard rules to follow. We should remember to call Mom, donate money to charity, and treat people kindly, instead of losing our temper. Today, choose a rule, make a resolution to follow it, and stick to it.

* *Rules are an important part of some spiritual practices. Pick a rule that is good for you and stick with it, remembering Spirit each time that rule is called into question.*

Day 106: Thinking about Ethics

Ethics are systems of behaviors within a community that are deemed right or wrong. An ethical person always conducts himself or herself with the right behavior. But who decides which behaviors are right and wrong? Usually, a person's culture, society, community, and family decide what's right and wrong and teaches the person. In many cases, scriptures have instructions about right and wrong. Many times an individual has to decide for herself or himself which behavior is right or wrong, and hope that other people agree.

Today, think about the ethics that govern your own life choices. Who told you what was right and wrong? Do these ideas of right and wrong conform to what you truly feel inside? Are there any ethical behaviors that you have that others think are wrong, or even silly? You can even write down your own code of ethics for walking through life. Write down what it is to ethically deal with others. How do you know when you are behaving ethically? What should you do when you behave unethically? Is there any way that Spirit can help guide your ethics or help you learn when ethical mistakes are made?

* *Write down your own personal code of ethics.*

Day 107: Trusting Your Gut Instinct

Trusting your gut instinct can be a difficult form of intuition. One's gut instinct is usually the first impression of a situation. It's called a gut instinct because this form of intuition is often visceral. A sense of fear or anger or happiness might be suddenly felt, causing us to feel the impulse to take action. Some examples of gut instinct might be the decision to walk instead of take a car to work because of a dream about a car crash, or the choice to ask a potential date for his phone number because you and your dog both seem to like him.

Gut instincts happen many times a day. The tough part about them is catching those feelings before you second-guess them. This can be easy when the stakes are low, such as deciding to take the next elevator because a person inside this one gives you the creeps. Gut instincts can be more difficult to follow when they involve buying a house that perhaps gives you a strange feeling of being at home. Today, keep alert for any gut instincts you feel while you're out and about.

* Be alert for your gut instincts today,
  and write down your first impressions.

Day 108: Listening to Warnings

Sometimes, intuitive impressions can be warnings from Spirit. These warnings may come as those gut feelings that immediately slam you. These warnings can also be more subtle, and take the form of patterns of negative things happening to get your attention. It's up to you to decide whether or not to heed the warning. A friend of mine who is a Vodou Priestess told me a story about a client who came to her for divination services. The client was a young man with a family, and he was told that he would need to leave his home city of New Orleans and buy a new house and make a new life somewhere else. He heeded the Priestess's warning and later was vindicated when Hurricane Katrina hit.

What an amazing show of faith to follow warnings from Spirit. In the above story, the man may have felt foolish if something bad never happened after heeding the warning. Of course, you still have your own free will and can change bad things that seem to be happening in your life. However, warning signs from Spirit can at least help you figure out what you're up against. Today, think about warnings from Spirit that may have come in your life before bad things happened. Whether you heeded or ignored those warnings, write down what they were. You may find they take that same pattern later in life.

* *Think back to some negative events in your life. Were there any intuitive warning signs or feelings from Spirit that you could have heeded?*

Day 109: Being Compelled

....

Blessed are the impulsive. It's not yet a famous spiritual quote, but it really should be. Impulsive people immediately follow those gut instincts from Spirit. Naturally impulsive people are easily compelled by choices in life. I'm one of those "leap before you look" types, and so as a result I've followed the call of Spirit down some pretty strange avenues.

You don't have to pick high-stake choices in order to follow those compelling feelings from Spirit. Here's a simple exercise that will hopefully help you to follow your instincts. Go somewhere where there are a lot of rocks, like a riverbed or a gravel pit or even a store with a bin of semiprecious gemstones. Ask Spirit to guide you to a rock. Walk around and allow yourself to grab hold of the rock that compels you most from among all the others. Pay attention to the feeling that draws you most. Is it a feeling like magnetism? Is it simply a matter of your attention being arrested? Does it feel like energy on your hands like a prickling or fuzzy, warming sensation? Procure the rock and bring it home to place on your altar or in your sacred space as a gift from Spirit.

* *Figure out what it feels like when you*
  are compelled by Spirit to do something.

Day 110: Figuring Out Your Concept of Spirit

Today, let's dive into the hard stuff and start thinking about the nature of Spirit. This question can be a wild one, because differing answers can start wars. Let me share with you a common Indian parable about a group of blind men who were asked to describe an elephant. One man walked up and touched the elephant's legs.

"An elephant is like a tree," he said.
Another came and felt the trunk of the animal.
"An elephant is like a snake," he cried.
A third touched the elephant's tusk.
"An elephant is like a sword," he said with certainty.

This story shows how each of us only sees a small piece of the big concept called "Spirit" in this lifetime. Some believe in one god. Some believe in several gods or even infinite gods. Some believe that the gods are so infinite that they are like the many facets on a single diamond, bringing them back to one being. Others believe that things in this world are either of the one true god or not of the one true god, and there is no confusion or grey area. How do you conceptualize Spirit?

* Write down your concept of Spirit right now. If you're
  unsure, that's okay. Write down a few good guesses that
  feel right to you. These guesses may change over time.

Day 111: Thinking about Afterlife
....

One of the great comforts of spirituality is the concept that there may be an afterlife. This, too, differs from person to person. One religion's comforting thought may be another religion's nightmare. Today, think about the concepts of afterlife with which you are familiar. Think of the ideas that you had as a child about where people went when they died. Think about your greatest hopes and your greatest fears regarding what comes after death.

Write down your thoughts about the afterlife today. Do any stories come to mind that you've been told that give you a sense of hope, or maybe even dread? Do you think that a paradise afterlife is in store for you? Would Spirit remove all pain from a perfect world such as that? Do you believe in reincarnation? What sort of reincarnation do you envision for yourself in the best-case scenario? In the case of any afterlife, do you think that you will meet your loved ones again? Do you believe that your identity will be preserved after death, or will you dissolve into an anonymous sea of Spirit? Which ideas give you hope and which give you fear?

* *Write about your present beliefs in the afterlife, if any.*

Part Four

Prayer

Day 112: Types of Prayer

I've given prayer an entire section of this book because I believe that it is one of the most important ways of connecting to Spirit. If you're new to prayer, or feeling a little rusty, or even feeling a little antagonistic toward the idea of prayer, hear me out. Your prayer life doesn't have to be like anyone else's prayer life. If the prayers said by others or that you've had to say in the past leave a bad taste in your mouth, by all means avoid them. That is why this section of the book is going to be a quick tour of the many types of prayer.

The basic types of prayer come from the reasons we pray and the sort of spiritual listener we feel like addressing. For example, many people pray intercessory prayers. Those are the types of prayers where we ask Spirit to intervene in our lives and change things for the better. Another type of prayer is that of praise or worship. Yet another is sometimes called an affirmation, because it speaks aloud the notion of agreeing with Spirit and then affirms that Spirit wants the subject of the prayer to happen. We'll explore some of these types of prayer and others in the coming days. For now, think about the types of prayer you've tried. Have you memorized rote prayers? Have you asked for help from Spirit? What other types of prayer have you tried?

* *Write down some of the types of prayer that are familiar to you. This is the start of your prayer toolkit.*

Day 113: Format of Prayer
....

The different faith traditions in this world have many different formats for prayer. Some are songs, some are memorized prose, and others are made up on the spot. For somebody new to prayer, it can be tough to come up with a prayer format that feels comfortable. Here's a sample one that you can use.

*Hail, [Name of goddess(es) and/
or god(s) or just "Spirit" or "to the universe"],*

*You who are [list three positive
attributes of Spirit], I praise you!*

*Thank you for [health/money/love/
other specific blessing for which you need to ask],*

[NOW!/other time limit],

*With harm to none, and for the
highest good of all, so may it be.*

*In return, I offer you [my eternal gratitude/
my love and devotion/other offering or sacrifice].*

*Blessed be. (Pause, take three deep breaths
and be silent and alert for a sign, an answer,
or any other physical sensation or mental feeling.)*

Thanking Spirit for something that you're requesting is an acknowledgment that you're visualizing and manifesting what you want through Spirit. Give thanks in advance, and you'll find that you draw success. You can remember the seven components to Pagan prayer through the mnemonic of the letters in the word *PRAYING*, which stand for: Person listening, Raise praise, Ask for help, Your deadline, Imperatives for safety, Note of thanks, and Gracious attention.

* *Try out a basic prayer format or write your own.*

Day 114: To Whom Are You Praying?

The first part of the prayer I suggested yesterday was to name the person or persons listening to your prayer. Were you able to pick a good name? This may make you think back to the last section of the book, in which I asked you to ponder the true nature of Spirit, and whether it is one person or many or something else entirely. It's okay if you have no idea how to answer this question. Perhaps you and Spirit haven't yet been properly introduced. It's okay to grasp, reach, and strive to learn this ultimate mystery. Not having any clue is no worse off than picking a random name.

Today, if you haven't yet been properly introduced to Spirit, I encourage you to do so. In some cultures, this is a ceremony of some sort. You can make it a big ceremony of your own, if you like, or you can just speak aloud to Spirit as if you were talking to a new stranger. It may feel awkward, but that's okay. Many first official greetings are. Tell Spirit your name and ask to get to know Spirit in your own words. You can ask Spirit to give you a name or to tell you about its nature. Then you can follow your intuition or pay attention to your dreams to learn the answers for yourself. It may take a little while to get to know Spirit, but an introduction is a good start.

* *Introduce yourself to Spirit and try to figure out the nature of Spirit.*

Day 115: Frequency of Prayer

How often one is supposed to pray is another concern to people who are new to prayer. Some people worry that they're not praying enough. Not praying enough may feel like you're not devout enough or like you should be doing more for Spirit through prayer. On the other hand, praying too much can also feel wrong, as if the prayer becomes frivolous or somehow phony. Both of these worries may be entirely unfounded, but it's still nice to find a happy medium between the two that works for your own life.

First, ask yourself what you believe about Spirit. Is Spirit something to be respected and feared, and so honored only occasionally when you feel you're properly prepared? Or would you prefer a relationship with Spirit that is more like a best friend, a lover, or a parent? This sort of spiritual relationship would entail frequent close conversations and saying your prayers while washing dishes or doing other unimportant tasks. With this in mind, choose whether you want to set prayer on your schedule as a daily occurrence, a weekly prayer marathon, or something else.

* *How often do you feel is right to pray? How often is comfortable for you right now? What can you do within your schedule to get your prayer life closer to what you want it to be?*

Day 116: Importance and Urgency

How important does a prayer have to be before you will pray it? Another worry of those new to prayer is that praying about little tiny problems bothers Spirit. After all, if there are so many troubles in the world being lifted up in prayer, it may seem silly and selfish to pray about getting a new car or even to pray just to start a conversation with Spirit. Does Spirit have time to chat? The answer to this quandary is refreshingly similar across many religions: It is okay to talk to Spirit anytime, so long as it is done in earnest and with respect.

Knowing that it's okay to pray about every little thing, you might still pass by prayer as one of the options open to you. If prayer is new to you, it's not going to be your first resort when you find yourself in a predicament, no matter how small or large. So, your duty today is to search for insolvable problems, and then try out prayer as a solution. The caveat is that the problems need to be insolvable. It's no good to sit around struggling with the right prayer when you could be doing what's necessary to actually fix something. However, these insolvable problems can be small and almost trivial. Spirit will still listen.

* *Find an insolvable problem and try to solve it*
  with prayer as soon as you become aware of it.

Day 117: Praise and Worship

Praise and worship are often touted as the highest forms of prayer. Why is this so? Some people believe that Spirit needs prayer. We may be in some sort of symbiotic relationship with Spirit. Spirit may enjoy and feed off of our worship. Others believe that's not the case, and that Spirit will continue to thrive and flourish without worship. Why, then, should praise and worship continue to take place? Because praise and worship are good for us as well. Taking joy in Spirit brings an unlimited well of happiness to our lives.

Today, praise Spirit in prayer. This may be tough to do if you're at a challenging time in your life. Think back to when I asked you to find ways to bring an attitude of gratitude into your life. You can start by thanking Spirit for the little things. Branch out to praising some of the bigger things about Spirit that affect our universe as a whole. Notice how this sort of prayer makes you feel. Try praying this sort of prayer more often and see how it changes your demeanor over time.

* Praise Spirit today in prayer, and see how it makes
  you feel during the prayer and afterward.

Day 118: Intercessory Prayer

Here's one of the most common forms of prayer: the sort of prayer in which you ask for stuff. Intercessory prayer may seem selfish after performing a prayer of praise and worship. Some people may feel a bit guilty treating Spirit like some sort of rich uncle or Santa Claus figure. However, another way of looking at this quandary is that Spirit loves us and wants us to be happy, but we need to be brave enough to know what we want and state our intentions. The universe is filled with abundance, and it is there for the taking if we just allow ourselves to be open to it.

With this theory in mind, try some intercessory prayer today. You can ask for help with a problem that is large or small. This time, it can be a problem that can be solved and you can simply ask for help solving that problem. For example, if you want to get a new job, you can pray for Spirit to lead you to the right new job for you, and then get out there and pound the pavement looking for that great job. In that way, you and Spirit are working together.

* *Try intercessory prayer.*

Day 119: Praying for Others

Praying for others is a major form of spiritual expression. Once you find joy and even success in praying intercessory prayer, you'll naturally want to share this power with others. There's a right way and a wrong way to do this, however. Many of us have been the victims of being prayed for by others in a way that felt manipulative or condescending. If you fling about your prayers for others in a way that is self-aggrandizing or rude, you'll find that you won't be spreading the joys of Spirit in the way that you desire.

If you want to pray for others, the best thing to do is to go to the other person in question directly. Don't ask Aunt Sally, for example, whether her son is doing well in school after his trouble with the police and whether you can pray for him. That's just using prayer for gossip purposes. Instead, go to the son directly and ask if you can pray for him. Permission is important because it can allow the person to work with Spirit. Then, you can ask what he or she would like you to pray about. You might be surprised at the avenue of prayer that person prefers.

* *Offer to pray for someone else.*

Day 120: Free Will

The world religions have a consensus that we all have free will. This may not seem to fit with the intuitive concept of "destiny." If there is a destiny, and some of us can intuitively sense future events or have premonitions, then how can there possibly be free will? I often like to think of destiny as a framework, like a system of roads. There are many times you can go right or left or even slow down to make a choice. However, there certainly is a structure from which some people seem unable to break. What do you think about destiny? Write your thoughts down.

Another problem with free will is that it can often not mesh well with the concept of Spirit being omniscient or omnipotent. If Spirit is that powerful, aren't we mere playthings and our free will is only allowed to the extent that it conforms to Spirit's wishes? Here are two common solutions from religious minds. Firstly, it could be that Spirit is not that powerful and is struggling along with us. Secondly, it could be that Spirit is that powerful, but graciously gives us free will to make our choices, and grieves along with us when those choices are poor. What do you think?

* Meditate upon the nature of free will.

Day 121: Chanting
....

Chanting is a prayer said repeatedly. It is often short and said audibly, although chanting can also be done under the breath. The point of chanting is not only to say the prayer, but to raise energy or enter a meditative or trance state. In this way, the chant serves both the chanter and Spirit. Chanting can also be an excellent way to memorize prayer. You can chant while breathing in and while breathing out in order to give your chanting a seamless quality. Some people choose to chant a specific number of times, such as the sacred Hindu number 108, counted with prayer beads. Others choose to chant for a set period of time. The choice is up to you.

The phrase or word chanted is called simply a chant or a mantra. You can choose your own chant that expresses worship and praise, or that asks for intercession, or simply affirms something good in your life. Perhaps the most chanted mantra in the world is the word *om*. Om represents the entire universe, and can be chanted with praise and awe. The act of sounding the word represents creation and then the cycle of ending when the end of the word comes about. It is said to contain all the vowels within that seed sound. Try chanting it today.

* *Try chanting the word* om *or write your own chant.*

Day 122: Prayers for Forgiveness

Many forms of spiritual expression are built around finding ways to deal with guilt. We all make mistakes in our lives and have regrets. Some of these regrets can become entangled with our spiritual identities. If you're feeling bad about something that you have done in your life, you might be ashamed to pray to Spirit due to low self-esteem. Conversely, you might even be angry with Spirit for letting you get away with what you've done. Throughout history, prayers for forgiveness to exonerate sinners of all types have been given and taught and passed down through generations.

Self-forgiveness may be the most challenging prayer for forgiveness. If you have a life choice that you still regret, consider bringing it to Spirit. The first step is owning that choice and meditating upon the lessons that it taught you. The second step is to pray and ask Spirit for forgiveness, as well as for an opportunity to make things right. The third step is to attempt any restitution that is possible. If you need to forgive others, try praying for the ability to let go of any form of personal justice that you feel you require. Release it to Spirit.

* *Try a prayer for forgiveness for yourself or for others who have committed wrongs.*

Day 123: Prayers for Wisdom and Guidance

One of my most frequent prayers is for either wisdom or guidance. I think of this as a sort of halfway intercessory prayer. I'm not asking Spirit to do all the work involved with solving a particular problem in my life. I'm simply asking for a sense of direction and for help making the right choices. Prayers for wisdom and guidance are a good way to pray if you're uncomfortable with the idea of Spirit coming in and taking care of everything for you. For example, some people are not comfortable praying for a political candidate to win an election, but are fine with the idea of praying for wisdom and guidance in choosing the best candidate for a vote.

In order to pray for wisdom, you'll have to listen for that guidance afterward. Whenever I pray for guidance, I always ask for gentle wisdom, like the kind that comes to me when I'm having a cup of tea, not the kind of wisdom that comes from learning a hard lesson. I also like to take some time after prayer to meditate quietly and receptively. This gives me a chance to try to receive some of that guidance for which I asked, and to integrate it into my understanding.

* *Try a prayer for wisdom or guidance on a confusing issue or duty.*

Day 124: Prayers for Healing
....

There's much to be said about healing. Many spiritual traditions include the laying of hands for healing, using energy centers in the palms to heal oneself or others. Praying for healing can be tricky business. Of course, whenever you pray for healing, you should always also go through the appropriate channels to get medical help if needed. Hospitals have spiritual care departments to pray with the sick because prayer works well in conjunction with medical intervention, rather than as a substitute for it.

There are several schools of thought regarding praying for healing. One is that any illness or injury is an illusion and not of Spirit. Thus, when you pray for healing, you should actually avoid talking about the illness or injury altogether. Instead, pray to see past illusion to what is true Spirit, and everything is perfect Spirit. The other school of thought is that illness and injuries are real indeed. However, one should visualize already being healed to bring that state of being into life while praying for healing. Whichever method of prayer you choose, pick one and stick with it to see if it works. Remember to ask permission before praying for healing for others.

* *Try praying for healing for yourself or someone else.*

Day 125: Unanswered Prayers

A country singer once wrote a song about unanswered prayers. In that song, he relayed a story in which, in his youth, he had prayed for what he thought would be best in his life. Of course, at the time he was not seeing the truly right outcome. When God did not answer his prayer, he was allowed to stumble across the best outcome for all concerned. In this case, the unanswered prayer was actually Spirit declining to give him the intercession that he wanted in favor of a better blessing.

But why do bad things happen to good people who pray to avoid those bad things? There's no way to know for sure why the universe is balanced with joy and suffering, and why people range from the terrible to the tender-hearted. It could be that this balance is needed in order for the purpose of the universe to play out or even for happiness to exist in a state of necessary contrast. Today may be a difficult writing activity. Write about a time when a prayer or a wish in your life went unfulfilled from your perspective. How do you rationalize that?

* *Write about an unanswered prayer and your reaction.*

Day 126: Listening for Answers
....

Meditation after prayer gives a good opportunity for a person to listen for answers to prayer. But, if you're totally new to prayer, what are those answers like? This depends on the person and the situation. Some people may get a feeling or a sense of knowing for certain that the prayer has been heard and answered. Other people may look for signs that happen around them. If an opportunity for success presents itself, this sign is taken as a sign from Spirit that must be followed to its conclusion.

Practice meditating today after prayer and listening for an answer from Spirit. You can even ask in your prayer for Spirit to give you a sign. That sign might be as simple as a dog barking during your meditation or as complex as a check being mailed to your home later that day. Remain vigilant and mindful throughout your day after the prayer. Observe everything happening to you in the context of Spirit working in your life. Look for potential signs and signals. Write down what you prayed for today. If your prayer is later answered, write that down as well. The issue being completely resolved may be the first sign you get.

* Pray today and then remain vigilant for signs from Spirit.

Day 127: Offerings and Thanksgiving

In life, one has to give and take. One reason that prayer may feel uncomfortable to some is that it feels like we're constantly asking things of Spirit without giving anything back, aside from praise and worship. Intuitively, it can feel like the real world doesn't work this way. There must be some way to pay Spirit back for all the blessings that are given to us. Throughout history, people have strived to do just that, with sacrifices. Now, I'm not going to ask you to sacrifice a goat or anything. I'm a vegetarian! But, I will ask you to think about what you could sacrifice in your life to get your prayers answered.

Material sacrifices are still used today: incense, food, and drink are the most common offerings. Food and drink can be placed outside in order for wildlife to act as proxies for Spirit. You can also give less-tangible offerings like a song, heartfelt thanksgivings, a labor of love of some kind, or by giving up a vice that you enjoy. Today, take an inventory of your offerings. You'll want to have some ideas on hand if you have a desperate prayer that you'd like answered.

* *Write down an inventory of your potential*
  offerings of thanksgiving to Spirit.

Day 128: Five-Minute Devotionals
....

Prayer doesn't have to be an hour-long affair that involves ritualistic entreaties, elaborate offerings, and plenty of time spent in meditation. Of course, those prayer sessions are fun and highly effective for me, but I don't always resort to them. Prayer can be something done while sweeping the house, washing dishes, or driving a car. Here's an example of a daily five-minute devotional that you can use when you're driving to work as an impetus to thank Spirit.

As you're driving your car or walking around town, go on a spiritual scavenger hunt with your eyes. Look for blessings that Spirit has given that cannot be bought or stolen. These bounties might include things like a smile from a stranger, a feeling of energy and excitement in your bones for the day ahead, or an act of kindness spotted between two people. Each time you catch one of these moments, say a brief prayer of thanksgiving as an offering to Spirit. By the time you reach your destination, you should feel uplifted. Spirit may get a boost and some encouragement to leave more blessings around you for you to find.

* Perform a quick devotional today, under five minutes,
  while you perform some other daily task.

Day 129: Prayer as Conversation and Connection

Some people aren't content with a relationship with Spirit that simply entails a few random prayers and wishes granted. These people desire a friendship with Spirit that is like that of a best friend or lover. Prayer can also act as a conversation with Spirit that connects you with Spirit. Prayer can be a thread woven through your day with ups and downs and questions. You can bounce your ideas off of Spirit like you would with any trusted partner in life.

So, how can you have a conversation with Spirit? Well, first you need to augment your listening skills. You can practice feeling answers in your gut, observing patterns and signs, or using tools like a pendulum or others that you've tried in this book. You'll also have to be a good conversation partner. Spontaneously initiate prayer as soon as you have a mind to. Talk freely and openly, allowing yourself to change your mind or correct yourself as you speak. Talk through your worries and your troubles, and openly celebrate your blessings. Don't forget to ask questions. Spend time listening and respond instantly with thanksgivings when you sense any response.

* Practice having an ongoing conversation with Spirit today.

Day 130: Is Any Prayer Too Silly?

My spiritual teachers instructed me that I should approach Spirit with both mirth and reverence. You've already learned some ways to be respectful to Spirit: bathing or cleansing yourself before coming in contact with Spirit, praising and worshipping, always giving thanks and offering sacrifice, asking permission from others before praying for them, and coming to Spirit with sincerity. However, if Spirit is going to have an ongoing conversation with you throughout the day, there's certainly going to be some levity and relaxation in your relationship as well.

What if the only beverage offering you have to give Spirit is half a can of energy drink? What if you want to pray to win an ultimate Frisbee competition? Are any of these situations too silly for Spirit? If you like to characterize yourself as a child of Spirit, remember that your family sees you at your best, worst, and most silly. Resolve to seek a balance between silliness and respect, rather than trying to eliminate the laughable. Don't take yourself too seriously.

> * Is your prayer life balanced between moments of joy
>   and levity, and moments of awe and reverence?
>   If not, seek to relax or tighten up accordingly.

Day 131: Sacred Space as Prayer without Words

One reason altars and sacred spaces are so helpful is that they allow you to talk to Spirit with symbols instead of with words. I like my family altar at home because it's a place we can all use to commune with Spirit. For example, if I get a bill that worries me or a birthday card that makes me happy, I can place it on the altar. If my husband builds something and is proud, he can put it on the altar. If my daughter finds a pretty rock and is thankful, she can put it on the altar.

There's no need for other fancy words or gestures. The items themselves say everything that is needed. Today, keep an eye out for things that you can place on an altar or in your sacred space. If you find yourself troubled, choose a symbol for that trouble and place it on your altar. If you spy a pretty bird feather or flower, go ahead and place it on your altar. Of course this is also a good opportunity to look for offerings and place them accordingly.

* Pray with symbols instead of words by placing token objects on your altar or in your sacred space.

Day 132: Prayer Beads
······································

Prayer beads are a necklace or bracelet or string of beads strung together for the purpose of being handled during prayer. One can run through a list of repeated prose prayers, or one can simply chant a word or phrase for each bead. You can choose the number appropriate for your prayer beads. You can use numerology or select a number that feels right to you or that works with a spiritual tradition of choice. If the number is large, consider making a smaller prayer bead set and then just counting through the prayer beads multiple times. For each prayer, hold a bead and then move on to the next when you are done. In this way, you can count with your eyes closed and with your mind focused on the prayer or chant.

Go to a bead shop or buy a bead set from a craft store. In a pinch, knots in a length of string can work as prayer beads. Select beads according to the meaning of the prayers, if possible. I have a friend who made a set of prayer beads with letters on the beads, reminding her which prayer goes next in line. I made a prayer bead necklace based mostly on the prettiness of the beads. Try praying with your prayer beads and see if it helps you relax more into the prayer or chanting process.

* *Make a prayer bead necklace or bracelet, or tie some*
  knots in a string to try out the prayer bead concept.

Day 133: Prayer at Different Times of Day

Many spiritual traditions portion up the day with little moments for prayer. This has a number of benefits. It adds structure, predictability, and familiarity to one's day during an otherwise hectic lifestyle. It punctuates the day with excuses to set aside petty, worldly arguments and think of Spirit. And finally, it helps get the body and soul in tune with natural rhythms, in a world where lights can keep us up around the clock. The most common prayer times for these daily sorts of prayers in such religions are marked by stations of the sun, such as sunrise, sunset, and noon. Consider praying at those specific times to create a habit for yourself.

Planetary hours are another way to choose a good prayer time. The planetary hours begin at sunrise with the planet of the day. Then, they roll through in the same lineup over and over again until sunrise the next day. Here's the order:

Saturn (First at sunrise on Saturday)—
   best time for prayers about duty or ridding yourself of things.

Jupiter (First at sunrise on Thursday)—
   best for prayers about leadership.

Mars (First at sunrise on Tuesday)—
   best for prayers about conflict or surgery.

Sun (First at sunrise on Sunday)—
   best for prayers for the divine masculine, success, and health.

Venus (First at sunrise on Friday)—
   best for prayers about love and comfort.

Mercury (First at sunrise on Wednesday)—

best for prayers about business and communication.

Moon (First at sunrise on Monday)—

best for prayers about cycles, the divine feminine, and magic.

  * *Choose the best time for daily prayer for you.*

Day 134: Sleeplessness

Humans didn't always sleep for one eight-hour stretch at night. Before electric lighting made lamps widely available and affordable to all, most people went to bed relatively shortly after sundown and awoke at sunrise. Even rich people could not always afford to burn oil lamps to light entire rooms for hours on end. This meant that there was often a longer stretch of sleep, but it was punctuated by an hour or so of quiet wakefulness, often spent in bed. This was thought to be a prayer time. After this, sleep would resume until morning.

When you find yourself waking in the night, consider it a call from Spirit to pray. Be prepared with some supplies at your bedside. Have a flashlight or a candle or small lamp nearby. Have a pencil and your journal handy, in case you feel compelled to write. You may choose to have a small book of prayers or myths by your bed to read during this time of wakefulness. When you're ready to return to sleep or after five minutes, whichever is longer, extinguish any lit candles and go to sleep.

* *Jump on periods of wakefulness at night as opportunities for prayer.*

Day 135: Keeping a Prayer Record

Keeping a prayer record can be tough business if you pray a lot. It may also seem a little bit repetitive. However, it can be fun to be diligent about prayer records, because you can see which prayers are answered and which prayers are still on your to-do list and which ones have been abandoned in favor of different prayers. This can be a very interesting map of your spiritual journey.

How should you keep a prayer record? Here are a few methods I've tried. Firstly, I have a log of all of the major prayer sessions I've had with others so that we can see which of our wishes come to pass. Then, I also keep a prayer record for each of my family members for prayers that I pray for them. I hope they will be keepsakes for my kids someday. I also keep a journal filled with thanksgivings and praises for blessings. It helps me notice more of them. For myself, I keep a jar full of rocks. Each time a prayer is answered, I thank Spirit and add a rock to the jar. My faith grows as the jar fills. Plus, it doesn't saddle me down with even more writing to do. Any or all of these methods might work for you. Pick one and try it out.

* Choose a method of keeping some sort of
  record of your prayers consistently.

Day 136: Prayer Stance and Hands

If you're new to prayer, the very practice of speaking aloud to Spirit may feel awkward. How do you stand? What do you do with your hands? If you're praying with a group of people, it's easy to follow along. If more than two people in the prayer group are doing something, it's pretty safe to say that you can do the same thing. If you're alone, however, you can do what feels natural.

The most common prayer stances are standing, kneeling, and bowed. Try each of these in prayer, to the best of your ability. When bowing, you can place your hands on the floor first and then touch your forehead to the hands. No need to get too up-close and personal with the floor. You can use your hands as a barrier. Hands can be folded together in a pleading gesture, palms together or facing outward in a blessing gesture, or lifted upward or placed on the floor to receive blessings from Spirit. Try other hand or body positions if you like.

* *Choose a favorite stance and hand position for prayer.*

Day 137: Written Prayer

Prayers don't have to be spoken aloud or even whispered under one's breath. You can write out your prayers and never speak them at all. This prayer book becomes your prayer record. This is also a good way to try out some serious poetry. Some people even choose to write out their chants or mantras over and over again, page by page. This can become an automatic and meditative act. You can also choose a long prayer that you find beautiful from a faith tradition and write it down as a way to commit it to memory.

In your spiritual journal, try praying by writing. You could write a brand-new prayer of your own prose, copy down a favorite prayer, or try writing a chant over and over again for a designated period of time or a certain number of times. As you pray in this way, ask yourself if it takes less time or more time. Does it feel more comfortable or less comfortable than praying aloud? Is this a method of prayer that you want to use regularly, or is it something you might save for special occasions?

* *Try writing a prayer, either one you've made up or a preexisting prayer.*

Day 138: Memorized Prayers

Memorizing prayers is preferred by some but rejected by others. Some believe that memorized prayer results in perfunctory and emotionless prayer, done by rote as a matter of course. Such people keep memorized prayers only for very special occasions, and strive for most of their prayers to be spontaneous and made up on the spot with words from the heart. Others believe that memorized prayer can be a tool for getting one's mind outside of the words and experiencing the moment for all that it is worth. I find that memorized prayer is useful when there are no real words for the mysteries, and I want to simply evoke the feeling that I get from prayer in the moment.

Today, choose a prayer to memorize. You can search for one online that matches your values or your wishes. You can flip through a prayer book at the library. You can choose a common mantra, or a verse from scripture. Memorize that prayer by reading it aloud over and over. You might try writing it down, or using marked prayer beads as a memory aid. After you've memorized the prayer, keep it fresh in your mind by using it whenever it is appropriate.

* Choose a prayer to memorize and begin
  working on learning it by heart.

Day 139: Speaking from the Heart

Spontaneous prayer spoken from the heart should be a vital part of your toolkit. Even with the myriad of beautifully written prayers available, there may be moments in your life in which you don't have time or the inclination to look up an appropriate prayer. If you prefer memorized prayers, it is also good to get outside of your comfort zone and try praying spontaneous prayers as well. This can help you initiate the sort of conversation-style relationship with Spirit that can help a person through confusing times.

If you already talk to yourself, it's an easy transition to start talking to Spirit in the same way. However, if you're the type of person who feels silly talking to a pet or to a baby who doesn't talk yet, this may be an uncomfortable practice at first. Make sure you have privacy when you try praying in this way. Use your normal speaking voice. Close your eyes if you wish. Talk to Spirit as if Spirit were a best friend. Don't worry about any flubs in your words. Think aloud to yourself, and talk through the thoughts even as you're trying to organize them.

* *Try spontaneous prayer from the heart, talking to Spirit as if Spirit is a friend.*

Day 140: When You Don't Know What You Want

It can feel frustrating and hopeless when life takes a turn for the confusing and you're not even sure what you want. I felt this way when my father was dying. I knew that he was ready to die and that I wanted his pain to end. At the same time, I knew I was going to miss him and didn't want him to leave this realm any sooner than necessary. What to pray? Praying to prolong his life might be cruel, but praying to release him felt too difficult at first.

When you don't know what you want, it's okay to use spontaneous prayer to talk it out with Spirit. Go ahead and tell Spirit that you are just thinking things through, and not to hold you to any desperate, confused wishes at the moment. This is also an excellent opportunity to pray for wisdom and guidance, if you feel that you are ready for it. You can also simply pray for comfort and peace of mind. Give yourself time to think of the right prayer for the situation. Have faith that timeframes may operate differently in Spirit's world.

* *Think of a time in your life when you didn't know what you wanted. What would be the right sort of prayer for a moment like that?*

Day 141: Smells and Bells
....

Incense makes an excellent offering to Spirit, and so does the ringing of bells and playing of beautiful music. Those who had an upbringing in a religious tradition that makes use of a lot of pageantry in rituals may miss the showy smells and bells of such services for Spirit. There's no reason why you can't bring a little bit of that pageantry into your own home and your own spiritual life. Decorate your sacred space or altar to be showy. Dress yourself with jewels or robes for prayer. Go all out if you wish.

Today, think about what you imagine as the grandest expression of worship. This will be different for different people. A person who yearns for a simple life will have a completely different mental picture than a person who wishes to one day build a lavish cathedral for Spirit. Sketch your idea of the perfect sacred space for you on a piece of paper. Imagine that you are creating this space on the astral plane. If you wish, you may go there in meditation, or you can begin to furnish your real sacred space to live up to your dream, integrating some pageantry into your prayer sessions.

* *Create a prayer space on the astral plane, either simple
  or complex according to your own sensibilities.*

Day 142: Prayer Space

Your sacred space may not be big enough for prayer if you live in a small or shared place with little room. You may also have to create new prayer space when you travel, or when you find yourself needing to pray throughout your day. Carving out space for prayer can be difficult if you want your space to be both private and to have an atmosphere conducive to prayer.

Today, carve out a prayer space in your home. If you already have a sacred space, it's okay to pray outside of it, of course, but try to make a habit of retreating to that space for prayer whenever possible and convenient. If you don't have a sacred space, create a space and time when you can be undisturbed. At your bedside, for example, with a "do not disturb" sign on the door. Be on the lookout at your workplace to find good prayer spaces. A bench in a courtyard or a spare conference room can serve as a sanctuary. Make it a point to escape to your little prayer sanctuary whenever it is appropriate. Notice how these retreats affect your demeanor and your day.

* *Find prayer spaces and use them.*

Day 143: Prayer Shawls

Sometimes all it takes to have a good prayer session is to get in the right headspace. Earlier, you learned how getting into special robes and jewelry can be one way to prepare for connecting with Spirit. But sometimes it is too much to don lots of gear for a simple prayer session. A prayer shawl or stole can be a special garment you can keep on hand anywhere in order to immediately be dressed for the occasion and get in the mood.

A prayer shawl or a stole can be merely a scarf or simple cloth draped over the shoulders. Ideally, you can make this yourself as an offering to Spirit, if you knit or sew. If you're not very crafty, you can go to a fabric store and choose an inspiring fabric and then use an iron-on bonding product to hem any ends to keep it from looking frayed. Don your prayer shawl before prayer and then immediately remove it afterward. If you only wear it during prayer, it will remind you of prayer and will collect the energy of your prayers. A prayer shawl can make an excellent gift for somebody who has asked for prayer from you.

* *Make or obtain a prayer shawl and try wearing it during prayer.*

Day 144: Repeating Prayers
....

Picture this: You have a sore throat coming on and you really don't want to be sick all week. You say a quick prayer for healing and then go about your day. When nighttime comes around, you feel even more run-down. Do you say another prayer? Or are you worried that might show a lack of faith? Different spiritual traditions might answer this question differently, no matter what the subject of the prayer. Some embrace repeated prayer, and encourage repeating a prayer every day for a set number of days for best efficacy and to give the prayer more oomph. Other spiritual traditions advocate releasing all your worries to Spirit with the prayer and not thinking about it anymore.

Each style of prayer has benefits. If you let go of your worries and give them all to Spirit, you may feel a certain level of stress relief and can build your faith. However, if you repeat your prayers, you give yourself a sense that you're actively doing something to solve the problem, and you give yourself more opportunities to open a conversation with Spirit. Decide your stance on the matter today.

* *Do you believe in repeating your requests to Spirit, or letting go and allowing Spirit to do what Spirit wills?*

Day 145: Angry Prayers
....

Sometimes we get angry with Spirit. We may think, "That's okay, Spirit is big enough to take it." Nevertheless, in the moment it can cause a serious spiritual crisis. It hurts to be angry at someone you love, and it can cause a loss of faith or even fear that Spirit will no longer share blessings or affection. While practicing as a chaplain at hospitals, I had the opportunity to see a lot of anger toward Spirit during times of suffering. I even got to be the target of such anger, in my role as a representative of Spirit. Here are my tips for being angry with Spirit.

Realize that it is okay to feel anger. It is how you react to that anger and behave that matters. Choose to react in a way that is appropriate to the context. If you are in a situation in which you must restrain your behavior, try counting to ten and breathing slowly. Take time out for yourself. If you are in a situation in which it is appropriate to express your anger, you can do so by crying or yelling at Spirit if you want. If you feel concern about sharing your words, share your anger through movement or art.

* *Think of a time in your life in which you were*
  angry with anything and everyone, possibly
  including Spirit. How did you act during that
  time? Is there anything you wish you had done?

Day 146: Affirmations
....

Affirmations are prayers or statements to the higher self that are positive in nature. Sometimes, affirmations state what is possible to achieve, but not a reality right now, in order to create that new reality on the astral plane. Other times, affirmations are a positive view of the present objective reality. For example, if you are single and want to find a new relationship, there are two sorts of affirmations you could try. The first is to visualize yourself already in the relationship you seek. You could speak an affirmation such as, "I am in a loving relationship and feel fulfilled as much as I fulfill my partner." The other sort of affirmation would affirm the present: "I am a beautiful person worthy of love, and can attract a loving relationship into my life."

Pick which sort of affirmation suits your beliefs and comfort level. Think of something you'd like to emphasize or draw into your life. Write down an affirmation. Speak it aloud. Perhaps write it down many more times. Visualize your affirmation in meditation. Write it on your mirror. Do what you can to make that affirmation a prominent part of your life.

* *Write an affirmation.*

Day 147: Invocations
·····································

An invocation is a special sort of prayer in which one calls Spirit to come and be present in a sacred space or even inside a person. Invocations are common throughout many religions, but they certainly depend on a specific belief—the belief that Spirit can be both imminent and transcendent. What that means is that you have to believe that Spirit's presence or effect in your life can vary; in one moment Spirit can feel close or at one with yourself and in another moment Spirit can be more abstract or diffuse or distant. For some people this is never the case, and an invocation may seem unnecessary. Even so, it doesn't hurt to try. You can use the following basic prayer format as an invocation, or try your own.

*Hail, [Name of goddess(es) and/
or god(s) or just Spirit],*

*You who are [list three positive
attributes of Spirit], I praise you!*

Thank you for descending to/within me,

NOW!

*With harm to none, and for
the highest good of all, so may it be.*

In return, I offer you [my eternal
gratitude/my love and devotion/
other offering or sacrifice].

Blessed be. (Pause, take three deep breaths
and be silent and alert for a sign, an answer,
or any other physical sensation or mental feeling.)

* *Attempt an invocation of Spirit.*

Day 148: Evocations

....

Evocation is different from invocation, because it means to bring out from within the self, rather than to draw down into or toward the self. An evocation makes another belief assumption: that Spirit dwells within the self and can be expressed through the self. Again, those who believe in an exclusively transcendent Spirit will find this concept silly or impossible. If you're unsure, evocation can be a worthwhile experiment.

An evocation can be done like an invocation, or it can be done in a more subtle way. Think of the characteristics within your view of Spirit. Is Spirit compassionate? Then pray for Spirit to work through your hands and go volunteer in a soup kitchen. Is Spirit beautiful and pleasing? Pray for Spirit to sing through your voice and write a song. Find ways for Spirit to live through you with skills that you already possess. You don't have to go outside of your comfort zone for this one. The simplest form of evocation is to recognize the gifts that Spirit has already given to you. Express your true self and Spirit at the same time, and see if others are able to recognize Spirit in you.

* *Try evoking Spirit today.*

Part Five

***

Getting in Touch with the Divine Feminine

Day 149: Your Feminine Side

Is Spirit male or female? Is it genderless and, in being such, does it contain all genders? An exploration of the divine feminine is in order because of all the spiritual potential the female represents. Don't worry if the male view of Spirit is more familiar to you; the very next section of the book will dive into the divine masculine. For now, let's think about what femininity means to you. This will differ from person to person and between cultures.

If you're a man, you may have to dig deep. If you're a woman, you might have to dig deep as well if, like me, you're a tomboy who takes womanhood for granted. What symbolism does the divine feminine evoke in your mind? Brainstorm on paper some words that you think of when you think of goddesses, spiritual women in your life, and feminine values. Write down words and don't be afraid to free-associate. Are any of the words you think of virtues that you have within you? Are there any feminine influences that you would like to see more of in your life, from yourself or others?

* Brainstorm some feminine virtues and
  symbolism to seek in your life.

Day 150: Other Women

Seeing the Divine in others is one way to connect with Spirit. Giving Spirit more personifying aspects, such as a gender, makes it easier to see Spirit in others who share that characteristic. If every female is a goddess, then every female should be treated with respect, like a goddess. If the divine feminine dwells within every female, this gives us many more people from whom Spirit can be evoked. Blessings from the divine feminine could come from a barista or doctor who embodies the goddess for you in that moment.

Today, imagine that each of the females in your life is a goddess. Your mom, your sister, your daughter, and even the mean lady at work. It may be challenging to see Spirit through this lens. For one thing, real women are imperfect, which might not mesh well with your usual assumptions about Spirit. It may be difficult to respect people who are sometimes a pain in our lives. As you practice this perspective, think about what lessons some people may be teaching you. Are you accepting these lessons graciously, even when they are challenging? Is it difficult to think of Spirit in these forms?

* *Attempt to see the divine feminine in every woman today.*

Day 151: Maiden

....

One of the symbolic representations of the divine feminine is as the archetypical maiden. The maiden is a young, unmarried female. You can think of the maiden as a girl full of promise and innocence. The maiden is a girl laughing in the springtime. The maiden is naïve, sweet, and gentle. She has not yet realized her true creative force. She has not yet realized all her roles in the world. Her time is happy and carefree.

Do you see the maiden represented in the young ladies and girls in your life? Are there any projects in your life that are in the "maiden" stage of development? That is, are there any that are fresh and new in their development, so that you are still full of passion and curiosity at all the potential? Do you feel the maiden inside yourself at times? Have you ever played the role of the young, pure, and innocent? How can you bring more of the maiden's energy into your life, if that is what you wish? You can draw or paint a picture of the maiden if you wish, giving her attributes that you imagine from this archetype.

* *Meditate on the divine feminine as a maiden.*

Day 152: Mother

The mother is a widespread goddess form because this archetype is so familiar. So many people have had a mother figure in their lives who has influenced them strongly with positive energy. The mother is nurturing, at times kind and other times stern. The mother is a powerful and mysterious creative force. Who can fully understand the amazing miracle of a person being formed in the womb of another person? The power of this miracle exists in every mother. This creative force can also be seen as a metaphor. The mother has realized her role in the world and can impact all through her manifestation.

Do you have a mother figure in your life? How can you honor her like a goddess? What do you visualize when you think of the epitome of a mother? Can you create a drawing or a painting of a mother goddess? How can you nurture others in your life like a mother? How can you be a mother in order to give birth to creative ideas? The mother is all about manifesting the potential the maiden had within her all along.

* *Meditate on the divine feminine as a mother.*

Day 153: Crone
....

Crone is the word for an old woman. Though it colloquially has a negative connotation, in some cultures it is known as a term of respect. This wise woman has already lived through the roles of maiden and mother, and she has those collective experiences on which to draw for her decisions. As a result, the crone can be a healer, a storyteller, and someone who knows the true mysteries of Spirit. Though the crone approaches the end of her life and the inevitability of death, she faces this unafraid and with faith.

Have you reached the point of being the wise crone in any area of your life? Do friends come to you with questions about something with which you have extensive experience? Do you know anyone who embodies the wise crone? How can you live up to the image of the wise crone in your golden years? What can you do now in order to become respectable, wise, and still useful to the world? Draw or paint a picture of the crone. How can you honor elders in our society and thus honor the divine feminine in living crones?

* *Meditate on the divine feminine as a crone.*

Day 154: The Necklace Worn By the Divine Feminine

One symbol of the divine feminine is the necklace. Of course, women wear necklaces most prominently in Western culture, and a necklace can be a very feminine piece of jewelry. The necklace is a circle, without beginning and without end, representing the endless cycle of maiden and mother and crone that makes up life and death. In some cultures, necklaces are received as a sign of initiation into the spirituality of the group and are worn in rituals. Necklaces can be made of prayer beads or numbers of stones or seeds that have special significance to you.

Today, make or procure a necklace to either wear yourself in prayer or to give to somebody who is like a goddess in your life. You can make a necklace out of beads, seeds, other natural materials, or even by rolling up triangles of newspaper and gluing them into cylinder-shaped beads. Just like a prayer shawl, try using these beads while you pray or meditate or are involved in another sacred activity. You can leave the necklace on your altar or in your sacred space when not in use. Meditate on the endless cycle of death and rebirth as mediated by the divine feminine.

* Create a sacred necklace to represent Spirit as the divine feminine.

Day 155: Creation and Mother Earth

The creative force of the female is a miracle and a mystery. There are many instances of creation that are beautiful and mysterious in our universe. For example, the creation of the universe in general is a beautiful mystery. Present evidence shows that there was a big bang at the initial creation of the universe. But what existed before the big bang and what initiated the big bang? This is where the faithful get to run wild with their imaginations. Since there is not yet any consensus on this issue, it is a good time to have faith and to dream.

What do you think happened at the time of creation? Was the Creator male or female or both? Is creation part of a cycle of growth and destruction? What is the ultimate purpose and course of the creation of this universe? Write down your thoughts on the matter. Consider writing your own creation myth. Explore the creation myths of other cultures. The contemplation of the creation of this universe and of life in general is an opportunity to allow your belief in the unknown and the unbelievable to soar—because, honestly, this stuff is cool!

* *Meditate on the creation of the universe
   and the impetus for creation.*

Day 156: Life and the Life-Giving Divine Feminine

Life is amazing. Out of the primordial ooze, the first life took root and evolved into the panoply of living things that we see today. The only difference between us and amoebae are many years of evolution. What is this fire of life that lives inside us all? No matter how far we scientifically advance, we are as yet unable to jump-start life in the same way as the original Creator or Creators. Some people believe that life is the essential nature of Spirit.

How do you think life began, if you have any guesses at all? Do you believe that life is sacred because of its uniqueness and miraculous nature in the universe? If so, does the sacred nature of life affect any of your ethical choices? Today, meditate on the true nature of life and death. Spirit gives life, but are humans allowed to take life away? Is one life more or less sacred than another? How can you honor the sacred nature of life? Is there any way to desecrate or profane life in general, or is life just life the way it is?

* Meditate on the sacred nature of life.

Day 157: Love and Sexuality as a Sacred Feminine Power

You've already thought about how sex fits into spirituality. Today I want you to think about love and sexuality as a symbolic act, rather than literal. If Spirit is male and female in nature, then the two can be joined in sexual union. If this is true, then some people believe that this sacred union is the ultimate expression of Spirit. In the real world, everything is separate and categorized for people. There are somewhat clear delineations between black and white, up and down, and sometimes even right and wrong. But when union happens in the name of love, the world becomes paradoxically less clear and also perfect just the way it is.

Do you believe that love is sacred? Do you believe that sex is sacred? What is the difference between sacred and profane sex? Is there a difference? Today, meditate on the true nature of love and sex. How can you bring more sacred union in your life, metaphorically or literally? Is there a way to dishonor sex in the eyes of Spirit? How can you conduct yourself in order to bring more sacred love or sex into your life?

* Meditate on the topic of love and sexuality.

Day 158: Nourishment as a Motherly Trait

The first form of nourishment for most people comes from the mother. From the breasts of the life-giving mother, milk and nourishment flow into the baby. Before the breast, the umbilical cord furnished all nutrients for the fetus, through the lifeblood that connected the two. In our culture, often the mother, as well as the father, continues to nourish children throughout childhood. Nourishment can be thought of as an essential function of the divine feminine. In a sense, Spirit continues to nourish us all with spiritual food.

For many people, spiritual food is something that feeds the soul even when the body goes hungry. There are those who even believe that humans can live off of light and spiritual nourishment in the same way they can live off of food. Of course, such experiments are dangerous when practiced by ordinary people and not mythological figures and experienced yogis. However, it is worth asking Spirit to nourish you in prayer. This spiritual nourishment can build upon your physical nourishment and help you to feel stronger in life overall. Today, think about the true nature of nourishment. Ask for Spirit to nourish the parts of you that are frail and weak and in need of care.

* Meditate upon the true nature of nourishment. Pray
  for Spirit to nourish the parts of you that are weak.

Day 159: Beauty

Beauty is a mysterious human ideal. Beauty is a vital factor in human existence, since it is often noticed when two people fall in love and have children. Yet, beauty ideals differ significantly from culture to culture. Some people believe big is beautiful, while others revere thin as the ideal. Various beauty ideals shift across time and space. Yet, in the individual's experience, beauty seems like a fixed and unexplainable experience. When you see something beautiful, you don't have to debate it within your own mind. Beauty slaps you across the face and shakes you to your core.

Today, meditate on the true nature of beauty. Think about various beautiful things that you have seen in your life. Beautiful landscapes, beautiful children, beautiful women, and beautiful acts. What feelings or senses unite these beautiful ideas in your life? What thread weaves these beautiful things together into one whole, if anything? How can you bring more beauty into the world? Can you create something that is objectively beautiful? If not, can you create something that is guaranteed to be beautiful to you? If so, get started.

* Meditate on the true nature of beauty.

Day 160: Compassion and Empathy

Compassion is a spiritual ideal that spans many faith traditions. Compassion entails feeling a sense of sympathy and empathy for the suffering of others. If you don't know anyone who is going through a hard time, compassion would be largely unnecessary. However, most of us know somebody we love who has gone through a great deal of suffering. In those cases, compassion can help us to connect with the loved one and treat them kindly. When the person suffering is a stranger, compassion is more difficult to find and to hold.

Think of a time in your life when you were able to feel empathy for somebody else who was suffering when you were not. Was this person close to you? How were you able to link your own experience into the suffering of that person? Was there anything positive that could come of that compassion? Have you ever been able to feel compassion for a complete stranger? How could you compel yourself to feel compassion for more strangers more often? What are the downsides of feeling compassion, and how can any negative feelings be mitigated?

* *Meditate on the true nature of compassion. Find more opportunities to show compassion for more people in your life. This can be harder than it seems and can be an ongoing process.*

Day 161: The Quest for Youth

The spiritual value of youth can be a controversial subject. After all, none of us are getting any younger. There's no way to get younger in this lifetime, no matter how devout you happen to be. Nonetheless, youth continues to be an ideal across many forms of religious expression. Youthful worshippers are honored as beautiful expressions of Spirit. Youthful people are protected by their elders, and fiercely defended when put in danger. The youthful virtues of purity and innocence are revered as joyful and sacred states of being. The energy of young people is certainly something to be envied.

Today, meditate upon the nature of youth. What are the benefits of youth over age? How was your spiritual experience or expression different in your youth? How can you bring some of your youthful energy back into your present spiritual practice? Since you aren't getting any younger, how can you encourage youthful people in their own personal spiritual expression? You might have the chance to become a mentor to somebody younger than yourself, who can in turn inject youthful energy into your own spiritual life.

* Meditate on the nature of youth. What is the
  benefit of youth? How can you emulate that?
  How can you bring real youth to Spirit?

Day 162: Kindness

....

Kindness is a universal spiritual virtue. You can't do wrong by being kind, even when you have to be firm, be stern, and set boundaries in your life. The worst that can come about from being kind is that your enemies become confused. And yet, kindness is one of the most difficult virtues to fake. If you're used to defending yourself with cruelty or aloofness, kindness can seem like an impossible virtue to emulate. After all, kindness springs from compassion. If you have no compassion, you will have a difficult time producing kind behavior.

Today, meditate on the true nature of kindness. What makes an action kind? Is it the intention of the act that truly makes it kind, or is it the outcome of the action that makes it kind? Can a kindness that is impractical for a community or a corporation be encouraged or accomplished by an individual? Is there any way to stop keeping count altogether and execute kind acts simply because you're a good person? It's always a valuable decision to try to bring more kindness into the world, so go for it.

* *Meditate on the true nature of kindness. How can you encourage kindness in others? How can you compel yourself to act with more kindness every day?*

Day 163: Gentleness

....

One virtue that is consistently characterized as female is gentleness. Consider the character of the southern ideal of womanhood. She's kind, pleasing to listen to, and always ready with a hand on the shoulder and a fresh glass of cool lemonade on a hot day. What is the true nature of gentleness? Any parent of a two-year-old knows that teaching gentleness involves a lot of explaining about a light touch. Touching another person with gentleness involves moving slowly and resting only lightly. Gentleness can be less tangible as well. Gentleness can include a "soft eye." Look at people with a smile on your lips and a hopeful thought in your mind.

Meditate today on the true nature of gentleness. When is it right to be gentle? How can you exemplify gentleness in your home? How can you embody the ideal of gentleness in your workplace? When you are feeling aggressive and defensive, how can you be as gentle as possible in your self-expression? Catch yourself being gentle throughout the day. Who helps you to be the gentlest version of yourself? What intrinsic rewards do you notice when you are gentle? How do you feel? How do others treat you?

* *Meditate on the true nature of gentleness.*

Day 164: Humility

....

Humility is a strange virtue to contemplate. It's a common virtue associated with women and spiritual people throughout the world. At the same time, it is also one of those tricky states of being to achieve. The more you try to be humble, the faster it flees from you. You can't very well stand on a rooftop shouting about your humility without looking like a braggart. Essentially, humility comes from achievement, sure. However, humility also comes from a life well lived, and a healthy sense of self-esteem.

Today, meditate on the true nature of humility. When have you been praised and yet at the same time felt satisfied? Who was the person (or persons) giving you accolades? How was your journey to the achievement? How was your success recognized? How can you encourage yourself to do the same sort of thing in your life now? It may seem silly to force yourself to achieve something and then be humble. Instead, try to catch yourself in the act. Is there anything you've recently done that you haven't yet celebrated?

* *Meditate on the true nature of humility.*

Day 165: Reverence Around the Sacred
···

Earlier in this book I asked you to contemplate whether anything was too silly for Spirit. Today, I'd like you to think about being reverent and showing respect for Spirit. You've already learned some practical ways to show respect to Spirit. You can address Spirit respectfully in prayer. You can dress especially for Spirit and you can clean yourself and prepare your sacred space for Spirit. But what is the true reason behind it all? Why treat Spirit carefully like a potentially angry grandparent when Spirit is also supposed to be your best friend?

In all cultures, there is a strange dance of respect that is done to show power differentials. It may be impossible to say whether the chicken comes before the egg here. Is your mom more important than you in your life because you treat her so, or is it because she imposes her will upon you and so it becomes true? In most religions, Spirit takes the high rank over people. Though there are a few traditions in which people threaten Spirit until they get their way, most people tend to step aside and let Spirit take the lead. Decide now what choice you will make.

* Meditate on the true nature of reverence.

Day 166: Abundance

When many people pray to Spirit asking for blessings, they ask for abundance, whether that means abundance of wealth or love. Abundance isn't a virtue, but a blessing. We know that a rich person isn't necessarily better than a person who is in poverty. A person with many loved ones is not any better than a person who only holds a few people dear to his or her heart. However, we all want sufficient abundance in our lives. When I pray for wealth, I ask that my life be blessed with enough to provide for myself and enough to share.

It's tough to get a handle on how much abundance you want and need in your own life. Witness the many people who seem to have it all but are still unhappy and wanting more. Don't spend your whole life chasing one goal after another without finding the true abundance of Spirit in your life. Even those who seem to have nothing can be truly happy if they find spiritual abundance.

* *Meditate on the true nature of abundance.*

Day 167: Sweetness
....

Today's challenge is tougher than it seems. More than kindness, sweetness is also a virtue at times attributed to Spirit. Let us carefully analyze the difference. While it may be more kind to tell someone that his beloved pet needs to be euthanized, sweetness comes into play with the gentle delivery of this bad news. The difference between the two is very subtle. You may have to practice sweetness a good deal even if you are a pro at choosing kind words and delivering tactful messages.

Today, think about how you can be sweeter to people in your life. The good news about sweetness is that kindness is not always necessary. Even if you have to give somebody bad news or if you have to do something challenging, you can do so while being sweet to all concerned. Try smiling and drawing from the joy of Spirit, even if you must pull it from the earth through grounding. Whenever you need to communicate a message, try to do so with gentleness, kindness, and sweetness. Observe the reaction you receive. Is your news received more quickly and smoothly when you are sweet?

* *Meditate on the true nature of sweetness.*

Day 168: Reciprocity

....

The divine feminine represents receptivity toward spiritual energy, and the divine masculine represents projection of said spiritual energy. The phallus is an expression of energy while the vagina accepts the spiritual gift. Even the female electrical outlet is receptive. This doesn't mean that women are always passive. However, it does mean that the goddess represents the ultimate expression of perfect acceptance. Whenever you send out prayers or energy into the universe, the goddess is guaranteed to receive it. This is why she was made. This is the perfect expression for which she was built.

Today, meditate on the nature of reciprocity, or the exchange of Spirit. Think about a time in your life when you were grateful that you accepted an idea or a person. Have you experienced a moment when you were happy that somebody was approachable? How can you encourage others to be more open to your spiritual energy? How can you be more welcoming to the spiritual energy of others? Imagine that spiritual energy is the perfect gift. One that can never really be returned, but can be exchanged for any gift you could want in the entire world. How can you be the most grateful recipient of this gift?

* *Meditate on the spiritual nature of reciprocity.*

Day 169: Perfect Love and Perfect Trust

Love is such a strong attribute of Spirit in many cultures that some believe that Spirit and love are indistinguishable. The concept of love is also inextricably bound with trust. Ideally, for faith to be present, one should develop both love for Spirit and trust in Spirit. This is easier said than done, and certainly both feelings may falter at different points in life. That doesn't mean that your sense of love and trust are flawed.

Do you feel love for Spirit? Do you feel trust in Spirit? You already know that one way to demonstrate your love for Spirit is to show love for a person in your life. Make time to do that today. It follows, too, that you can demonstrate your trust in a trustworthy person in order to grow your faith with Spirit. This can be very challenging for people with trust issues. Think of a trustworthy person you have in your life. This could be a best friend, a partner, a child, or someone else. How can you open up your trust to trustworthy people more? How can you thank these people for being trustworthy?

* Meditate on the topics of love and trust.

Day 170: Mirth and Joy

Being a spiritual person takes a lot of work and dedication. However, spirituality should be fun as well. The same Spirit that created the world in which you live also created love, laughter, and joy. In many religious traditions, showing joy and experiencing pleasure are expressions of worship in and of themselves. Some faith traditions go so far as to prescribe joyful singing, dancing and whirling, and other outward signs of mirth as daily worship. Spirit can be an enjoyable part of life, not a chore.

Everybody wants more happiness, but joy can be a fleeting thing. I can't give you homework to be happy today, because the issue can't be forced. Sometimes one has to come at happiness sideways and gently, like approaching a timid animal. Look back on your spiritual practice so far and recall which forms of spiritual expression make you the most joyful. Also think of the happiest moments in your everyday life and how you might interject more Spirit into those. Give yourself a break from anything you can that kills your joy today. You can return to such unpleasant duties tomorrow. Today, give an offering of your playful mood to Spirit.

* *Meditate on the nature of joy.*

Day 171: Feminism

It's easy to see the power in ordinary women if you honor the divine feminine. When considering the divine feminine, many people take note that there's an overwhelming emphasis in world religions on the idea of god as a masculine archetype. Seeing this imbalance, some choose to advocate for the divine feminine. This can be seen as a form of feminism. In fact, some religious people combine feminism as a political movement with spirituality. You don't have to exclusively honor female notions of Spirit, although some choose to do so, believing that is the only way to truly find balance.

Do you consider yourself a feminist? Do you believe in an equal balance between the divine feminine and the divine masculine? How can you promote this balance in your spiritual practice? Do you think that your own spirituality is currently gender-skewed in any way? Today, meditate upon the place of feminism in society and spirituality. You may notice more places they intersect in your own life experience. You may feel compelled to align your spiritual goals with feminism or you may not. Either view is okay. In fact, many actively distance themselves from feminist ideology in order to focus on building up the divine masculine as well.

* *Meditate on the place of feminism in spiritual practice.*

Day 172: Staying Down-to-Earth
....

Female archetypes and societal roles can be confusing. A single person can embody completely polar opposite ideals within a lifetime. In the real lived experience of spiritual women, the sacred and the profane dance together in everyday life. A mother can be sexy. A flirty person can be nurturing. A girlfriend can be a vixen and the sort of lady to take home to meet Mom. In our society, people tend to either devalue women or place them high on a pedestal, treating them with so much grace and gentleness that their humanity is obscured.

When you think of the divine feminine, which archetypes do you tend to gravitate toward? As you progress through this book, you may naturally find yourself opening up to seeing the divine in every person and in every woman. How can you show honor to women while also acknowledging their ordinary humanity? Allow yourself to think of the less honorable traits of women you respect in your life as well. How do their flaws highlight their human nature and their potential for growth?

* *Meditate upon some ways that you see the divine feminine
  as greater than the ordinary. How can you reconcile the two
  images of femininity, the sacred and the less-than-honorable?*

Day 173: Correspondences

....

At the beginning of this section, I asked you to brainstorm some ideas about the divine feminine. Looking back on those notes may help today. Correspondences are symbolic associations that can be used in spiritual working. For example, when you worked with the elements, you learned that a bowl of salt in your sacred place can represent the element of earth. This is an example of a correspondence. You can also come up with correspondences for the divine feminine. These correspondences might vary from person to person and especially between cultures. For example, the divine feminine may be represented by flowers, the color purple, the earth, the moon, a necklace, and many other things.

Today, meditate on other correspondences for the divine feminine. What are some objects you can place on your altar or in your sacred space to represent the divine feminine to you? What are some representative foods, incenses, or gestures that you could add to your prayer time? How can you add a bit of the divine feminine touch to your household? Use these correspondences to keep yourself more mindful.

* Brainstorm and free-associate some
  divine feminine correspondences.

Day 174: Goddesses

You may already be familiar with some specific goddess names in mythology. For example, Aphrodite, the goddess of love in Greek mythology. Artemis, goddess of the moon, the hunt, and chastity. Athena, goddess of wisdom and war. You may have already been able to explore other pantheons while reading myths. Today, I want you to drill down deeper and get specific with goddesses. You can read about goddesses online or pick a good book from the library. You can even reread an old favorite myth, this time paying careful attention to any goddess characters.

As you read and research, notice attributes that are common to many goddesses. You can ponder whether all goddesses are aspects of a single goddess, or whether they are each individuals in their own right, or whether these are merely stories to help people understand female roles in spirituality. Are some goddess archetypes more believable and appealing to you than others? Are there similarities between the stories that contain goddess figures? If you were to write a myth about a new goddess, what would she be like and what would she do? Do any of these goddess myths inspire your spiritual practice?

* Read goddess mythology.

Day 175: Matron
....

Some people who honor the divine feminine choose a matron goddess. Some people believe that a matron goddess chose them. As you read through goddess mythology, you may have found one goddess who stood out for you more than others. Or, perhaps a goddess came to you in a dream or during a meditative vision. There are many ways for the divine feminine to reach out and touch your life. You may have to go seeking, or you may have already found her right where you are.

So, what do you do with a matron goddess once you've got one? Well, that depends on your beliefs and preferred practice. You could print out a picture of the goddess, decorate it, and display it in your living space. You could begin directing your prayers to that goddess. You could simply use that goddess as a meditative focal point and contemplate her myths and attributes. Is the goddess real? The good thing about myths is that they always hold within them a little bit of human truth, no matter how fantastic. You can bring to life some of your matron goddess's attributes by integrating them into your own life.

* Choose a matron goddess.

Day 176: Goddess Planets

When I first introduced astrology in this book, I had you take a look at some of the planetary aspects and your own sun signs. Imagine that the planets are a cast of characters, and the sign is the stage. The aspects are the dialogue between them. Today I'd like to introduce you to some of the planets. Venus is the Roman goddess of love. Whenever Venus interacts with another planet, there's sure to be love or passion going on. Even though the moon isn't a planet, it is considered one in astrology. The moon belongs to the goddess Diana, and represents mystery, cycles, and magic.

Look up an astrological calendar. You may have to search for a key if your astrological calendar uses signs to represent the planets. Pay special attention to the moon and Venus, and look at what is happening with them this month. In which star sign is Venus right now? Look up the characteristics of that star sign. What would it mean if those characteristics were supercharged with love right now? Try the same exercise with the moon and its mystery. If you have access to your natal chart, you can take a look at how these two planets influence you. If you find this interesting and want to jump into the male planets as well, you can look up the Sun, who belongs to Apollo, the god of healing. You can also look at Saturn, the god of chaos and destruction; Jupiter, the god of leadership and duty; Mercury, the god of business and communication; and Mars, the god of conflict.

* *Investigate goddess planets.*

Day 177: Herbs and Flowers
in the Garden of Mother Earth

Herbs and flowers are often associated with the divine feminine. There are those who believe that herbs themselves are divine. Devas, the spirits of plants, dwell in gardens. If you build a garden suitable for herbs and flowers, consider adding some to your garden that remind you of the divine feminine. Meditate near herbs or flowers and see if you can feel the divine energy emanating from them.

Flowers are a frequent offering to Spirit. Cut flowers and place them in a bud vase on your altar or in your sacred space. You can purchase flowers in the supermarket or paint or draw a picture of a flower. If the flowers have a good scent, breathe in the beautiful fragrance and sip some herbal tea while you meditate. You can visualize yourself laying the flowers at the feet of a goddess if you wish. Leave the flowers in the sacred space when you are done. Later, when they begin to droop, you can discard them, preferably outdoors, perhaps in a compost pile, to return to the earth. Try not to have wilted flowers on your altar. However, you can place dried flowers as a permanent feature in your sacred space.

* *Use flowers or herbs as an offering to Spirit.*

Day 178: Tarot Archetypes

The tarot is a deck of seventy-eight cards originally designed as a game and political satire and later used as a divination system. If you lay out the tarot cards from the first to the last, they tell the classic story of the hero's journey. When you shuffle tarot cards and lay them out carefully in arrays called spreads, they can tell your own story. In forthcoming days, we'll investigate several tarot card archetypes one by one, as well as further exploring the hero's journey.

In the coming exercises, you can look up pictures of tarot cards online, but ideally I encourage you to get your own tarot deck. You can buy a tarot deck sight unseen, but if you're lucky enough to live near a metaphysical bookstore, you can pick one out in person. Most metaphysical bookstores have sample decks so that you can look through the cards before you buy. Flip through them and see if any of the imagery speaks to you. You might even sense the energy of a deck by simply holding it and decide that tarot deck is right for you. If you already have a tarot card deck, flip through it today and take special note of any divine feminine archetypes.

* Begin to explore tarot card imagery. Consider
  purchasing a tarot card deck of your own.

Day 179: Birth and Death

....

The divine feminine is the gateway to birth, since every human who is alive today once gestated within the womb of a mother. The cycle of birth and death is one of the greatest spiritual mysteries. As mysteries, birth and death are often best explored through symbolism. The divine feminine is an important symbolic key for understanding these mysteries for many people.

Today, meditate on the true nature of birth and death. Do you believe that birth and death are a cycle? Is death necessary for birth? What do you think happened with your personality and identity before birth? Is the afterlife also a place where our souls dwell before birth? Explore your beliefs surrounding birth and death. One symbol for this is the labyrinth. During your walking meditation, I suggested that you see if there is a labyrinth near you, or build your own. You can also meditate upon a smaller labyrinth model. You can print out a picture of a labyrinth and trace its path with your finger. You can think about any issue while journeying through the labyrinth, but the issue of birth and death is especially well suited to the labyrinth.

* Meditate on the topics of birth and death.

Day 180: Earth

....

The earth is associated with the divine feminine in many myths. Mother Earth is a nurturer, because she nourishes all life as we know it. The Gaia hypothesis, named after the earth goddess, suggests that the earth itself is a giant organism. We are living upon this goddess, and she may in fact be sentient. The earth is also associated with the element of earth. Green, growing things; financial abundance; and a sense of stability all come from the earth. Financial abundance comes from the elemental energies of earth that have to do with material things, stability, and the abundant wealth of fruits and vegetables that spring forth from the earth.

Today, practice your grounding during meditation. This time, be especially mindful that the refreshing and renewing energy that you receive through grounding is coming from the earth. Visualize the earth as a mother who takes care of you. Next, visualize yourself as a part of Mother Earth. You are but one cell in her body. Imagine that you are loved by her as much as you care about your own two hands. Feel the divine feminine energy flowing through you, washing and refreshing you, and filling you with love. When you have finished grounding, thank the earth and any being that may embody it. You have come from the earth and one day you shall return to it.

* Practice your grounding while staying mindful
  that the energy comes from Mother Earth.

Day 181: Oceans, Rivers, and Bodies of Water

In mythology, goddesses are often associated with oceans, rivers, and other bodies of water. Why is this? The element of water is thought to be feminine. The waters of the womb bring forth life. In many cultures it was thought that after death, souls went over the water to an afterlife. Just as goddesses are mediators between life and death, so is the element of water. In some cultures, every body of water is thought to have its own spirit. I am lucky enough to live at the edge of two creeks. Whenever I like, I can go rest at the side of the flowing water and gaze into it. It is a peaceful experience and the pattern of the water flowing over the rocks can easily lull me into a trance.

Today, you can practice your water scrying, preferably while visiting a natural body of water. Scrying is the practice of seeing psychic visions within a divination tool such as water. It doesn't matter if it's a lake, a pond, or a stream. Hopefully you'll be looking into something that is a little bigger than a puddle. Imagine that the Divine Spirit that dwells within this natural feature is what gives you the images you see during your meditations.

* Try water scrying in a natural body of water.

Day 182: Blood Symbolism

Blood has long been a symbol associated with women's mysteries. After all, women bleed once a month, often coinciding with the moon's cycles. Blood coming from the womb, the place of birth, represents life. And, of course, exsanguinations can cause death. To primitive peoples, blood must have seemed like a mysterious, magical, and sacred substance indeed. Thinking in this way, it's amazing to know that there is an intricate system in your body that allows this sacred substance to constantly circulate within you. If you choose to donate blood, you are literally giving life from this spiritual essence of yourself. If you happen to be the proud owner of a uterus, it is thought that your psychic abilities are increased during the time of menstruation.

Today, meditate on the topic of blood. Consider grabbing some red paint and creating art. If you're a little squeamish about blood, you don't have to be so visual with your meditations. Instead, you can feel your pulse and the heat of your blood flowing in your veins as you meditate. Try to focus on your own blood movement, visualizing it helping the energy move around your body.

* Meditate upon the topic of blood.

Day 183: Wise Women

Before the advent of modern medicine, every village and hamlet had its wise women. Indeed, in some rural communities in the world, this is still the case. Such wise women were crones old enough to have experience with various illnesses and conditions. Wise women would make herbal preparations to treat various maladies. When younger women were giving birth, wise women did their best to get the mom and baby through the ordeal alive. Historically, wise women were sometimes persecuted by those who disliked strange old women on the fringes of society, or who were threatened by their role and station in the community.

Even in this modern world, we are blessed with wise women. Luckily, we now have the opportunity to take advantage of the wisdom of these ladies in addition to the miracle of modern medicine. Do you know a wise woman in your life? Would you like to take on some of the attributes of a wise woman? Today, meditate on the wise woman as a symbol and a representation of the divine feminine. The wise woman is the embodiment of the divine feminine walking and acting on this earth.

* *Meditate on the archetype of the wise woman.*

Day 184: The Cup and the Pentacle

....

Today we will look at two symbols often found in altars and sacred spaces and also seen in the tarot cards. First, the cup. The cup represents the cauldron of death and rebirth. It is the womb or vagina as a symbol. You can place a cup of water in your sacred space as a representation of the divine feminine, or you can even pour yourself a glass of wine when you sit down at meditation to honor the divine feminine. The myth of the Holy Grail represents the divine feminine and the eternal life that she can bring. The cup can also act as a representative of the element of water in your sacred space when filled with water.

The pentacle is both a symbol and a tool. A pentacle is a five-pointed star inscribed in a circle. The five points of the star represent earth, air, fire, water, and Spirit. The circle represents cycles and also protection. In the tarot, the pentacle is the symbol of material abundance. You can make a pentacle as a tool to keep in your sacred space. Cut a circle out of paper, or get a circular piece of wood. Paint or draw a pentacle on the circle. This can be a representative of earth in your sacred space.

* *Procure a cup and a pentacle for your sacred space.*

Day 185: Woman Warriors, the Fierce Side of Women, and the Fire in the Belly

Goddesses are often painted in myth as receptors of the seed of life, and so they may appear passive. However, there are plenty of warrior goddesses in myth as well. This archetype may seem to go against the passivity and gentleness often associated with the female form. Of course, in real life we know that every person has the capacity to be violent or peaceful. The same fire of creativity that rises up within the divine feminine can also be a fire of destruction. Creators can be destroyers.

Today, meditate upon the archetype of the female warrior. You can choose a goddess like Athena, or you can think of a woman warrior in your own life. You can even think of a woman who is battling cancer. Draw strength from this image in your meditation. Imagine this divine warrior within you. The nurturing gentleness of womanhood and the strength of a warrior are combined in this image. Do you find a conflict in these two roles? Are you drawn to the juxtaposition of peace and war? Do you ever have to play both of these roles?

* Meditate on the topic of woman warriors.

Part Six

⚹

Getting in Touch with the Divine Masculine

Day 186: The Creative Force

In this section of the book we will explore the divine masculine, which may be more familiar to some. However, we'll do so with the same lens as we used to explore the divine feminine. So hold onto your hats. As the divine female represents receptive energy, the divine masculine represents active and dynamic energy. Though goddesses are the womb of creation in which new things are formed, gods are the spark of creation that gets things started.

Think about projects in your life that never really got off the ground. You may be missing the motivation that gets you over that initial hurdle or inertia. Even if there are barriers preventing you from starting one of these projects, the divine masculine force can help you power through them and get started. Today, pray and meditate to ask for help getting things off the ground. Then, you must feel and listen for the motivation. Run with it. The creative force can have a sort of snowball effect with your own energy. The more you help things along, the more energy you will receive. Think of it as the big bang.

* Receive assistance from the creative force in meditation.

Day 187: Projective Energy

The projective energy of the divine masculine can be helpful in many ways and is often the power sought in intercessory prayer. In fact, it may help you to think about each of your wants and needs in life in terms of receptive or projective. For example, if you want to increase your psychic ability and intuition, turn to the divine feminine for receptive energy. If you want to ask your boss for a raise, you'd do best with the projective energy of the divine masculine. You'll need the impetus to call your boss and make the appointment. You'll need the energy to project your best self during the meeting and to deliver the message.

Today, make a list of some plans and projects in your life. Try to order this list in two columns: one for receptive energy and one for projective energy. While you pray or meditate today, try praying down the list of projective energy items. As you do so, visualize divine energy welling up within you and giving you the motivation and power to accomplish what is on your list. If you have a project on your list that you've already started, visualize yourself seeing it through to its completion.

* Pray using projective energy.

Day 188: The Prince

....

The divine masculine has archetypes that differ from those of the divine feminine, of course. Over the next few days, we'll explore some of them. The prince is the counterpart to the maiden. He is youthful and exuberant. Sometimes called the Green Prince in folklore, imagine him running around in the springtime like a young buck. He is the greenery of the forest world, but he is also "green" in the sense that he is new and inexperienced. He wants to take in the entire world all at once. The prince has so much to learn.

Today, meditate on the archetype of the prince. Have you played the role of the prince in your life so far? When would the prince's youthful energy be useful in your life? When might that energy be more of a liability than a help? Do you know anyone in your life who embodies the young prince? Draw or paint an image of the young prince. How do you envision him? What would he be holding? What is he up to? Imagine the young prince meeting the maiden. What sorts of exploits might they tackle together?

* *Meditate upon the archetype of the prince.*

Day 189: The Father

The father is, of course, the counterpart to the mother. The father god is a comforting image. He is patient and loyal. He is strong and skilled. The father is a great protector. However, this father figure isn't all fun and games. He also sets limits when limits are needed. He can be stern and strict, teaching harsh lessons when necessary. The father joins with the mother to be a strong team of archetypes. He is a loving husband to the mother, and can provide the support his family needs. No wonder so many prayers of the world religions address the father god. This guy gets things done.

Meditate upon the archetype of the father god. How would you visualize the father god? What is he doing? What is he holding? Paint or draw the father god. Do you have a father figure in your own life? Recall instances in your life when you felt enfolded in the father energy of that person. Try to perfectly recreate those feelings in your mind and heart. In what pursuits in your life would father god energy be helpful to you? Do you have a bit of the father god inside yourself? When do you find yourself playing that role?

* Meditate upon the archetype of the father god.

Day 190: The Bearded Old Hermit in His Cave

The hermit is the counterpart to the wise old crone. This character, however, is solitary. He lives up in the mountains or deep in the forest, where he whiles away his time with hobbies and ponders life's deepest mysteries. He is close to death and yet is entirely unafraid. He and the reaper are close friends, and are honestly one and the same. Occasionally, the hermit will reach out to the world with his wisdom, or will have some young seeker come knocking on his door. He may be curmudgeonly, but he will help if you ask the right questions.

Today, meditate on the hermit. Draw or paint a picture of how you might imagine the hermit to look. What is he doing? What is he holding? Look up the Hermit tarot card. He is often depicted holding a lantern. This is his way of reaching out to the world while remaining aloof. He shines the light of his wisdom out from his dark and cold hideaway. Have you known some wise old hermits in your life? When do you take on the role of the hermit? Certainly anyone who has taken a spiritual retreat of any kind has become the hermit, if only briefly. Is there a situation in your life in which hermit energy will help?

* Meditate on the archetype of the hermit.

Day 191: Strength and Muscles

Strength is an essential characteristic of the divine masculine. This strength can be both physical and emotional, or can be a figurative characteristic of something else. So many of the world's scriptures encourage disciples to be mentally strong and to encourage the strength of the physical body as well. In Western culture, heroes are defined by their strength. It is often strength alone that allows them to overcome trials. There is no such thing as being too strong. However, there is such a thing as not knowing your own strength.

Do you know your own strength? Today, meditate on the concept of strength. How can you strengthen your mind? How can you strengthen your emotions? How can you strengthen your body? If it is right for you, consider undertaking a physical strength-training regimen. Strength is gained through experience. Thus, many emotional challenges bring with them the blessing of strength. Remember a time in your life when you had to use your strength to get through a challenge. Recall the strength that you felt. How can you quickly bring that strength to mind without having to suffer?

* Meditate upon the topic of strength.

Day 192: Power of Place and Physical Power

Power is the ability to get stuff done. Power can come from strength, but power can also come from cunning, collaboration and teamwork, taking on a role, and from many other sources. One could say the power of the divine masculine is limitless, simply because there are so many ways in which it can be expressed. Power is yours for the taking. One reason why people seek spirituality is to get closer to the power of Spirit. Power calls to us because we can use it to solve our problems and the problems of others.

Today, meditate upon the concept of power. How do you acquire power? What do you do with power once you have it? What power in your life comes inherently from the roles you play? For example, if you're a boss at work, you have power over your subordinates. If you are a father at home, you have power over your children. If you're a pet owner, you have power over your pet. When do you find yourself seeking more power? When do you find yourself avoiding power? As you meditate, try to feel the power of Spirit. Know that you can tap into that power at any time.

* Meditate upon the topic of power.

Day 193: Ranks of Honor

To be honored is to be held in high respect or esteem. To be honorable is to be worthy of that respect. This is a value seen time and time again in religious practice. It may seem strangely out of place. How is it that the opinions of other people matter to Spirit? If you think about this capacity for respectability as a character trait, however, it may make more sense. We live in a societal context, no matter how much the hermit archetype may sometimes appeal. Each person does the best he or she can to be a proper member of that society. One's honor doesn't always precisely correlate with wealth or success.

Is being respected and held in high esteem a value of yours? Certainly, everyone wants to be treated with respect. But do you embrace your desire for status, or do you hold it at arm's length so as to not take yourself too seriously or be too full of yourself? Think of the people in your life who are honorable. What characteristics make them worthy of your respect? Who holds you in high esteem and why? Are there any areas in your life where you think you may be given more credit than you deserve?

* *Meditate on the nature of honor.*

Day 194: The Sword of the Soldier

The sword is often the weapon of gods in mythology. The sword is also an entire suit of tarot cards. Unlike the cup and the pentacle, it may be difficult to get a sword for your sacred space. However, you can still meditate upon images of swords within your tarot deck when the real thing is not available. Not only is the sword a weapon, it is also a symbolic representation of cutting intellect and the ability to communicate. Some spiritual traditions associate it with the element of air. The sword can defend and can create a boundary between the world of Spirit and the world of men.

Today, meditate upon the image of the sword. Visualize a sword in the hand of a god. If you were to write this story, how would it begin and how would it end? How is the god standing? Strong? Defensively? Fearfully? Angrily? When do you defend yourself with your words? When is your communication cutting, just like a sword? In these moments you may have an opportunity to conduct yourself in a spiritual way, instead of losing control and saying things that are hurtful for the sake of being hurtful.

* Meditate upon the symbol of the sword.

Day 195: The Wand of the Magician

The wand is another symbolic weapon of the divine masculine. When wielding the wand, the mythological god takes the role of the magician. He is in control of his environment and changes the world around him by sheer force of his will. The wand that he waves to punctuate his power is merely a way to add flourish to his inner strength. It is no coincidence that the wand looks a little like a phallus. However, both men and women can symbolically use a wand in spiritual practice. Hold the wand when you wish to direct your will. The wand is sometimes associated with the element of fire.

Today, consider making your own wand, or meditate upon the power of a wand if you already have one. To make a wand, find a stick about the length of your forearm. If you must cut a stick from a tree, you can ask Spirit's permission first. One way to do this is to tie a ribbon around the branch you're about to cut, knock on the trunk to tell the tree's spirit to hide in the roots, and then thank the tree after cutting the branch. Various branches will feel differently as wands, so it can be fun to experiment.

* *Create a wand and meditate upon it.*

Day 196: The Dark Side of Spirit and Your Shadow Self

Just as some men are good men and some men do bad things, Spirit allows difficult things to happen in this world. For some people, god is vengeful and jealous, and unleashes his rage on the world. In other cultures, god is a terrifying god of the dead and the underworld. Being god-fearing is certainly a valid path to take, but it may be a confusing one. It's hard to love somebody you fear, but it is certainly possible. Even our own selves have a dark side from which we often hide. Exploring your shadow self may be something you avoid, but it can be a transformational experience as well.

Today, meditate upon the dark side of Spirit and your shadow self. What are the dark and scary things you fear in this universe? What are the dark parts of yourself? What triggers your darkest thoughts? Is there anything positive or constructive that results from this darkness in the world and within yourself? How can something terrifying but powerful be made into an asset? If that is impossible, can you access it from a safe distance?

* *Explore your shadow self.*

Day 197: Warrior

....

The warrior archetype of Spirit can be a tough one to comprehend. It may be that this warrior archetype has started wars. When people believe their god is calling them into battle, they respond wholeheartedly. So, why should a warrior god be revered? Aren't spiritual people supposed to be peaceful? At the same time, going into battle may be unavoidable at times. Battle may be waged to protect good people. Battle may be waged within the self in order to become a better person. The warrior god dons his armor and walks into battle alongside us whenever appropriate.

Today, meditate upon the archetype of the warrior and visualize Spirit as being at war. This is a metaphorical war, and can be fought in any way you imagine. Draw or paint a picture of your warrior god. What is he wearing? Does he hold any weapons? How does he conduct himself in battle? Does he attempt to negotiate? Think of the battles you are currently fighting in your own life or within yourself. How can you properly prepare yourself to win? Can there ever be peace in these wars?

* Meditate upon the archetype of the warrior.

Day 198: Animals and the Wild Hunt

While earth and plants are the realms of the divine feminine, animals are often assigned to the divine masculine. Because he is the hunter, he is also associated with the hunted and other creatures in his wild kingdom. The divine masculine is the hunter and the hunted. While the divine feminine is the earth itself upon which the wildlife frolics, the divine masculine is the animalistic spark within those living beings. God can be seen inside every animal, large and small. Some find animals so sacred they pray before killing them, or even refuse to eat animal meat altogether. Do animals have souls? Do all dogs go to heaven? These are questions you can look into your own heart to answer.

For today's exercise, observe an animal in meditation. It's ideal to use a pet such as a sleeping cat, but this exercise can even be performed while watching a wild bird. Relax and observe the animal from afar. Try synchronizing your breathing. Try seeing the aura of the animal. Imagine this animal is a creation that belongs to the divine masculine. Pay attention to any emotions you feel or any messages you receive from this animal. Write down any impressions that you get.

> * Connect with an animal today, and think
>   about its relationship with Spirit.

Day 199: Resurrection of the Divine Masculine

The divine masculine is associated with new life even though he can't physically give birth like a feminine archetype. New life happens in many god myths through resurrection. An eerily similar story is told and retold across cultures. A god dies in the prime of his life. He is then reborn and brought back to life. Spirit resurrects this god because he still has work to do and still offers aid and joy to this world. This myth parallels the seasons, in which we alternate between periods of growth and periods of culling and reaping.

Today, ponder the nature of resurrection. Why do resurrection myths involving a god happen across many cultures? Thinking of the current season, in what stage of death and resurrection are the crops and herds? Think about cycles that happen in your work or school or relationships. How can you instigate a sense of renewal and rebirth in your life? Read resurrection and rebirth myths for inspiration. Becoming reborn through Spirit is one way that many have kick-started their own lives.

* *Meditate on the concepts of resurrection and rebirth.*

Day 200: Protection and the
Divine Masculine as Protective Force

God is a protective force for his followers. We are surrounded by dangers every day. Our current society seems obsessed with risk. We have safety precautions, features, and procedures everywhere in our cars, homes, and workplaces. Yet the media is full of stories about dangerous people and things. Our daily life experience may as well be as fearful as the lives of primitive people. Like them, we can turn to Spirit to protect us when all other precautions have already been taken. God's protection is one way to overcome fears that might otherwise keep us from rolling out of bed in the morning.

Today, formulate a prayer for protection you can use in the morning before leaving the house. Personalize this prayer for your own situation. If you drive to work or school first thing, you might say a prayer while walking around your car and checking the tires and mirrors for safety. If you work with a particular occupational hazard, say a prayer that speaks to that. If the environment around your home has specific dangers, name them and ask for protection.

* Create a prayer for protection that can be used daily or as needed.

Day 201: Sacrifices
....

Some gods die as a sacrifice so their human followers can live closer to Spirit. Today I'd like you to think about sacrifices. This time, we're not talking about offerings such as incense or food given during worship. This time, I'd like to discuss sacrifice in the sense that you lose something or give something up in order to make great gains in life. God can be a force that limits, and god might also be perceived as demanding great sacrifice from you. At other times, you may willingly make a great sacrifice for Spirit or somebody you love. For example, in order to be dedicated to prayer time, you'll have to sacrifice time you could otherwise spend relaxing or getting caught up on work.

Meditate upon the nature of sacrifice. Do you believe in a deity who asks a sacrifice of you? Have you been called upon to make a sacrifice for Spirit? Is there something you know you should give up, and yet you have a tough time making that sacrifice? Is there any way you can make that sacrifice for Spirit, and in doing so, give yourself motivation? Sacrifices are tough to make, but many sacrifices in life bring greater joy and fulfillment down the road. Try to willingly make sacrifices to your loved ones and to Spirit with an attitude of hope and love so you don't breed resentment in your heart.

* *Consider sacrifices yet to be made in your life.*

Day 202: Control

....

Is god a control freak? If you believe in an all-powerful god, perhaps he's controlling by nature. Part of the greatness we covet in Spirit is the ability to have control. This higher power has a degree of control over fate, people, and events about which we can only dream. Part of tapping into that power means hoping to have control over an otherwise chaotic world. Control over one's own mind is also a vital spiritual practice. This is why I give you so many meditation exercises. Spiritual disciplines like having a daily prayer life, meditating for twenty minutes or more, and keeping a dream journal when you'd rather be sleeping are all ways to increase your mental control.

Today, exercise control in some way over yourself and your life, and in doing so become god-like. Choose something difficult. For example, if you're addicted to the Internet, turn it off for the day. If you struggle with quiet and receptive meditation, tack on a few more minutes to challenge yourself. Or, pick something else like vigorous exercise or fasting.

* *Exercise control over your life and ask for Spirit*
  to give you help with that sense of control.

Day 203: Metal and Wood

··

You've already learned about the four elements: earth, air, fire, and water. The Chinese omit air, but add a couple additional elements to this list that are both masculine: metal and wood. Metalworking and woodworking are often attributed to men. These materials are also strong and unyielding. Items made of these materials can be used as meditative tools. Hold them during your meditation and feel their energy.

You may already have some tools of these materials in your sacred space. For example, a wand made of wood. You may not have a metal object in your sacred space yet. A ritual knife is often placed in sacred spaces in religious traditions. It's not a sword, but it can represent the same things. Get a piece of metal to add to your sacred space, remembering this represents the strength of divinity. It can be a knife or a ring or a bracelet to represent the eternal nature of divinity. Or, it can be a pretty piece of metal that speaks to you.

* *Meditate upon metal and wood, two spiritual elements associated with the divine masculine.*

Day 204: Conservation of Energy

The divine masculine is energy, and you've seen how he can energize the potential in your life in many ways. Scientific principles teach us that energy in the universe is conserved. That means that energy can't just disappear without affecting something. Likewise, energy can't appear out of nowhere. Energy flows, going from one thing to another and changing forms. Spiritual energy is different, of course, but as a metaphor it is similar. In fact, some people say that money is energy. It changes forms, it changes hands, and it always moves around, doing no real good when it stagnates in one place.

Recycling is another good metaphor for the conservation of energy in life. It honors the earth by reusing materials that might otherwise cause damage to creation. Some people find that honoring the earth by recycling can be a simple form of spiritual expression. Today, commit to this practical activity. If you've saved items in your home to reuse, reuse or donate them today. If you recycle, look over the rules of your recycling company to make sure you're not missing anything that could be reused and put back into circulation. If your community doesn't recycle yet, think about starting a program in your area.

* Recycle as a practical way to keep the
  flow of energy going in your world.

Day 205: Wood and Woodland Places

By now, you've seen several correspondences built up for the divine masculine that have to do with wood and woodlands. You know that wood is his element. There are mythological stories of a god conducting a wild hunt in the woods at night. You know that woodland creatures are all created and loved by god. All of these things make the woods a special place for Spirit. In fact, god shows up in art as the Green Man, the face of god formed by leaves. This Green Man of the forest is a more kindly and peaceful image than the mysterious god of the wild hunt. This is the face of god I'd like you to ponder today.

Pray and meditate in some forested area today. If you're in a region without woodlands, you may have to fudge things a bit. Try to find natural wood and an area that is wild enough to have wild creatures living there. It could be a tiny park with woody shrubs and insects or a genuine forest. Pray to the god present in this woodland and then meditate, listening to the sounds of the area. Does he give you any signs?

* *Meditate upon the woodlands.*

Day 206: Destruction before Creation and the Divine Masculine as Destroyer

···

I remember when I was a little kid and I first learned things don't last forever. It was bad enough to learn I would someday die. Around the same time, I realized the house in which I grew up would also one day grow old and crumble. Worst of all, I learned our very sun in our solar system will die one day. I ran to my parents crying. As an adult, I know bodies must die and decompose in order for the world to continue working the way it does. People can't live forever. In the same way, I know that things must be destroyed in order for whatever will come after to happen.

Destruction, thus, is not always a terrible thing. In fact, it is a sacred thing, even when it is distressing or not in your own best interest. Today, meditate on the sacred nature of necessary destruction. Think about things in your life that must one day be destroyed. This may be a lot of things. In a way, destruction is comforting. Think about how many of your life's worries won't matter in 100 years.

* *Meditate upon the true nature of destruction.*

Day 207: The Divine Masculine as the Loving Force that Limits

··

Running up against limitations in life is frustrating and sometimes deeply depressing. On the other hand, knowing one's limits can be sacred. Spirit seemingly presents to us unlimited abundance and opportunities; however, there are limits and obstacles placed in front of us. It's okay to acknowledge that some obstacles are insurmountable. Just like the unanswered prayers you may have had in your life, god may set limits for you. Remember destiny is a framework. It may support you and protect you at the same time. When one way is closed to you, it may be there are other opportunities needing to be pursued.

Today, meditate upon your own limitations, trying to reframe them as gifts or opportunities for other things. Allow yourself to experience feelings of regret or disappointment, but then let those feelings go. Imagine the strong force of the divine masculine has placed those limits in your life like a loving father trying to help a child avoid the wrong path. Try to find gratitude for your limitations. Think about other paths in front of you that are not currently blocked by obstacles, and make your way forward.

* Embrace your limitations.

Day 208: The Hunter
....

Another archetype of god is as a hunter. This archetype of the divine masculine has many attributes. He is strong and he may be part of a tribe or family.
Most of all, he is a provider. In a world that is chaotic and full of many battles,
he fights those battles and brings home food for his people day after day. At
the same time, the hunter must be fierce to kill an animal, especially if it is an
animal larger than himself.

Today, meditate upon the hunter archetype. Draw or paint a picture
of a hunter deity. What does he look like? How is he standing? What is he
holding? What quarry does he seek? Imagine your own mythological story
about a brave and heroic hunter. How does the story begin? What happens
in the end? Can Spirit provide for you in your life? What sort of bounty
would you like Spirit to make available every day? Can Spirit fight some of
your battles, or teach you how to fight those battles yourself? How can you
embody the spirit of a hunter?

* *Meditate upon the archetype of the hunter.*

Day 209: The Sun

....

Many ancient cultures saw the sun as a deity, usually masculine. At the time, they did not have our modern knowledge that the sun sustains all life on this earth. It was a mysterious orb in the sky giving light and heat and whose movement seemed to dictate the days and the seasons. Now we know the sun's energy feeds plants, which in turn feed us, and gives the earth the heat it needs in order to survive. The sun has power over us, and still remains a symbol of transcendent power today.

Meditate on the topic of the sun. If you have a tarot deck, find the Sun card and gaze upon its image. When the sun is shining, seat yourself where it shines upon you. Some believe the light of the sun directly nourishes us with spiritual energy as a counterpart to the energy we gain from food. Breathe in and out deeply, and imagine you are getting all the spiritual "food" you need from the sunlight. This works even if it's an overcast or cloudy day.

* *Meditate on the sun.*

Day 210: The Hammer as a Tool of the Divine Masculine

The hammer is a tool of mythological gods. My husband's favorite hobby is blacksmithing, and he feels close to Spirit while he works on forging treasures and tools. The hammer makes a sound like thunder, and it can be used as both a weapon and a force in shaping things. Spirit metaphorically hammers us into the beings that we are supposed to be. This process is necessarily violent and unpleasant at times. The more resistance we put up, the longer the hammering goes on. The hammer metaphor teaches us to withstand the suffering required to forge something beautiful while relaxing into the form we're meant to have.

Today, meditate on the tool that is the hammer. Visualize it wielded by a god. What is the god forging? Think about processes in your life that take patience and effort in which you are metaphorically a blacksmith. Think of yourself as the metal being worked by god. Is time and suffering building you to be a better person in your life? Ponder these metaphors while you listen for god's advice to you.

* *Meditate upon the hammer as a symbolic tool of god.*

Day 211: The Lightning Bolt

Several gods in mythology have been associated with lightning—either causing lighting when angry, or holding the lightning bolt as if it were an easily wielded tool. Lightning represents the active force of the divine masculine. It is the energy that can bring light and destruction. Modern people know electricity has useful power, helping us get work done in our lives. A lightning storm has a certain spiritual energy to it. The next time you experience a lighting storm, pay attention to the energy surrounding you. You might sense humming or buzzing or a prickly sensation in the air. You might even have a feeling of excitement. Safely stay indoors if you can, but marvel out the window at the power of god in the sky.

Meditate today on lightning as a symbol for Spirit. Visualize god having power over lightning, able to send it wherever he wills. Think about how that level of power might have frightened or awed ancient people, and try allowing yourself a taste of that awe, even if in your imagination.

* *Meditate upon the symbolic meaning of lightning.*

Day 212: Initiation as a Metaphor
and the Divine Masculine as Initiator

Religions all over the world have initiation ceremonies welcoming new adherents to the faith or young people into adulthood. An initiation is a ritual in which a person is invited into a community by its community members through an experience, often including trials. Initiations can be intense and life-altering for all people involved. The divine masculine represents the sparks of change settling over a person during initiation. He is also the mythological hero who goes through initiations himself. If you feel called to initiation within a specific faith tradition, today is a good day to pray to the god of initiation to draw you and your initiators together.

Today, meditate on the topic of initiation. Which metaphorical initiations have you been through in communities in your life? Which sort of initiations, if any, do you seek in the future? More about worshipping in fellowship with others will be included in the last section of this book.

* Meditate on the topic of initiation and, if called
  to do so, pray about it in your own life.

Day 213: Comfort and Consolation from a Loving Father

....

The divine masculine is what consoles and comforts us in times of angst and despair. This is one of the roles of god that has served me well in life, when I might otherwise have lashed out or dragged others down with my suffering. Instead, I reach out to god as my comfort. I visualize him as a father figure. Like a child, I can come to him at any hour of the day or night. I can metaphorically curl up in his lap and cry my eyes out or talk through any situation happening to me. He listens well. I feel infused with the warmth and love of god, and it gives me the strength to carry on.

Today, call to mind something troubling you. It could be a problem in your life or a worry about someone you love. Take a moment to own that concern, especially if you've been in the habit of dismissing it or running away to avoid being hurt. Pray and call upon god to comfort you. Some people experience this as giving the worry to god and others as having god aid and assist you emotionally. It may depend on the problem. Take note of any feelings you sense. Try to make a habit of turning to him in times of need.

* *Reach out to god for consolation.*

Day 214: Relinquishing Possessions or Relationships that No Longer Serve You

Giving things up is difficult. Letting go of people is even harder. The divine masculine has the discipline to help with this task. Many spiritual paths promote the idea of letting go of attachments. How can this bring happiness? When I first read about this phenomenon, I had an immediate visceral reaction. I like my material possessions and relationships. But, one can enjoy those things without clinging so tightly it causes inevitable grief.

Today, become aware of the things you cling to in life that you will one day give up. Realistically, this is nearly everything, knowing you will die one day. How can you enjoy every moment of your relationships and ownership of belongings and then joyfully part ways? If you have any objects cluttering your home you know you can give up to have a simpler and happier life, try the following: Choose one item that is difficult to get rid of, although you'd be better off for it. Donate it or throw it away and check in with your feelings.

* Clear some clutter out of your home to practice relinquishment.

Day 215: Discernment of the Powerful Divine Masculine

By now, I hope you're working on developing your ear for listening to god. At this stage, it may feel like intense words or thoughts entering the mind for some people. For others, it may be a more subtle feeling, like a memory or a sense something is significant when no other evidence points to that fact. You may worry how you can tell god's voice from your own. After all, each and every one of us has an internal monologue. If god's words are lost in that mental chatter, how can we sort them out? How can we keep from mistaking our ideas for those of god?

There are several commonsense logic filters that most people use. First, ask yourself if the thought from god sounds more like something you would say? Next, ask if it's something god would say. Check it against your knowledge of god. A kind and loving god isn't going to ask you to do something that would hurt somebody. Finally, you can always double-check a message from Spirit. Ask god to give you another sign, wait for additional messages, or ask a spiritual friend to pray on the issue and give you his or her impressions.

* *Think of your last experience with Spirit. How did*
  you know it was Spirit and not just your own mind?

Day 216: Have a Cup of Tea with God

If you've been working on these 365 days consecutively, you've hopefully got a routine down pat in which you regularly connect with Spirit. If not, it's understandable if you try to fit prayer and meditation into spare moments of your day. In such cases, a busy life can push spiritual dedication out the window, at least for a little bit. But now it is harder to get back into the swing of things. Sure, you can set your alarm an hour earlier or schedule an hour into your calendar, but what if, after all that, you feel uninspired or clueless?

Today's exercise is one you can do to add a little fun to your time with god. Have a cup of tea (or coffee) with him in the morning. Pour an extra cup for god as an offering and set it at an empty place at the table. Talk to him as if he were an invisible friend named god. Be casual, if you like. If you want to be able to reach out to god during tough times, you may need to know him on this casual basis, just as you trust the friends whom you tease at times and around whom you don't mind flubbing your words. After your chat with god, place the offering on your altar or pour it out outdoors.

* Chat with god over a cup of tea in the morning.

Day 217: Masculine Confidence

God is confident, because he is god. Whenever you show confidence in your life, you evoke a virtue of god. Though being humble has its place as a virtue, it's important to not be humble to the point of rejecting your best qualities. Confident people can let their light shine in ways that are subtle but honest. Lifting your confidence to the world can help you realize the gifts that god gave you to use in this lifetime. If you lack the confidence to fully express your spirituality, you're missing out on a lot of what god has to offer.

Today, tackle something in your life for which you lack confidence. If you're shy speaking in a room full of others, sign up for a public speaking class at a community college. If you're ashamed of your deplorable cooking skills, invite a friend over to help you learn a potluck recipe you can always use to impress. Turn a lack of confidence into pride, and then don't shy away from that feeling. Know this confidence is god's doing, and you can channel that energy into being a positive influence in others' lives instead of merely bragging.

* *Choose an area in your life in which you lack confidence.*
  Make a plan to improve yourself to the point of feeling
  confident.

Day 218: Fake It Until You Make It

Believe it or not, one way to increase faith is to play a bit of make-believe. In fact, some think a true faith can be built out of simply wanting to believe. Wanting to believe gives you the hope and motivation that miracles can come true. Playing pretend with god may seem a little disrespectful, but remember he is the god of your hopes and imagination. You're using gifts from god to get in touch with god. Even if you know full well that you're pretending, each time you practice this make-believe, you're giving opportunities for real and believable experiences to happen.

For today's exercise, think of something to do with Spirit you'd like to believe in, but about which you're skeptical. This might be from a bit of scripture, or from somebody else's faith that you envy. Now, begin your game of make-believe. Try to act as though the belief is true. For example, pray to god as if this is something you are certain he will grant. It may not happen right away, but changing your attitude about things can have a marked effect over time.

* *Give yourself permission and pretend that*
  something you want to believe is true.

Day 219: Waiting and Its Place in Life
....

Sometimes, life seems to be put on hold for a long time. For example, perhaps you can't get preapproved for a loan to buy a home. Perhaps you struggle with infertility while trying to start a family. Maybe you are stuck in a dead-end job or a lack of money put your higher education on hold. At some time in your life, you've probably experienced a time when circumstances brought the progress toward your goals to a screeching halt. Even the most patient person finds this frustrating, and an impatient person like me finds it maddening.

Today, think about something in your life that is being put on hold against your will. If you like, think of something in your past where a period of waiting was significant to you. Imagine god placed that waiting period in your life for a reason. Meditate upon the image of the Hanged Man tarot card. The god in this card hangs upside down from a tree, with a funny smile on his face. This waiting time for him is enjoyable, because it gives him a chance to think about what he really wants.

* Meditate upon a place in life for long periods
  of waiting, postponement, and hesitation.

Day 220: How to Make God a
First Resort in an Emotional Crisis

You've learned a few awesome benefits the divine masculine presents in your life. You've learned about intercessory prayer, which can grant you blessings from god. You've also learned how god consoles and comforts you when you feel overwhelmed. That alone helps make you better able to deal with life's problems. However, you'll still need to gently train yourself to turn to god as a first resort when it's appropriate. If you're new to prayer and spirituality, you'll naturally go into panic mode when things go awry. After you're done wringing your hands and possibly turning things into an awful mess, you might find yourself thinking, "Why didn't I pray to god in that moment?"

In order to train yourself to turn to god, first give yourself permission. Remind yourself it's okay to take time to pray when there's absolutely nothing else to do that's practical and useful in that moment. Then, assign yourself a prayer position or plan to use when experiencing your next crisis. For example, if you have a prayer or quiet place you can retreat to, plan to walk there immediately. Plan to take a knee or immediately clasp your hands when praying in crisis. These cues will hold you to your wish in your time of need.

* Make a plan for prayer for your next moment of emotional crisis.

Day 221: Service to God

Earlier you learned volunteering and service to others can be one of the greatest expressions of service to god. Many religious traditions take acts of worship as service to god. There are faiths that require praying at certain times every day, regardless of other activities or human interactions going on. There are religions that believe their holy rites must be observed for the world to keep turning as it does. And some spiritual practices require care and feeding of a deity's shrine that rivals that of the most complicated pets.

Today, choose your own service to god in the best way you feel it can be delivered. It might mean giving him sacrifices of food, incense, or beverages. It might mean committing yourself to regularly offering him special prayers. It might even entail taking on another volunteer duty that serves the world at large. Remember, once you decide this act of service, you should strictly hold yourself to it. It is a big responsibility to be a servant of god, and shouldn't be taken lightly.

* *Choose a way to serve god and turn it into a regular duty.*

Day 222: Traditions
....

By means of segue into the next part of this book, which deals with how to infuse Spirit into your everyday life, I'd like to speak to the importance of traditions within spirituality. The divine masculine is often in charge of traditions, because he marks out the days and years with the sun. Traditions help us mark our lives with holidays, daily routines, and special occasions. Your own life draws tradition from your spirituality, your culture, your family, and more. Traditions can be difficult to start, but are fun to continue once past the initial awkwardness and logistics. This is another fake-it-until-you-make-it thing.

Today, meditate upon the traditions in your life. Think of traditions from your childhood. Which ones filled you with the greatest joy or sense of purpose? If you no longer follow some of these traditions, why not? You may have very good reasons for no longer practicing your childhood traditions. Can you brainstorm traditions that could take the place of the childhood traditions you miss? Are there any traditions you've been a little unenthusiastic about or too preoccupied to continue? How can you infuse new spiritual interest and motivation into such traditions?

* *Meditate on the topic of traditions, and*
  commit or recommit to one of them.

Part Seven

Infusing Spirit in Your Everyday Life

Day 223: Bedtime Prayers

Bedtime is the classic prayer time. Imagery of children kneeling by bedsides, closing their eyes, and earnestly praying graces art and popular culture. If you're not already using bedtime prayers, you're missing out, and here's why. Firstly, it's a great way to always remember to say your prayers. Secondly, it's a good psychological trick to unpack your day while relinquishing worries before attempting sleep. And finally, it becomes a cue to your body and mind that sleep is soon coming, allowing you to fall asleep more quickly after saying your prayers.

Today, commit to saying a bedtime prayer. Choose a bedtime prayer from scripture or one you already know. You can search the Internet or library for prayers or poems that speak what you'd like to say before bed. Or simply choose a prayer position and speak from the heart, making up what you want to say as you go. Think of what you'd like to accomplish during a bedtime prayer. Do you want intercessory prayer to relieve your worries? Do you want to pray for your safety and protection in the night? Do you want to pray for rest and preparation for the new day?

* *Choose a bedtime prayer and memorize it or make up your own.*

Day 224: Grace
....

Grace is the prayer of thanksgiving traditionally said before meals. In many religions, this prayer acknowledges the food is made possible by Spirit. Many grace prayers also ask for the food to grant blessings to all those who eat it. Grace can also include a food offering or a word to ancestors who would enjoy the food in Spirit. Some people say grace while cooking the food or immediately afterward, including all the cooks in the praying. Others say grace once the food is on the table but before eating, often including those seated around the table holding hands. And finally, there are those who say their prayers while eating, going around the table so each person can say special thanks.

Think up a grace tradition appropriate for your lifestyle. Can you include everyone in grace whenever you eat, or would you rather silently say grace by yourself? Commit to saying grace at every meal, even if it's only in your head. If you're new to saying grace, you may find you forget on a regular basis. In those cases, say the grace as soon as you remember after you've eaten, blessing the food already in your body. Even if it feels silly, it will bring you closer to remembering to say grace at the appropriate time.

* *Choose a grace prayer and memorize it or make up your own.*

Day 225: Prayers for Family

....

There are many ways to include family in your prayer life. If you live with your family, or honorary family in the form of friends or lovers, invite them to pray with you. If you don't live with family, invite them to a regular prayer circle or add them to your prayer list. Today is meant to be a brief introduction to these concepts. After all, many people want to include their closest loved ones in the joy and blessings that prayer can provide.

Ask your family members if they'd like to join you in prayer. If they agree, frankly discuss which practical time is best for them. Do they want to pray grace with you at mealtimes, or do they want to expand prayer time to other parts of their day? If your family does not want to pray with you, ask if you can pray for them. Create a written list of those you'd like to pray for on a regular basis. Pray down the list, personalizing it for each person's current issues.

> * *Find an appropriate way to pray for your family*
>   *or chosen loved ones, if possible and desired.*

Day 226: Making Room for More
Offerings During Your Holidays and Meals

Giving back to Spirit is a vital part of many people's practices. It's intuitive that without giving, we may not be able to receive. Thus, it's important to build a tradition of offerings to Spirit. You don't have to make a huge show out of these things. That said, if you don't plan for them, they might not happen. Here are some suggestions for seamlessly building offerings into your life. You can adjust them for your own life as often as you like, or only for special occasions, if needed.

First, decide on your offering. For example, you may wish to burn a scented candle as an offering at every meal. If you drink wine at dinner, you may wish to pour out a libation of wine each evening. Or, you may wish to offer a bit of every meal. If you offer food, you don't need to give Spirit a human-sized helping. A small crumb of each food eaten is enough. Designate a container or two for the offering. You might choose a tiny decorative saucer. Or you might choose a porcelain cup or serving plate with a lid to conceal the contents. Also choose where the offering will go afterward, preferably outdoors for woodland creatures to eat as proxy.

* Plan for moments of offerings and thanksgivings
  during holidays or daily meals.

Day 227: Including Ancestors in Your Life

So far, I've had you interact with your ancestors on a few occasions. You've looked up some ancestors and said their names aloud. You've also had the option to set up a shrine for your ancestors. Keep in mind, though, that regularly including your ancestors takes planning. If you don't make time to connect with your ancestors as an expression of Spirit, then they will be easily forgotten, especially in the haste of holiday traditions.

Today, choose how often you'd like to connect with your ancestors. Do you want to make it a daily occurrence, or do you want to make it an event for special occasions? How often do you want to call your mom, or your great-great-great-great-grandmother? Setting up the ancestor shrine and an offering plate during holidays is one option. Near the end of October and the beginning of November is a traditional time to honor ancestors in many cultures. If you like, you can try to communicate with their spirits during this time.

* *Decide how much ancestor work you'd like to include
  in your life and create a plan for doing so.*

Day 228: Choosing a Peaceful
Attitude in Moments of Chaos
....

Confession time: I'm the mom of two very small children. My eldest is three years old and my youngest is experiencing the terrible twos. Even on a good day, I am driven to the brink of madness. It is important for me to find my rock in Spirit. I need to anchor myself in the Divine to get myself through the day without yelling as loudly as my toddler and behaving as immaturely. Recognizing Spirit as the source of peace and strength is one way I get through the day. You too can use this, drawing on the power of Spirit to calm the storms of your day.

The key to successfully tapping into the peace of Spirit is to realize a peaceful demeanor is a choice. I know. If you have a temper like mine, this is one of those cases where you'll have to pretend and want to believe. When you run into a stressful moment in your day and chaos seems to reign, pause and tell yourself, "I can choose to experience peacefulness now instead of what I'm currently experiencing." Sometimes, when I tell myself this, I can feel the peace wash over me. The choice is real. I can choose something different. If that doesn't work, you'll have to escalate to your prayer crisis plan.

* When you feel life is at its most chaotic today,
  consciously choose a peaceful state of mind.

Day 229: Building More Thanksgivings into Daily Life

By now you know there are good reasons to be thankful. You know being overtly thankful can help bring your attention to the best parts of your life, thus making you happier. You also know being thankful can encourage Spirit to give you more blessings. Today, you should make a plan to be thankful more regularly in your everyday life. This will combine some of the strategies you've already learned.

Firstly, make a plan for regular thanksgivings. You can build vocal moments of giving thanks to Spirit into your grace or bedtime prayers, whichever one is most appropriate. Since giving offerings is a way of giving thanks, this is one way you might choose if it works for you. Most of all, you'll need to train yourself to thank Spirit for good things happening in your life as soon as they happen. This rewards Spirit, but also rewards yourself and allows people to be a part of that thanksgiving, if you choose.

* Make a plan to build more opportunities
  to be thankful into your life.

Day 230: Mindfulness

Let me tell you another story about being a mom of two small children. Oftentimes I'm interrupted throughout my day. When my kids interrupted me for the zillionth time one day, I found myself snapping, "I'm busy." This came back to bite me later when I asked my small child for her attention while she was coloring. She told me, "No. I'm busy, Mum!" Being busy is not a spiritual virtue of mine, but being mindful is. Thus, I adopted a different frame of mind. Now, when my kids interrupt me, I try to ask them to be mindful. When my daughter is asking for a trip to the playground, I tell her to be mindful of me helping her brother eat his snack. I'm pleased that now when I say something to my daughter, she often replies, "Be mindful that I'm coloring right now."

Being mindful means not only paying attention, but caring. It is challenging to find ways to be mindful in your life. The best advice I can give is to notice when you are dissatisfied with your level of attention or your way of interacting with a loved one. If you find yourself distracted and distant, find a way to reframe your state of mind. Set an alarm, if you have to, when you need to be especially mindful.

* Meditate on the topic of mindfulness.

Day 231: Creative Expressions of Spirit at Home

....

Hopefully you've found ways to make sacred spaces by now. You can have an altar hidden on a shelf or in a cupboard. You can turn a closet into a secret prayer or meditation space. You can retreat to a place in the forest, a courtyard, or a garden when you need to be with Spirit. Today, I'd like you to branch out and bring Spirit into all other areas of your life. Allow Spirit to reach tendrils into your working and living space. These could be decorations designed to draw the eye of others or subtle reminders akin to tying a string around your finger to remember Spirit wherever you go. Whether you choose an ostentatious statue of a deity or a discrete drawing of a rune on an index card, the reminder of Spirit can enrich your life whenever you're near it.

Today's exercise is to bring a representation of Spirit into your home or, if appropriate, office. My suggestion is to find a spiritual quote that inspires you. It could be a verse from scripture, a direct quote from a guru, or simply a quote by your favorite author that gives you spiritual inspiration. Write it out in a decorative way or print out in a stylish font. Post it prominently and reflect upon it each time it catches your eye.

* *Add a quote or other representation of Spirit*
  to your regular living or working space.

Day 232: Holidays

....

Holidays are special times to celebrate Spirit, seasonal changes, and traditions. Sometimes they are associated with great mythological events. When I was a teenager, I attended a religious fair with booths from local spiritual groups. Cheekily I asked each booth which religion had the most holidays, thinking it would be fun. I ended up involved in some pretty fun and deep discussions. Obviously, the frequency of the holidays doesn't have any impact on the piety of the person. You'll only need to commit to holidays important to you.

Today, plan for spiritual holidays in the year ahead. Think of the holidays you already celebrate and how you can infuse them with spiritual traditions. Think of holidays from your childhood you might want to resurrect in your life. Consider researching holidays in a religion, nation, or culture of your choice. Adopt some of those holidays as your own, or look for local cultural celebrations that welcome public participants. Mark the holidays you'd like to celebrate on the calendar. Mark your calendar ahead of time if you need to procure supplies to make the holiday special.

* *Research and choose some holidays to celebrate.*

Day 233: Finding the Divine in Chores

Chores can seem like dull and mundane tasks and the least spiritual. This is so true that many scriptures and religious leaders encourage injecting chore time with worship and other spiritual activities. After all, if you clean the entire kitchen and your family comes in and messes it up, you may feel angry and discouraged. If you spend your kitchen cleaning time in prayer and song, chanting and blessing your home, you won't regret that time spent with Spirit no matter what happens afterward.

Today, change an ordinary activity into an act of worship. I'll give you a good suggestion. If you sweep any area of your home, it can be an act of special spiritual significance. The broom represents the combination of male and female divine energies. Ancient people hopped on brooms in fields to show the grains how high to grow. Jumping over a broom is a blessing used in wedding ceremonies. The broom can be used to clear the room not only of dirt, but also of negative spiritual energies in your home. As you sweep, imagine sweeping out the negativity. Sweep out your home, bathroom, garage, or front sidewalk today.

* *Turn a chore like sweeping into an act of worship and blessing.*

Day 234: Daily Devotionals

Daily devotionals are a specific way to spend daily time with Spirit. You've already tried several ways to set aside time for Spirit. Daily devotionals are another way. Typically, daily devotionals involve a daily appointment with Spirit at the same time. They include prayer and learning components. In fact, many of the daily entries in this book work as daily devotionals. Today, I'd like to teach you to build your own daily devotional so that you can continue when you're finished reading this book.

To form a daily devotional, you'll have to plan ahead for your learning component. I suggest choosing a big book of mythology, scripture from a faith tradition, or another book on spiritual topics. Pick the time and place for your daily appointment with Spirit and place the book nearby. Next, choose your prayer component. It might be a prayer book. Or you can choose to meditate. You might ad lib prayers from the heart, or memorize a prayer for each day of the week. As an example, a friend of mine goes through a list of loved ones to pray for every day in the shower.

* Make a plan for daily devotionals when you're finished reading this book and implement them in your life if you wish.

Day 235: Taking Advantage of Waiting Moments

When I made an appointment with a local clinic yesterday, they had appointment slots in fifteen-minute intervals to choose from. I assumed the wait wouldn't be very long since they packed the appointments so close. Wrong. My appointment turned into an ordeal of waiting. It's often disheartening to have sudden and unexpected waiting periods. An appointment running long when you need to pick up your kids. A ridiculously long line at the post office. These things can be stressful. But if you interpret these delays as surprise invitations from Spirit to connect, they may seem less painful, and your time and attention will be occupied.

Firstly, seize the moment as soon as it comes. Wherever you are, take deep breaths to control your breathing and relax. Ground yourself. If it's appropriate, you can close your eyes for a few seconds. Silently "speak" to Spirit in your mind. Praying for patience might be the first order of business. If you carry prayer beads or a worry stone in your pocket, you can surreptitiously reach for them. They can serve as a reminder to turn to Spirit as soon as you find yourself waiting and fretting.

* *Seize your next waiting moment as a way to connect with Spirit.*

Day 236: What Is in a Name?

The more you know about something, the better you can connect with it. This basic spiritual truth extends to Spirit when it comes to names, both the name of Spirit and that of the practitioner. Some religions believe it is very important to call Spirit by its true name. If you don't address Spirit by name, they suppose, how will you know you're contacting the correct entity? If you don't know the name of Spirit, do you ever truly know Spirit at all? Some faith traditions have practitioners choose a new name for themselves when they become adherents of the faith. This name can be taken on in everyday life or only used during official rituals and ceremonies.

Today, think about what name you take on when connecting with Spirit. Do you want to have a secret name only shared between you and Spirit? Do you want to have a spiritual name known by your community members as a tribute to your relationship with Spirit? Think about the names by which you know Spirit. Which names do you use for Spirit while praying? How did you come to know Spirit's name? Have you been properly introduced using your names yet?

* Today, meditate on the name(s) you have for Spirit and the name by which you would like to be known by Spirit.

Day 237: Bathing Meditation

We've already talked about how ablutions and cleansing can be an important part of worship for many. Likewise, you can turn any bath or shower into a sacred act. For me, the mother of two small children, my baths and showers are often the only time I have to myself. I have to turn these moments into tiny spiritual retreats. Time spent cleaning yourself can also be time to talk to Spirit about things you'd like removed from your life, like smudges of dirt wiped from your skin.

Instead of merely taking a bath, use it as time for meditation. Light candles and sprinkle nice-smelling herbs in the water to help set the mood. If you don't have a bathtub, you can still create this environment in your shower. Place a few candles on a nearby counter visible from your shower. Try purchasing soap or body wash containing fragrant herbs or make your own. As you cleanse yourself, think about what you'd like Spirit to wash out of your life.

> * *Take a bath or shower today and make it into*
> *a mini-retreat to have time alone with Spirit.*

Day 238: Starting Your Day on the Right Foot

Today's exercise combines some of what you've already learned. I don't know about you, but I make a subconscious assessment of what type of day I'm going to have within an hour of waking. If things go smoothly, my mood and expectations lift. Adding a dose of Spirit to your morning routine ensures things start off on the right foot, allowing you to focus on your attitude of gratitude. Being mindful as soon as you get up can also help rouse you and make you feel more ready for your day. Overall, Spirit and early morning are a winning combination for many.

Try combining some of the morning suggestions I've given you. Choose a prayer to say as soon as your eyes open, or as soon as you roll out of bed. You can learn sun salutation yoga or keep it simple. If you shower first thing in the morning, use that time as you did yesterday to have a moment with Spirit. As you put on your clothes and any accessories, visualize yourself placing the virtues of Spirit upon yourself. If the morning is a good time for your daily devotionals, make time for that as well. The goal of today's exercise is to create a plan that seamlessly integrates with your routine.

* *Plan a morning routine that integrates Spirit. Watch
  how it affects your attitude when implemented.*

Day 239: Listing Your Gifts

Today's activity is similar to when you actively counted your blessings. When you assign yourself to seek good things, you'll attune your attention to life's great things. This naturally snowballs into spiritual blessings. This time, I want you to look inward and list some of your own personal gifts. These can be personality traits, skills, or opportunities you've had to help someone.

Open up your spiritual journal and reserve a page to list some gifts that Spirit has given you. Also think of some of your negative traits and how they might be gifts in your life. Think how each of those gifts could have been given to you by the special design of Spirit. You can also use this technique with your family and loved ones in an effort to encourage them during their life challenges. Review the list in your journal when you feel blue or lack self-confidence.

* Make a list of your gifts from Spirit. Some of your
  gifts may appear as vices or problems because you
  haven't yet learned to properly express them.

Day 240: Painting a Spiritual Target on Your Back

Many people seek Spirit for stability. To have a rock to cling to, even when life is chaotic. However, Spirit can also be an initiator and instigator in life. Spirit can really shake things up. Take a look at the Tower tarot card. In it, lightning strikes a tower and the entire foundation is rocked. It can look pretty miserable for all concerned, but sometimes a foundational shift is needed to get life back on the right track. This is why some people seek a radical conversion, rebirth, or initiation.

Since I practice an initiatory spiritual path, I encourage you to carefully think before asking Spirit to make big changes and bring focus upon yourself. Your life can turn upside down and, even if it's for the best, it might be awkward or bad timing. If you are ready for more from Spirit, ask for more in small doses. Consider saying a prayer to ask Spirit for more responsibilities and challenges. Praying for strength and wisdom often results in similar blessings, since challenges can grant you wisdom and strength.

* Decide whether you are seeking radical change in your life.

Day 241: Incense and Other
Aromatherapy in Everyday Life

You've learned that incense can be an offering to Spirit. Incense doesn't have to be burned only in the context of a specific meditation, prayer session, or celebration. There are some good reasons to bring sacred scents into your everyday life. Not only are pleasant smells an excellent way to make your living space a better place to occupy, but the scents can put you in a spiritual state of mind. Your sense of smell is closely tied to memory. If you smell something every time you are in a state of ecstatic worship, then sniffing that scent at another time may be enough to recall that emotional state.

How can you bring scents into your everyday life? The best place is at home. Talk to people with whom you share the home before introducing new scents on a regular basis. I like to light incense after the kids go to bed and before my husband gets home so he can enter a nice-smelling home. If incense isn't practical for your household, you can use fresh-cut flowers or essential oils. At the very least, you can always add a scent to your skin in the morning before going about your day. Try perfume or cologne, as some essential oils can irritate the skin.

* Add some pleasant smells to your life.

Day 242: Music and Ambiance in Your Life

Another way to make your surroundings more pleasant and spiritual is to evaluate the sounds and sights that stimulate you in your environment. Do you listen to music at home or at work? Which sounds do you hear during your days and evenings? Do they feed your soul? Take a look at other aspects of your surroundings. Do you see natural light from where you sit most of the day? Is the lighting harsh or gentle? Can you relax by candlelight in the evenings?

Take stock of your everyday environment and decide what is spiritual and what is not. Play inspirational music, if you like. Take note of things that detract from your spiritual frame of mind. This could mean clutter or other messes. You might have things in your home to fix that remind you of your to-do list. Piles of paperwork, for instance, do not encourage someone to take time for meditation. Instead, mundane tasks constantly beg attention.

* *Take note of what makes you feel spiritual*
  in your home and workplace environments
  and what does not. Make changes accordingly.

Day 243: Refraining from Foolish and Vain Conversation

In some magical practices, one is encouraged to very carefully watch words in the days or weeks leading up to an important ritual. In many religions, being careful with topics of conversation is a constant duty. For example, gossip is a conversation topic that is widely reviled in spiritual circles. Gossip directs one's attention away from Spirit and one's own self-improvement. Besides, it isn't very nice and can make people feel bad about themselves.

Being prideful or vain in conversation is typically a no-no in spiritual circles. Bragging about one's achievements steals the spotlight from Spirit. It also increases one's motivations to do things for oneself instead of serving Spirit. Foolish conversations are best avoided in general. Nobody wants to speak in an uninformed and ignorant way, and most want to achieve respect in spiritual and other communities. Try opting out of conversations you find detrimental to your spiritual state of mind. You don't have to tell others to stop talking, but you can hold your silence or gently bring up other topics.

* Choose topics of conversation you want to avoid in order to
  nurture your connection with Spirit. Practice refraining from
  those topics.

Day 244: Being the Person
You Want to Be in Relationships

Most of us have read the quote commonly attributed to Ghandi that says, "Be the change you wish to see in the world." A subset of this idea is to be the person you want to be in all of your relationships. This goal may be more difficult than the former. All one has to do to change the world is be the best possible expression of the self for one or more world-changing achievements. Being the best person you can be in relationships is a tough order of business. You must be the best you can be every day, and since relationships are dynamic, the best is often a moving target.

Today, think of a relationship in your life right now that is either troubled or very important to you. Imagine what that relationship would ideally look like. Then, try to act like the person in that ideal relationship. Play that role to encourage the other person to join in. This practice may be difficult, because often we come from a place of resentfulness that the other person isn't trying as hard. But when you take the first step, you can lift the relationship. And, if not, you can be proud of yourself.

* *Choose a relationship in your life for spiritual improvement.*

Day 245: Spending Your Time Aligned with Your Values

Many people have a mid-life crisis based on how they have spent their time. If you've spent decades of your life working at a job you hate, it's easy to see why you might have a spiritual crisis. If your job hasn't aligned you with at least one of your core values, you may likely feel completely unproductive and at a loss.

Today, write down a list of your deepest values. Some of them, like health and spirituality, may be easy. Some of them may present as broader values. For example, if you value traveling, it may be you actually value a sense of adventure. If you value money, it may actually be you value a sense of stability in the material features of your life. Next, evaluate how you spend your time and money in relation to your values. Are you completely ignoring some of your core values? Do you invest lots of time and energy in something that isn't even on your list of values? Modify your time and budget so you are living in closer alignment with your values.

* *Make a list of your values and try to align your life with them.*

Day 246: Connecting with People Who Matter

In the same way you can experience a mid-life crisis when you stay in the wrong job, you can have a spiritual crisis when spending time with the wrong people. You've practiced clearing out clutter from your life in order to practice relinquishment. Today, I want you to seriously ponder whether there are some people in your life you need to let go. It might be friends who have not acted like friends, an ex-boyfriend or ex-girlfriend, or any toxic relationship.

Next, think about the people you may neglect in your life. Maybe you don't call your mom as often as you should. Perhaps there's a beloved cousin or sister of yours whom you haven't visited in more than a year. Make a commitment to reconnect with those people right away. Try to make communication with important people regular and intimate. Share your spiritual struggles and triumphs with them, and allow them to share their own life trials and joys with you.

* *Release harmful people from your life and*
  reconnect with people important to you.

Day 247: Daily Journaling and How to Use Your Journal

Hopefully you're still journaling daily observations of the changing seasons, nature in general, your prayers, and impressions from your meditations. I'll discuss your dream journal tomorrow, so I hope you've been keeping up with that as well. Before that, I'd like to talk about making the most of your journal. The act of writing in a journal is a wonderful spiritual practice. If you never look at it again, though, you're missing out on so much it can teach you.

Read through your journal with an eye for improvement. Learning to listen to and interpret Spirit is as much a skill as a doctor reading medical charts. Over time, you should pick up more and more. You will discover you make notes more often over time. You may notice a voice of confidence develop in your writing. You might also see a record of prayers that have been answered. Keep writing in your journal, and keep looking back at how far you've come on your journey.

* *Review your spiritual journal and look for improvement.*

Day 248: Analyzing Your Dreams

Dream analysis is another skill that takes time to develop. There's no time like the present to start. When you first write down your dreams, you may have impressions about what they mean. That's good. Write them down as well. After you've recorded your dreams for some time, go back and read your dream journal. It can be shocking how many dreams you don't remember writing down. Reading old dreams can feel like peering into the mind of a stranger. Some may seem riddle-like. Others may seem to have greater significance over time.

As you go through your dream journal, circle words that could be symbols. These are typically nouns. Tally up how many times each common symbol occurs. For example, if you dream a lot about a raven, you might assume this bird has a specific spiritual meaning you'd do well to meditate upon. Highlight any dream events that later came true. These are called precognitive dreams. Make note of the date they came true, if possible. You may notice a pattern. Keep writing in your dream journal, checking it regularly for precognitive dreams as well as more symbols to add to your tally.

* *Review your dream journal.*

Day 249: Overcoming Inertia

Overcoming personal mental inertia can be the most significant hurdle to spiritual practice. Dream journals are a great example. When I wake up after having a dream with thirty minutes until my alarm goes off, the last thing I want to do is wake my brain up enough to write down the dream. I'd much rather close my eyes and snuggle down deeper into my blankets for the brief moments before I have to be up. However, the value I get from my dream records is so great that I work hard to record important dreams.

For you, inertia may make itself known in other areas of your spiritual life. Today, contemplate where you find the greatest degree of spiritual inertia. This depends upon your personal goals. For example, if your dream has always been to get up in the wee morning hours, before the household is awake, to converse with Spirit, your greatest hurdle may be getting out of bed. If you want to have a conversational relationship with Spirit, but still feel silly praying out loud, your greatest hurdle may be simply opening your mouth every day. Target your inertia and get rid of it.

* *Attack your greatest source of inertia in your spiritual life.*

Day 250: Seeing Signs in Ordinary Things

So far we've gone over some signs from Spirit you might expect. For example, you might sense that something is true, such as knowing whether an early pregnancy holds a baby boy or girl. You might "hear" an answer to a question from Spirit in your mind, just like you "hear" a song stuck in your head. You might notice patterns showing up over and over again, such as the number 111. You can ask for a sign, even a specific one. For example, you can say, "If my prayer is answered, let me hear the singing of a robin now."

There's a particular sign that is an odd combination of having a sense of knowing and spotting a requested sign. It's when you see significance in something that would ordinarily have no meaning. For instance, one day as a child I prayed to Spirit for joy. And it started raining. Far from seeing this as a bad sign, I felt Spirit's joy pouring down my face. I twirled and laughed in the rain. In that moment, the rain was confirmation Spirit was listening.

> * *Actively look for signs from Spirit today,*
>   *even in very ordinary occurrences.*

Day 251: Creating Keys to Unlock Experiences

Training yourself to be a spiritual person is a lot like training a pet. Seriously. You may have heard of the behaviorist Dr. Pavlov, who trained his dogs through operant conditioning. Every time he fed them, he rang a bell. After a certain amount of time, he rang the bell and the dogs salivated, even when food was not present. This conditioning is pretty amazing. It wasn't that the dogs were using their intellect to consciously think about food. Instead, their very body chemistry was trained to react to the bell. You can carefully train your body and mind to react to Spirit in the same way.

When I wrote how scent can trigger memory, I gave a clue for one key you can use. When you are consistent in your spiritual practice, you create more. The more you practice grounding, the more you practice getting into the meditation headspace. The more you pray at specific times of day with specific environmental cues like incense and bells, the more you train yourself.

* Create keys and cues to train yourself
  to snap into a spiritual headspace.

Day 252: Falling Asleep

Carving out a sacred moment each day can be difficult for busy people. If you haven't done anything spiritual by bedtime, you are probably relieved you can at least say your bedtime prayers. Your bedtime prayers can be a cue to help you smoothly fall asleep each night. They help you in the transition, or liminal state, between wakefulness and sleep. Today, I'd like to speak to the act of falling asleep, and how this can be a special spiritual time.

When you first fall asleep or just wake up, your brain begins producing the alpha waves associated with light sleep. These alpha waves can be deliberately produced by skilled meditators. Therefore, you can achieve well-trained meditation by simply catching those liminal times between sleeping and wakefulness. Some cultures believed that at this moment the body was detached from the soul, so extra protective prayers were said before bed. When I was a child, my mother told me the last thing I thought about while going to bed would often be the first thing I thought about upon waking. I used this as a study key in college, and now I use it to think about Spirit. Try this as you fall asleep, whether with repetitive silent prayers or just a state of mind.

* *Keep Spirit in mind in the instant you fall asleep.*

Day 253: Recognizing the Divine Hand in Events

Years ago, on a road trip, I was in an accident. My husband was driving while I dozed off in the passenger seat. Suddenly, my car had a major blowout. The tire was completely stripped off and rubber flew like ribbons onto the freeway. The car spun across four lanes of busy traffic, narrowly missing numerous cars. We flew across a large ditch and landed heavily in a grassy field. A woman pulled over to help us, shouting how amazing it was that we missed every last one of the other cars and ended up without a scratch or bruise. I remember my husband said, "Now I know why people say 'god had a hand in this.' There must have been three or four gods and a goddess involved in that miracle!"

Keep your eye out for the divine hand in events. Read the news looking for good news. Notice the amazing scientific advancements happening. Be aware of the lucky news people share with you. Raise up your thanksgivings for such things.

* *Actively search for the divine hand at*
  work in seemingly miraculous events.

Day 254: Consciously
Acknowledging Spirit with Immediacy

Another common spiritual rule of thumb is that you should say your thanks-givings and immediately raise your praise to Spirit when you feel the inclination. There are several reasons behind this. Firstly, out of respect for Spirit. You should show your appreciation right away to demonstrate to yourself and Spirit that these things are important to you. Pretend you're conditioning Spirit to feel encouraged to bless you. Finally, some spiritual traditions believe Spirit can indeed feel wronged by unappreciative people. Avoid hubris, or the sin of pride, and be thankful.

A friend of mine had a young daughter who found a penny. When her daughter picked it up, she was reminded to thank Spirit right away. "Spirit may not realize that you like money," her mother said, "so give your thanks. It doesn't matter to Spirit whether it's a penny or five dollars, so be appreciative of anything you get." The little girl dutifully thanked Spirit and later the same day found a five-dollar bill. When my friend tells the story, she declares, "She's sold on that one!"

* *Today, be sure to thank Spirit immediately*
  as soon as you receive blessings.

Day 255: Planning Your Day Around Spirit

Most days are busy. When I have two major things to get done in a day it can seem just as busy as though I had 100 things to do. Time fills quickly. Imagine you have a jar that you need to fill with different-sized rocks. These rocks represent all the things you need to get done in a day. If you try to cram them in the jar randomly, they might not fit. Likewise, if you fill the jar with the smallest rocks and sand first, the biggest rocks won't fit. This shows how the little things in life can take up so much time that the most important things are left out at the end of the day. The best strategy is to first put in the biggest rocks, then fill the gaps with the smaller rocks. For this reason, you should plan your day around your most important values and spiritual goals and then tackle the little things.

Today, make an assessment of how your days have been. Are there any important things you keep letting slide? Do you find yourself procrastinating on the things that are most important? Make a plan to move the important life tasks, like the spiritual ones, forward in your day.

* *Plan your day to include the most important things first.*

Day 256: The Divine at Work

Some workplaces are very accepting of spiritual diversity, but others are not. If you don't have to be discrete at your workplace, you might choose to implement many things you've learned in this book that you might have in your home. For example, place statues or altars or other ornaments at your workplace. If you need to be more circumspect, here are some suggestions you can combine for your workplace.

Try subtle reminders of Spirit, such as a quote or a picture of a beautiful sunset. The very clothes you wear can remind you of the spiritual energies you want to possess during the day. Set an appointment in your work day to take a break with Spirit. A ten-minute walking meditation in a courtyard can be enough. You can even set an alarm to go off every hour or so to take a moment to be mindful and check in with your energy. The best tip I have for any workplace is to use work as an opportunity to ground yourself. Most people deal with stress and other people at work, and both of those energetic influences can leave you feeling ungrounded. Getting your practice in at work can help improve your spiritual life at home.

* Find appropriate ways to express yourself spiritually at work.

Day 257: Injecting Your Reading List with Spirituality

Since you're reading this book, I can safely assume you have an inclination to read. As a frequent reader, I find it's easy to let my list of books to read become cluttered with junk reading. Just like watching the television and flipping channels, I can end up cycling through books that don't really matter in my life. It's okay to have some entertainment reads flowing through your life. But you will find that if you pepper your list with spiritual books, you will end up gaining knowledge about Spirit over the years.

First, decide which spiritual books would be good to read. You can use the old standbys of scripture or books of mythology, or look at the lists of best sellers to find popular books about living a spiritual lifestyle. Ask your librarian which new books are available. Keep a list of books you'd like to read so you can have a new one ready every time you finish a book. If some spiritual books are dull but you want to read them anyway, make yourself a captive audience. Only take that book on vacation or bring it to the gym to read on the treadmill.

* *Make a reading list of spiritual books you'd like to read. Sprinkle those books among reading you do for pleasure or school.*

Day 258: Finding Opportunities for Grounding and Meditation

Hopefully you've been practicing grounding and meditation when you find yourself waiting in line. If that's not a daily experience for you, however, or if you find waiting in line too aggravating to meditate, you can find plenty of other opportunities. Squeezing these extra chances for inner stillness into your day is good training to achieve a spiritual mental state under any condition. Have you ever tried to pray or meditate and just weren't feeling it? You can't always wait until circumstances are perfect. Train your mind to be able to snap into Spirit anywhere.

Every time a specific thing happens in your life, follow it with grounding and meditation as soon as you remember. For example, before getting into a car or getting on the bus, ground yourself. This daily activity can become a cue so it becomes automatic. If you forget, it's okay to ground yourself even when the wheels are moving.

* *Think of some daily routines and experiences*
  that could trigger grounding or meditation.

Day 259: A Prayer List of Daily Prayers for Family and Others

··

Imagine this scenario: Someone comes to you and asks if you will pray for him or her. You accept. The person walks away. Now what? You've just had somebody added to your prayer list. Today will cover how to manage a list of people so it doesn't get too long or confusing. The first step is to build your prayer list. People may ask, or you can offer specific prayer, or you might extend an open invitation for whoever would like your prayer. Write down the date, name, and purpose for each prayer. Tell each person you will include them in your daily prayers for one week (or another appropriate time frame), and to let you know how the problem evolves.

Each time you sit down to pray over your prayer list, group the people according to their needs. For example, everyone with health-related concerns can be included in a single prayer. Use a pretty prayer you find about healing, or make one up on the spot and insert the desired names. After you've prayed through the big categories, you're done. You can light candles for the people on your prayer list. When a name reaches the end of the time frame you commited to, check in with that person.

* Start a prayer list and pray through it according to need.

Part Eight

———— ✳ ————

Connecting with Spirit During Challenges, Milestones, and Rites of Passage

Day 260: The Hero's Journey

As the star of my life's story, my life seems unique. But it happens that the human experience plays itself out over and over again all over the world in similar ways. A classic format of this story is the hero's journey, as written about by mythology expert Joseph Campbell. The hero's journey is a classical myth format. The hero goes forth into a strange new world and comes back bearing treasures or lessons learned.

You can see the hero's journey played out in classical mythology in fairy tales like "Jack and the Beanstalk" and even in modern movies like *Finding Nemo*. You might see the hero's journey in your own life with strange metaphorical journeys and treasures. Over the next few days, I'll drill deeper into the various stages of the hero's journey. For today, meditate about some of the journeys, literal or figurative, that you've taken in your life, and how you might play the part of the hero in your story. Once you learn about the hero's journey, you might never look at a movie or storybook the same way.

* *Meditate upon the hero's journey.*

Day 261: Separation

....

The first major stage of the hero's journey is the separation. The separation has five stages of its own, which we'll go over in the next few days. Overall, separation is when life drastically changes and departs from the ordinary. Think of the separation as the hero heading off on his adventure, with packed bags and excitement in his heart. The separation can also be something against his will, such as being sucked into another world. Either way, things will never be the same for him again.

Today, meditate upon a period of your life that was a separation. It could be when you went off to college, joined the military, or moved to a different country. For some, this may be less literal. Separation could mean being diagnosed with cancer or becoming addicted to drugs. Think about how you prepared for the separation, if at all. Think about all the ways your life changed after this separation phase in your life. Do you think Spirit instigated this separation in your life?

* Meditate upon a phase of your life that conformed
  to the separation stage of the hero's journey.

Day 262: The Call to Adventure

In the mythological tale of our everyman hero, the journey begins with a call to adventure. This is the exact moment the story begins. It might begin with a foolish mistake or blunder in which the hero offends a god or falls down a hole into the underworld. It could begin when a goddess calls to him to go on an adventure and seek a treasure on her behalf. This might be a loud call that cannot be ignored or it might be a subtle encouragement for an already adventuresome hero.

Today, meditate on the call to adventure. When have you received calls to adventure in your life? How did you know your life was about to change? Have you ever received a call to adventure from Spirit? How did you hear that message? Was it a feeling inside you or was it a sign received from Spirit? How can you watch and listen for calls to adventure in your future? Have you ever had a call to adventure that was more like being forced into an adventure against your will? Do you think Spirit helped you with that adventure?

* Meditate upon a phase of your life that conformed
  to the call-to-adventure stage of the hero's journey.

Day 263: Refusal of the Call

Change is hard, and so at first even heroes may refuse the call to adventure. The adventure's road ahead might be too dangerous, too costly, or simply incredibly inconvenient. The hero may run away or say no to the deity. This may seem very foolish indeed while reading a story in which the hero is about to be smote by an angry goddess or god. However, in real life it's easy to see how even mundane duties can get in the way of divinely inspired adventure. How many of us would give up a well-paying job or leave our families for a significant period of time for a zany adventure?

Today, meditate on the idea of refusing a call to adventure. Was there ever a point in life when your sense of reason prevailed over your inclination toward adventure? Was there ever a duty you needed to perform that was simply too scary to attempt? Have you persevered through fear and gone on an adventure despite misgivings?

* *Meditate upon a phase in your life that conformed
  to the refusal-of-the-call stage of the hero's journey.*

Day 264: Supernatural Aid

Our hero has finally decided he is going on an amazing adventure to which he's been called. He finds next that he has supernatural help to get him started or to carry him through the quest. Perhaps a magical companion will aid him. Perhaps he has been given some sort of amulet or special weapon that helps. Or perhaps a goddess or god has committed to assist him throughout the entire adventure. We've seen these incredible helpers time and time again in stories and movies. However, the metaphorical equivalent to these helpers can be Spirit's intervention in your life.

Today, meditate upon the topic of supernatural aid. Have you experienced a miraculous moment in your life when Spirit gave you aid? When you pray for help from Spirit, what form do you hope that aid will take? How do you know when help comes from Spirit? Does it even matter? If you feel compelled to ask for supernatural aid, today would be a good day to do so in prayer. Remember that supernatural aid can take the form of an ordinary person who happened to enter your life at the right time.

* *Meditate upon a time in your life in which you may have experienced supernatural aid as in the hero's journey.*

Day 265: Crossing the Threshold

Crossing the threshold is the moment the hero truly begins his journey. This may be where he leaves his home to seek fortune. It could be the door to the underworld or some other strange and mysterious land. After he crosses this threshold, he'll never be quite the same again. In a sense, it is a point of no return, even if he physically returns to his point of origin some day. When he returns, he will be a changed man.

Today, meditate upon crossing the threshold. What are distinct moments in time when your life forever changed? It could be the day your first child was born, the moment you said "I do" at your wedding, or the day you moved out of your parents' house. Were you filled with anxiety, excitement, or both? Did you gladly cross the threshold, or did you hesitate or wish the moment could be drawn out to an eternity? Do you normally confidently approach change? What are choices you've recently made that could change you forever?

* *Meditate upon a time in your life that conformed to the crossing-the-threshold stage of the hero's journey.*

Day 266: Belly of the Whale

....

The belly of the whale is the stage of the story when the hero starts to think "uh-oh, this is real." The unknown swirls around, and he's thrown in a state of limbo. As with people trapped in the belly of a whale in the Bible or "Pinocchio," everywhere the hero looks is dark. This dark time is a bit protective, like a womb. However, it means that some ingenuity is needed to escape this temporary delay and return to the light.

Today, meditate upon the topic of the belly of the whale. Have you ever experienced a period of complete unknown? This could be the start of a new job or role when you had no idea what you were doing. It could be a time when culture shock or other ignorance of the world kept you from making immediate progress toward your goals. How do you react when you're in the belly of the whale? Do you struggle wildly to gain information and power over the situation, or do you shut down and wait things out?

* Meditate upon a time in your life that conformed
  to the belly-of-the-whale stage of the hero's journey.

Day 267: Initiation in the Hero's Journey

Initiation is the second main stage of the hero's journey after separation. There are six phases of initiation in the hero's journey, which we'll explore in the next few days. For now, we'll discuss what initiation means in the context of the hero's journey. Initiation is a transformation the hero goes through to truly become a hero. Before initiation, he is a mere ordinary person. After initiation, he has gained the wisdom and experience to be what Spirit called him to be.

Have you already experienced a metaphorical initiation in your life? For example, have you been initiated into parenthood by having a child, or initiated into the world of adult relationships by falling in love? There's nothing that can truly prepare you for these new states of being. People can talk themselves blue in the face about their own experiences, but your initiatory experience will be your own. Even though everyone's initiatory experience is unique, you still join the ranks of those who have passed through the same sort of initiation.

* *Meditate upon a time in your life that conformed*
  to the initiation stage of the hero's journey.

Day 268: The Road of Trials

Now our hero is on the road of trials, where our hero's limits are tested. He may have various tests, some of which are met with small successes, and others that seem to show initial failure. Sounds a lot like life, doesn't it? At this stage, our hero can make the best use of his supernatural aid. He may have to call on his Spirit for help and may be challenged listening to the advice Spirit gives. This might also sound familiar to you right about now.

Today, meditate upon the topic of the road of trials. Which trials are you experiencing right now? Which past trials have resulted in success? Which past trials have been met with failure? Can any of your present life trials be interpreted as tests from Spirit? What help have you received from Spirit so far, if any? Have you asked for supernatural help with your trials? Do you have any upcoming trials that you can prepare for at this stage of your life journey?

* Meditate upon the road of trials that is your life.

Day 269: The Meeting with the Goddess

The meeting with the goddess is the stage of the hero's journey when he falls in love. The goddess, in this case, represents love itself or may represent a female character who is the object of our hero's love. This love represents encouragement and motivation for our hero. Nothing will stop him from uniting with his love, even if there are trials that separate them. Consider whether the goddess overshadows the original quest, or if she was part of the plan all along. The goddess, of course, may also represent Spirit.

Today, meditate upon the topic of meeting with the goddess. When have you experienced love in your life that withstood any trial? Would you walk across hot coals for your boyfriend? Would you die for your sister? Is there a female love in your life who could represent the goddess herself? Have you had something stand in the way of love? How did you feel when you tackled those obstacles? Is there anything standing in the way of love in your life now?

* *Meditate upon a phase in your life that conformed to the meeting-with-the-goddess phase of the hero's journey.*

Day 270: Woman as Temptress

Imagine our hero is a knight in shining armor. He's supposed to fight a dragon, but a beautiful and seductive woman appears and takes his mind off his quest. An obstacle he's only too happy to see hopelessly waylays our hero. Not every story has a tempting woman, because the woman as temptress is merely a symbol. She is an example of physical temptations for our hero. Those temptations could easily be a bed to sleep in or a warm bowl of soup. Not all obstacles are ugly and evil. Some of them are downright pleasant.

Today, meditate upon the woman as temptress. Have you ever been thrown off life's path by pleasant distractions? Of course you have. We've all been seduced by the siren song of laziness, hunger, desire, sleepiness, and other barriers to our adventures. How do you pull yourself out of temptation? Can your supernatural aid help you when you feel tempted? Can your supernatural aid help you discern temptation itself?

* *Meditate upon a phase in your life that conformed to the woman-as-temptress phase of the hero's journey.*

Day 271: Atonement with the Father

Our intrepid hero has passed all of his tests and even got past temptation on his journey. With his love in mind and heart, he confronts an enemy—an enemy who turns out to be none other than his father. An authority figure, often represented as the father, is the hero's initiator at this stage. This authority brings about the transformation in the hero's life. The hero can reach out to his love-goddess or supernatural aid for help getting through the ordeal of initiation. The father simultaneously tears him down and builds him up. Our hero is forever changed.

Meditate upon the topic of atonement with the father today. Who or what is the initiator in your life? Is there a father figure who has used tough love to shape you? Has anyone or anything broken you down so you hit a new low in life and had to build yourself back up? To whom could you reach out to for help if this transformative experience happened in your life right now?

* *Meditate upon a phase in your life that conforms with the atonement-with-the-father stage of the hero's journey.*

Day 272: Apotheosis

....

This is the climax of our story. Our hero is dead! Or is he? At the very least, he seems a lost cause. He has moved beyond the realm of the living. He no longer lives in this world with good and evil, up and down, right and wrong, black and white. He is somewhere else. Somewhere that has none of those things. Our hero now resides with Spirit. If you're watching a movie during this phase, you'd hate if there was a commercial break. It may seem like you've reached the end, and yet you haven't resolved the original nature of the quest.

Today, meditate on the apotheosis stage of the hero's journey. How would you feel if you were removed from this world and its everyday rules? Would you feel relieved? Frightened? Angry? Have you ever had a near-death experience or felt this level of dissociation from the real world? If so, how did you come out of this phase? Is apotheosis something you want to achieve in this lifetime? If so, how can Spirit help you achieve this apotheosis?

* *Meditate upon the phase of apotheosis in the hero's journey.*

Day 273: The Ultimate Boon

Success! Our hero has won the ultimate boon of the story. He's completed every last one of his trials, passed all temptations, and achieved his original goal. Perhaps he's holding a magical prize he was sent to retrieve. Perhaps he's getting married to the princess he rescued. This high point of the story is a joyful chance for celebration. Everything looks up for the hero. In fact, some movies end here with no follow-up. In real life we know that plenty comes after each major success.

What are some of the ultimate boons you've had in life? Think of things you had to plan and prepare to achieve over time, with plenty of trials and tribulations. For example, you might have received a college degree, created something complex entirely with your own two hands, or won a prize in a tough competition. How did you celebrate those achievements? How did the world celebrate your accomplishment? How was Spirit involved in the aftermath of your goals being realized?

* *Meditate upon the times in your life that conformed*
  to the ultimate-boon phase of the hero's journey.

Day 274: Return
....

This is the final major stage of the hero's journey, after separation and initiation. The return is when the hero goes back to his original world. Things don't exactly return to normal, of course. Our hero is forever changed. It is as if he left as one man and returned another. The return may hold its own challenges. After all, he may have journeyed a long way. Many of the problems he encountered on the way through his journey may be equally problematic on his return.

Today, meditate upon the return. What sorts of return journeys have you made in your life? Perhaps you've made plenty of them. Have you been back to the home in which you grew up? Have you become nostalgic enough to visit an old hometown? Have you gone back to an ex-boyfriend or ex-girlfriend and tried to rekindle things anew after the two of you have become different people? What return journeys may be coming up in your life? How can you prepare?

* *Meditate upon the phases in your life that conform*
  to the return stage of the hero's journey.

Day 275: Refusal of the Return

Our hero initially refused the call to adventure, and now he's refusing the return. This may seem foolish of him, but look how he's made new friends and allies in this new world. He may have taken a wife and had children. His place of origin may seem strange and alien to him now. He may worry that the treasures he's found on his journey may not survive the trip back. What if a magic treasure crumbles into dust when he sets foot back in his old, mundane world?

Today, meditate upon the refusal of the return. Are there any return journeys that you have resisted or refused up until this point in your life? For example, I never confronted the high school teacher who said I'd never do well in college after I graduated with honors. Do you avoid nostalgic visits to the past for fear they will cause pain or negate your present achievements? How can Spirit help you bravely confront your fears?

* *Meditate upon the phases in your life that conform to the refusal-of-the-return stage of the hero's journey.*

Day 276: The Magic Flight
······································

Okay, this return is turning out to be harder than we thought. Just as the hero waves goodbye to his new friends and starts to journey home with his treasure, a monster awakes. The gods from whom the hero stole this treasure are angry, and they won't let our hero leave without a fight. This battle might be more difficult than all the challenges up to this point. Our hero will need nerves of steel and all the supernatural aid at his disposal to survive.

Today, meditate upon the magic flight. Have you had to come to the rescue of a person or a beloved project in your life? Remember that moment in your life when you would not let go of your prize, no matter what. How did you save face and save the object of your affection? Who came to your aid? Who opposed you? What sort of magic flight might be coming up in your life? How can you prepare for a magic flight? How can Spirit prepare you for your magic flight?

* *Meditate upon a phase in your life that conforms
  with the magic-flight phase of the hero's journey.*

Day 277: Rescue from Without

Uh-oh, our hero can't get back without help. He has monsters to fight that he can't fight alone. He may have been transformed into a brave hero, but he is not invincible. He may need to make some powerful new friends, or call upon some old ones. Perhaps he calls upon his old supernatural aid, or perhaps he forms alliances with new supernatural aids. Our hero may have to become part of a team.

Today, meditate upon the rescue from without. In what times of your life have you not had the strength to handle things and been brave enough to admit it? Who did you reach out to for help? Was it a therapist, a doctor, a trusted friend, a stranger? How was your request for help received? Which areas in your life do you need help with right now? Who can you ask for aid? Can Spirit help you find the right person to get you out of the current problem?

* *Meditate upon a phase in your life that conforms to the rescue-from-without phase of the hero's journey.*

Day 278: Master of Two Worlds

....

Once our hero returns, he is a changed man. In fact, he may straddle the two worlds he has come to know. He remembers the wisdom and friendships he made on his journey, and yet he is part of the old familiar world from which he came. In mythology, this can take the form of the enlightened master. He simultaneously lives in the world of Spirit and the manifested universe. In the real world, this straddling of two worlds may be complex. Like the war hero who must come back to his safe hometown and try to act like a civilian, it can be difficult.

Today, meditate upon the master of two worlds. In which ways are you a master of two worlds? Which other cultures, communities, or states of mind do you belong to? Do you feel different than everybody else? Do you ever feel like you don't belong? How can you fit in with others without giving up a part of your identity, knowledge, or gifts? Do you want to fit in, or are you satisfied with your differences? Do you know someone else who is a master of two worlds?

* Meditate on a part of your life that conforms to the
  master-of-two-worlds stage of the hero's journey.

Day 279: Freedom to Live

Freedom to live represents freedom from the fear of death. This is a power any of us can achieve. It is a function of spirituality to serve as a salve against the fear of death. When death is no longer feared, life can be freely and joyfully lived with Spirit. This is the ultimate treasure the hero brings back from his journey. He is changed from the fearful child, worried about being hurt, to the brave and invincible hero who has no fear, even of death.

Today, meditate on the topic of freedom to live. Do you know anyone who has freedom to live and from the fear of death? How free from fear is your life? Do media frenzies about terrorism, gunmen, or rampant pedophiles keep you from freely living your life? What sorts of daily actions of yours are driven by fear? Do these actions limit your life in a way that makes you want to give them up? It may not be possible to entirely give up the fear of death, and that's okay. That isn't necessarily the end of everyone's spiritual journey. Perhaps you have a new freedom to live that you will be given by Spirit in another way.

* *Meditate upon a blessing in your life that you may be able to associate with the freedom-to-live phase of the hero's journey.*

Day 280: Rites of Passage in Your Life

Now that we've completed our exploration of the entire hero's journey, you can see why rites of passage may be so spiritually important. You're not just throwing a party for a specific phase of life; you may be honoring or even instigating a phase of the hero's journey. Unfortunately, many rites of passage have been eliminated from our culture. Aside from getting a driver's license and being able to vote and drink, Western society doesn't have much of a way of honoring the transition from childhood to adulthood.

Today, consider rites of passage in your life. Which rites of passage have you experienced so far? For example, a marriage or a graduation is a common rite of passage in our society. Are there any rites of passage you think you may have missed out on? This might feel like passing through a significant phase of the hero's journey without any fanfare. Can you give yourself a rite of passage you've missed, however late it might be? Think about a rite of passage that is still to come in your life. Plan for a spiritual celebration of your upcoming rites of passage.

* *Ponder the rites of passage you've celebrated,*
  and plan for rites of passage yet to come.

Day 281: Milestones in Your Life

Milestones in life are different from rites of passage. When you learned to walk, it was a milestone, but not really a rite of passage. When you first cooked a meal for your family or when you moved into a new home, it was a milestone in life. These moments don't require huge community celebrations honoring them. However, you may still benefit from recognizing them on a spiritual level. In fact, you might feel a little sad or empty if you watch a milestone pass by without taking any particular action.

The remedy for the milestone blues is to take a moment to celebrate. You can do this all by yourself. It can be as simple as saying a prayer of thanksgiving to Spirit. Or, it can be as complex as going out with Spirit to walk in the park and ponder the milestone or have a celebratory dinner. Just like finding a penny and thanking Spirit can bring more abundance to your life, recognizing Spirit's hand in milestones can help your life progress in other ways.

* Reflect upon your life's milestones and give thanks.

Day 282: Challenges in Your Life

....

When challenges come up in your life, Spirit can help you face them head-on. We've already gone over a number of ways Spirit can give you aid. Accepting that help can be the hard part. Today we'll put some of those theories you've already learned together to create an action plan for life's challenges.

Your first course of action when encountering a life challenge is to assess the situation. If there's nothing that can be done practically in the moment, reach out through Spirit with intercessory prayer or by praying for wisdom and guidance. The next step is to have a good attitude and to turn to Spirit for comfort if your emotions get the better of you. Lean on Spirit and talk things out if you need to. Spirit is the perfect therapist. You don't need to make an appointment and it doesn't cost money. After you've overcome the challenge, whether it was by miracle or good old-fashioned hard work and waiting it out, don't forget to offer thanks to Spirit.

* Choose a challenge in your life and tackle it with Spirit.

Day 283: Quelling Anger with Spirit

If you're angry, it's okay. Spirit can take your anger like a patient parent calming down a toddler. Think of anger as a form of energy. You can transform anger from inaction or negative actions into positive energy through Spirit. There are two basic sorts of temper tantrums that people can have. The first is explosive anger, in which the urge comes to lash out. The second is implosive anger, in which hits can be taken to self-esteem and sadness may result. Make no mistake, both of these reactions come from anger at their core. So, it is important to address those angry feelings. Spirit can help.

Today, be on the lookout for frustrations or things that make you feel angry. Prepare a bowl of water as a focus point for meditation today. Meditate and allow yourself to feel outrage, even if it is at some abstract injustice in the world. Place your fingers in the bowl of water. Allow the energy of that anger to flow through your fingers into the water. Imagine the water cleansing and transforming the anger into powerful, positive energy. Pour out the bowl of water, perhaps on a plant, for renewal.

* Meditate upon angry feelings and use
  spiritual energy to transform them.

Day 284: Sadness and Spirit

....

Sadness is a more difficult emotion to transform than anger. The gray cloud of sadness can feel immovable and may sap all other emotions. For some, sadness feels like a lack of energy. Thus, the steps for dealing with sadness can be different than for anger. If you have a real problem with depression, you may have to reach out for help from a therapist or doctor. However, you can also use the following strategies for more transient sadness.

First, if there's nothing else you can do, pray intercessory prayer to be consoled or, if applicable, for the sad situation to be resolved. Then, talk out your feelings with Spirit. Treat Spirit as your therapist who will always listen and who will never get bored or run out of time. When you've talked and cried yourself out, use spiritual activity as a distraction. Try walking meditations, chanted mantras, elaborate rituals, or whatever gets your soul out of your head and into your body and the spiritual world. Be gentle with yourself and give yourself time to gradually pull out of your sadness. When you do, be sure to thank Spirit for the role it played in your transformation.

* *Think of something that makes you
  sad and use some spiritual remedies.*

Day 285: Fear and Spirit

Fear can be a crippling emotion. The point of the hero's journey, the story of many people's lives, is to overcome fear. One way to measure whether you're living a good life is to decide whether your hopes for the future outweigh your fears. Spirit can help that balance by either increasing your hopes, decreasing your fears, or both. Today, we'll go over a few methods for you to work through life's everyday anxieties using Spirit.

First, select something you feel fear or anxiety about in your life. If there's nothing practical you can do at this point, pray intercessory prayer for strength to overcome your fear. It may help to talk to Spirit about your fears. Sometimes saying the fears out loud makes them feel silly, especially if you're dealing with an irrational phobia. This can release the power the fear holds over you. Before you set out to confront your fear head-on, practice grounding. Allow anxious feelings to be transformed into helpful energy in the earth below your feet. While drawing up fresh energy after grounding, visualize an energetic shield protecting you.

* Use spiritual techniques to work with an existing
  source of fear or anxiety in your life.

Day 286: Confusion and Spirit

Confusion is a frequent spiritual problem. If you don't know what to ask for in intercessory prayer, what good does prayer do for you? Confusion can cause a sense of paralysis in one's spiritual life because it may seem like there is no hope for resolution. If all available paths seem like bad choices, what is the point of progress? This hesitation can cause a sense of spiritual crisis. Confusion can cause embarrassment and shame. Make a plan of action for areas in your life you haven't planned for yet, where things don't seem clear, or where all options seem blocked.

Since nothing will be done until you decide what can be done, first stop and pray for wisdom and guidance. Then, take your time and meditate quietly and receptively to seek answers. If the answers are not yet clear, ask for a sign. Pay attention to your dreams. Review your spiritual journal and your dream journal to seek answers. Some people search scripture for inspiration. Try to adopt an attitude of confidence that Spirit will help you find the right answer, and find comfort in that. When you get the first inkling of a solution, quickly follow up on it as a sign from Spirit.

* Use Spirit to address some confusion in your life.

Day 287: How to Ask for Blessings

Asking for blessings can feel awkward if you're relatively new to prayer. Even those who reached out with prayers of praise and worship, or who have prayed for intercession in times of need, may feel strange praying for wealth or happiness or other seemingly greedy prayers. However, everybody wants blessings, so it pays off to learn how to ask for them from Spirit, even when you're not in dire need.

The first step is to adopt a positive attitude toward receiving blessings from Spirit. Assume that Spirit wants to give you blessings, and that it gives Spirit pleasure to live in a symbiotic relationship with you. Assume the universe is filled with abundance, and that it doesn't cause harm for you to reach out and accept the abundance that can come to you. Then, pray and openly accept blessings. If you have trouble finding the words, try quietly meditating with your hands open to receive. Visualize yourself already blessed, and thank Spirit as if those blessings have already been given. Thank Spirit again when you see evidence of their impact on your life.

* *Ask Spirit for blessings.*

Day 288: Thinking Positively

Thinking positively is one way to help prayers come true. Don't get me wrong, sometimes bad things happen in life that are not your fault. Just because you let your sunny smile slip one day does not mean the world will crash down around you. However, a positive attitude opens doors for Spirit to enter your life. How? By giving you the motivation to pursue riskier avenues to success, and by allowing you to celebrate the little things in life.

Today, work on bringing more positive thinking into your life. There's no spiritual magic trick for this, although you can pray for success if you like. The first step is to observe when unhelpful negative chatter creeps into your mind. Note the circumstances or timing that brings these negative thoughts about so you can change things if necessary. Stop the negative thinking through sheer force of will. Immediately replace negative thoughts with a positive affirmation. Want a good trick? Your positive affirmation can be regarding a completely different subject. The point is to break the negative cycle and switch gears to a positive frame of mind.

* *Work to think more positively today.*

Day 289: Protection and Wards

You already know protection from Spirit is only a prayer away. However, you can always remind yourself of lasting protection from Spirit by performing a special protection blessing for your home or for a person. This type of exercise is sometimes called a ward because it wards away danger for a long period of time. The end of October and the beginning of May are two times of year when it is good to set up wards or to reinforce a previously created ward.

To set up a ward, first cleanse the person or the place. Sweeping a home would be appropriate, or using a sage smudge on a person or within a place. Next, add your protective blessing. Mix up holy water by adding salt to water to represent the elements of earth and water. Sprinkle this holy water while praying for protection. Your ward has now been placed, and you need not worry about it, but reinforcing it every six months can help.

* *Place a ward on your house or yourself.*

Day 290: Wealth

....

Money can't buy happiness, but I'd sure like to give it a try. In all seriousness, most people want enough money to take care of their needs and a
little more to share. You know praying for blessings is perfectly okay. There
are a few wealth-specific things you can do with regard to Spirit in order to
grease the gears. Here are some suggestions for bringing a healthy amount
of wealth into your life.

If you are already doing everything you can to obtain wealth, pray an
intercessory prayer for riches. Remember there's abundance in the universe and that you can accept some of it without harming anyone. Visualize your needs being met. You don't have to imagine the money coming
in, but rather the life you would like to lead. Allow Spirit to make that
life possible by whatever positive means are available. Then, spend money
to get money. Invest in yourself; give money to the more-needy, however
much you can afford to give. Allow that monetary energy to flow.

* *Consider using Spirit to bring more wealth into*
  your life or the lives of loved ones in need.

Day 291: Relationships
....

It may seem strange to go to Spirit with problems in relationships. It's almost like bringing a third person into a private conversation. Don't worry. Spirit is with you at all times, so you don't have to solve problems with a loved one alone. Remember, Spirit is the perfect therapist who will always keep things you share confidential. Here are some steps you can take to allow Spirit to help you improve a relationship that is in trouble, or simply solidify a relationship that is important to you.

If you've already done all you can to practically help the relationship, turn to Spirit with intercessory prayer. But what to pray for? Before you choose the words for your prayer, take time if you need to talk things out with Spirit. You can yell or cry or express confusion. Visualize how you would like the relationship to be. How can you become the positive person in the relationship? What characteristics would you show? What sorts of things would you say? Pray to be that person. If you feel any confusion, pray for wisdom and guidance.

* *Invite Spirit into your relationships today.*

Day 292: Celebrations

....

We've all seen sports heroes thank god after a good game or point to the sky and say "thank you" after winning a race. This might seem kind of cheesy, but you likely know why this is a good thing. Thanking Spirit after a victory encourages Spirit to give more blessings in that way. It also trains the worshipper to be more grateful and thus to see more happy causes for celebration in life. It's a win-win situation.

You've already thought about how to inject more spirituality into your holidays. Now I'd like you to think about how to invite Spirit into other celebrations. Think about the life celebrations that are coming up in the upcoming year, and how you can acknowledge Spirit in each of them. For example, if you're giving a toast at a wedding, consider adding a brief prayer or thanksgiving to Spirit. If you're writing something, add a dedication to Spirit. If you're out celebrating with friends, ask if you can say grace before you dine together. If you're blowing out candles on a birthday cake, take a moment to meditate.

* *Find ways to inject Spirit into upcoming*
  ordinary celebrations in your life.

Day 293: Tragedy

....

When tragedy strikes, spiritual people like myself can easily make fools of themselves. Attempts to console people experiencing tragedy by saying things like "everything happens for a reason" can be met with anger and rejection. Obviously, that's not the goal. During tragedy, we want to make sense of things with the help of Spirit, and ideally we'd like to share that wisdom and sense with those around us. Tread lightly. Here's a brief guide to using Spirit when you and others around you are experiencing tragedy.

When all else fails, pray. Pray for yourself first and foremost. You can pray to be an asset during the tragedy if you like. If it's appropriate, you can offer prayer to others involved in the tragedy, but honor their wishes if your offer is refused. A helpful hint is to talk to people who are a few degrees away from the tragedy. Those people in the outer circle may be in a more ready emotional state for prayer. Those closest to the tragedy are just struggling to get through each moment and may need their space. Use Spirit as your therapist during this time.

* Pray about a tragedy in the news or one
  that has happened to those close to you.

Day 294: Mistakes

····························

Mistakes can cause a big knock to the ego and an even bigger spiritual crisis. In fact, some religious traditions characterize many mistakes as sins against Spirit. Talk about pressure. If you're a responsible person, you'll feel guilty about your mistake and try to make things right. Inviting Spirit to help you solve the problem may help. Try not to pass spiritual judgment on your mistakes. That's not your job, after all. If there's going to be balancing in the universe, then Spirit will take care of that and it does no good to worry or punish yourself.

When you make a mistake, take time to own it fully. Know where it began, how it played itself out, and everyone your mistake affected. Apologize and make amends to those affected. Think about how you can avoid the same mistake in the future. Only after those practical steps are made should you seek spiritual forgiveness and self-forgiveness. Work to release the burden of guilt, because after a time it no longer serves anyone and becomes oddly self-serving.

* Analyze a past mistake and take spiritual
  steps to solve it, if necessary.

Day 295: What to Do with Negative Thoughts

When you worked on positive thinking, you practiced replacing the negative scripts in your head with positive affirmations. This can be a very effective spiritual technique, to a point. It is best used when you have a specific negative thought that is counterproductive in your life, one that appears over and over again in your mind. However, it is only possible to take positive thinking so far. With the power of Spirit, you don't have to worry any concerns popping into your head will come to pass. In fact, negative thoughts have a place in a spiritual person's life.

Today, assess some of your negative thoughts. Separate them into categories. Place negative thoughts that are safe to discard or overwrite in one category. Call this category "whining." We know whining when we hear it, even if it's not said in a nasally voice. These complaints are unhelpful and can be downplayed without harm. Call the second category of negative thoughts "warning." Give warnings serious consideration and prayer. Consult with Spirit for guidance about warnings and take immediate action. Speaking them aloud won't make them true.

* Separate your negative thoughts into categories
  of "whining" versus "warning."

Day 296: Creating Your Own Destiny

Today's activity will combine some of the skills you've learned so far. Recall the metaphor for destiny being a system of roads upon which you can drive. You can turn right or left at various intersections, though generally you can't go off-road. This is your destiny, and it is full of choices and free will. Each of those intersections is an opportunity to consult Spirit and ask for guidance. You have two intuitive tools at your disposal: You can step on the gas with positive thinking, or you can hit the brakes and slow down when you sense a warning.

Today, meditate upon your destiny. What is the destiny you wish to create in your life? How would you get there if you were to map out a path? From where you are right now, do you need to step on the gas with positive thinking or do you need to slow down and heed warnings? Give yourself some time for quiet, receptive meditation and listen for guidance from Spirit. Write down any guidance you receive. This is your current road map to your preferred destiny. It's not a promise, but it is better than drifting about and assuming external events are in charge.

* *Meditate upon how you can create your own destiny.*

Part Nine

—————— ✳ ——————

Your
Own Faith

Day 297: The Difference between Spirituality and Religion

The sign on the conference room door read "Spiritual NOT religious." It was a monthly meetup started by a friend of mine for people who actively rejected religions but embraced spirituality. For those like me who tend to use the words interchangeably, it was a little confusing. However, the lived experience of religion and spirituality can be different depending on your childhood and cultural associations with the words. Religion is essentially a re-linking with deity or with the ultimate. It often carries with it connotations of dogma or practices of others in a shared faith tradition. Spirituality, however, doesn't have to include a belief in deity or any sort of dogma. This freedom can seem welcoming to those who don't fit with any of the world religions.

Today, meditate on the difference between spirituality and religion. Do you follow a religion? Do you have a spirituality? Do you embrace both expressions of Spirit? Do you shy away from both labels? What connotations do you have with the words *spirituality* and *religion*? Write down your thoughts about whether you practice a spirituality, a religion, or both. Your thoughts may change over time.

* Meditate on the difference between spirituality and religion.

Day 298: The Difference between Meditation and Prayer

....

Another point of semantic contention is the word *prayer*. Some people balk at the word because of negative experiences in childhood when they felt forced to pray or felt prayer was otherwise faked. Such people may choose to meditate, send energy, or even practice magic. Magic is just a prayer with wings. The difference between prayer and meditation or magic is that the latter forms of spiritual expression use the practitioner's own personal power as a conduit for change. Prayer can imply passivity. The supplicant petitions with prayer and the Divine responds by doing all the work.

Hopefully, this book has shown you prayer can be more than that. Prayer can be a passionate action with the force of helping hands and moving feet behind it. Prayer can be a team effort with Spirit to guide a person to the right path of action. Prayer, magic, and energy working blend together at a certain point. It's up to you to choose your own terminology. Whatever inspires and encourages you is best.

* *Meditate upon the difference between meditation,*
  prayer, and other similar interactions with Spirit.
  Choose what language suits you best.

Day 299: Morality
·····························

Morality is a system of right and wrong that exists within the individual. Morals arise internally. Don't worry. You're not alone when deciding what is right and wrong. You can always consult with Spirit directly. You know when something goes against your morals when you feel depressed, guilty, or just plain wrong. Even if you "get away with it," morality can come around to bite you. That's a good thing. Morality can be a consistent lighthouse in your life that guides you away from danger.

Today, meditate upon your morals and write down your own personal moral code. The funny thing is that nearly everyone considers himself or herself a moral person. Your morals may be different from the next person's, but that doesn't mean that you're immoral. Think of instances when you felt proud doing the right thing, even if others thought you made a mistake. How did you know you were doing the right thing? Think of a time you were confused about what action was right. How can you use Spirit to guide you to the best course of action?

* *Write down your own personal moral code.*

Day 300: Ethics

....

Ethics are the code of conduct for a particular community. Ethics can vary from culture to culture. You were taught many sets of ethics from birth. People told you the right way to treat others and the wrong way to do things. When you think ethics, think of rules. You can be caught doing something ethically wrong, and a consequence is likely to result. If not punishment, subtle social consequences can result from being unethical. If you have to stop and think about whether something is legal, you can be fairly certain it is unethical. However, there can be some variation between contexts as to whether an action is ethical. Ethics require other people to evaluate an action in order to determine whether something is right or wrong.

Today, meditate upon the concept of ethics. Write down your own personal code of ethics. Do you believe in some form of the golden rule, that you should behave with others the way that you would like them to behave for you? How do you know when you behave ethically? How can you use Spirit to help determine ethical behavior in a situation where you're not sure how others feel? In contrast to morality, many people knowingly bend the rules of ethical behavior in order to do what they think is best for themselves or loved ones.

* *Write your own personal code of ethics.*

Day 301: Theory and Philosophy

You've gone through so many days connecting with Spirit. You've had some practical experiences and likely some failures. There are good days and bad days, just like anything else. It's time to begin thinking about theory and philosophy. You've already thought about the true nature of Spirit, so start there. Review your own personal view of Spirit. Is Spirit male or female? Are there multiple gods or one supreme essence? Review your own morals and ethics, and whether you believe you practice a religion or spirituality.

Today, meditate upon your personal philosophy about life and your theory about where Spirit fits into this philosophy. Combine the above ideas to write your own philosophy. This might take a few pages, so take your time. Your philosophy is based upon your experiences thus far in life and will guide your experiences from here on out. Write as if trying to explain your philosophy to a mentor, even if you're never going to share this with anyone. You can even chronologically write your philosophy, detailing your beliefs from birth to the present day.

* *Write your personal philosophy and theory about Spirit.*

Day 302: Your Values at Home and in Relationships

Look in your spiritual journal where you wrote down your core values. If you think of any more values, you can add them now. When you first wrote these, you thought about how you spend your time and money. This might cause you to seriously consider your career choice or decide to devote more of your free time to specific causes or pursuits. Today, I'd like you to turn that critical eye on your relationships and home environment. For example, if leisure and recreation is one of your core values, you might want to clear up all the work clutter from your home. If connecting intimately with others is one of your values, you might want to set aside a date night for one of your life's important relationships.

Today, meditate upon your home life and relationships. Take a hard look at how your time and effort may or may not align with your values. Are there any daily routines you have that don't contribute to your values? Can those routines be either eliminated or tweaked to include one of your values? Consider infusing problematic areas of your home life and relationships with spirituality.

* Meditate upon how your home life and
  relationships align with your values.

Day 303: Writing Out a Family Creed

Today's activity is related to yesterday's meditation on relationships and home values. It makes the most sense if you have children, but you can post a personal creed for just yourself. In fact, it can help you adhere to your values even when you're feeling stressed or too stuck in an everyday rut for self-improvement.

Take a look at your list of values and your personal philosophy. If you have family living with you, gather and share these with them if you like. Agree on specific values and philosophies you share. Write a sentence that acts as a mission statement about what your family believes and holds dear. You can also write rules for interacting with each other and the environment in your home according to your values. Try not to get laden down with a big list of rules; three to five rules is ideal. Place them somewhere you'll see them frequently. I put one copy in the garage so I can see it when I pull in, one copy in the bathroom where stressful arguments with small kids can happen, and one copy in my kids' room.

* *Write a personal or family creed to post as a reminder to yourself.*

Day 304: Labels

....

As a leader in my spiritual community, I get a lot of questions about Spirit. The most frequent question I'm asked by beginners is a puzzling one. It basically comes in the form of "What do I call myself?" Newcomers to Spirit immediately feel at a loss without some sort of specific label for their faith. There are several reasons for this. In America, we like our labels because spirituality can be an important part of identity. We want to be able to express ourselves as this, that, and the other thing. When no label is appropriate, it may seem like we don't know what we're talking about. The second reason is a desire for fellowship. The question of what to call oneself can also take the form of, "May I call myself one of you?"

Today, meditate upon which spiritual labels, if any, you may choose to apply to yourself. Do you follow a religion? Would other members of that religion accept you? Does it matter? Would you give modifiers to your label? Are there any subcategories of your chosen spiritual label? If you were to search for other people who believe and practice like you, what terms would you search for online?

* *Meditate upon any chosen spiritual labels for yourself.*

Day 305: Gaining Strength from Your Beliefs in Spirit

One of the major benefits of having a spiritual foundation is the strength you gain in times of need. What does it look like to have strength in Spirit? When I think of somebody with strength in Spirit, I think of people in my life who have shown bravery and peace of mind in the face of terrible circumstances. The rock-solid foundation Spirit provides is their calming influence. Think about how you might confront such challenges. How can you find peace and show courage in the face of extraordinary life circumstances?

Most of us survive hard times in life. The biggest difference between people perceived as strong and those perceived otherwise is strong people can still function. So, it does you no good to dive into Spirit to the detriment of real life when troubles arise. Today, meditate upon how to be strong for others during your next big life event. How can you turn to Spirit but still be available to those who need you? The answer to this question is different for different people. For some, it may mean bringing your loved ones closer to Spirit with you. For others, it may mean becoming the master of two worlds.

* Meditate upon how you can portray strength
  during your next major life challenge.

Day 306: Gaining Comfort from Your Beliefs in Afterlife

Belief in an afterlife serves an important purpose in this world. It is one of the things that staves off a fear of death. Your belief in an afterlife helps you in many ways. When you lie awake at night thinking about your mortality, thoughts of the afterlife can help you drift into sleep. When somebody you love dies, your belief in the afterlife can take away some of the pain of loss. For these reasons, it is important to nurture your belief in an understanding of the afterlife before you are confronted with loss or a brush with death yourself.

Think back to your beliefs in an afterlife, if any, that you established earlier in this book. How can you strengthen your understanding? For example, if you believe in reincarnation or heaven, there are plenty of scriptures in the world religions that can back up those ideas. Reading them can help. If you believe in Spirit communication, you can work on communicating with ghosts so you are encouraged that people will talk to you after you're gone. The possibilities are endless. Brainstorm activities that feed your soul according to your own belief system.

* *How can you strengthen your belief in the afterlife now?*

Day 307: The Place of Doubt

....

Does doubt have a place in spirituality? In our culture and media, there is a false dichotomy between science and religion. Science is supposedly the way of knowing that allows for doubt and experimentation. Religion is conversely thought to be full of mindless zombies who observe blind faith. In actuality, there should be more doubt in both of these ways of knowing. Doubt in science leads to further theory-building and testing. Doubt in religion can likewise be helpful. If you doubt your religion, you'll either come back to your faith stronger than ever or you will find something better.

Today, embrace doubt in your spirituality. If you follow a specific religion, think of a tenet that is the most unbelievable to you. If you don't belong to a religion, think of something you'd like to believe but cannot because there is too much doubt. Pray for Spirit to show you a sign or evidence that this is real. My religious practice involves me taking on a spiritual name. I thought this was silly, so I prayed for a name to come to me in writing. The next day I found a nametag on the ground and found a name card in a library book. Spirit gave me more than one name.

* *Embrace doubt today.*

Day 308: Conversion, Changes, and Evolution of Faith

Many people find the most honest expression of their faith when they convert. This seems paradoxical. If the only way to be born again into Spirit is to convert, then only people who are born into the incorrect faith would be able to have that experience. This seems to be an unavoidable conundrum unless you consider the hero's journey. In the hero's journey, everyone can have that initiatory experience. Nobody can be born knowing all the solutions to the world's problems. The initiatory experience represents the revelations anyone can have.

Today, meditate upon the evolution of your own faith. The easiest observation may be the labels you have taken on throughout the years. Any outright conversions will markedly stand out in your mind. More subtle, though, is the evolution of faith. Just as you didn't notice growing an inch each year as a child, it's easy to not notice how often you speak with and listen to Spirit at different points in your life. This is why you should keep a spiritual journal.

* *Meditate upon any conversions or evolutions of faith in your life.*

Day 309: Dedicating Yourself

At some point in your spiritual journey, you may want to give Spirit a ceremony to celebrate your commitment to the faith. This ceremony may not be an initiation, because it may have little bearing on your rank within any spiritual community. You can, however, dedicate yourself to Spirit with all your heart. Dedication has no need for any kind of community. A dedication can be as ostentatious or as humble as you like. I highly recommend you dedicate yourself to your faith.

To perform a dedication, first decide what sort of commitment you want to make. Are you going to dedicate yourself for a year or a lifetime? Think about what this sort of commitment means. Are you going to take a new name? If so, introduce yourself to the four directions of the world—north, south, east, and west—while identifying yourself to Spirit. Are you going to take on a new task such as feeding the homeless in your community? Make that vow in front of Spirit. Your oaths or vows become your motivation for the coming phase of your life.

* *Dedicate yourself to Spirit to the level you feel is appropriate.*

Day 310: Becoming the Proper Person You Want to Be

In my religious community, we have the concept of a proper person. A proper person is initiated into our community. A proper person becomes a vital part of the group. It all sounds a little pompous unless you understand a "proper" person doesn't mean "proper enough to marry my daughter." It means the correct fit for the job. You can become a proper person for anything as long as you know what you're trying to be proper for. If you're not proper for one role, it doesn't mean you're somehow damaged or wrong. It just means you're a better fit for a different role.

Today, meditate upon the role of the proper person. Think about what proper roles you'd like to be assigned. How would such a proper person think? How would a proper person act? How would a proper person feel? How can you express yourself as a proper person to those in your life? In the end it doesn't matter how proper we seem to anyone as long as we fit the right role for what we're destined to be.

* *Meditate on being a proper person*
  for the roles you want to play in life.

Day 311: Being Serious about Spirit

It's important to be serious about the world of Spirit. That doesn't mean you have to be solemn all the time. In fact, it may even seem to be at odds with the nature of Spirit to constantly be serious and solemn. How can you balance seriousness with joyfulness and celebration? It is important to be able to straddle the line. If you want to practice any sort of spirituality with other people, you have to pick up on when the situation is as serious as a funeral. Even if you're practicing alone, it can be fulfilling to experience both great joy and great solemnities with Spirit.

If you want to be serious about your spiritual experience, you merely need to put more effort into your practice. Seriously dedicate yourself to the parts of spiritual practice that you find most appropriate to you. Your dedication over time will amount to serious study. Anything you practice over a long period of time develops respectable skills. If you don't give the time needed for expertise, it will never happen. Conversely, anyone can build a little bit of skill with practice. Today, commit to a serious skill. Write down your goals.

* *Write down some serious spiritual goals.*

Day 312: Discretion and Silence

Secrecy is a value of many spiritual traditions and is associated with the element of earth. But why? It seems strange or even creepy. There are lots of good reasons for secrets, including:

1. It is part of the tradition.

2. It teaches loyalty and the discipline to stay silent.

3. Some things in the tradition cannot be spoken.

4. One should never spoil the surprise for any future initiates.

5. Words without context would not make sense.

6. Some things are private and intimate.

7. One is never obliged to share spiritual information with another.

8. An unshared concept can be internalized
   without diluting its meaning and associations.

9. The information may not be appropriate for everybody.

The ability to be discreet is often an attribute desired in spiritual gurus because of some of the reasons above. You might think of other purposes of your own. However, discretion in real life can be pretty challenging. The good news is that you can talk to Spirit about whatever you want without revealing any information that is not supposed to be revealed. Go ahead and pray aloud to Spirit if you know other people aren't listening. This affords you the opportunity to be less circumspect with information.

* *Meditate upon the potential virtue of discretion and silence.*

Day 313: Women's Mysteries and Men's Mysteries

The word *mysteries*, in a spiritual sense, means "shared experiences and rites of passage that express things that cannot be spoken." For example, I got my driver's license when I turned eighteen. Getting my driver's license sent me the message that I was an adult far more clearly than if someone had simply told me that fact. In many ancient cultures, women had separate coming-of-age mysteries than men. This makes sense because there are different cultural cues. For women, the coming of age is often marked by menses, the physical evidence that the young woman is now able to bear a child. For men, the demarcation between childhood and adulthood might not be as clear. His celebration of adulthood might be linked to his sexuality, his achievements, or something else entirely.

Today, meditate upon men's mysteries and women's mysteries, as they may have played a role in your life. Bring to mind the first time in your life you felt you represented an adult of your gender. What led up to this momentous event? What was the proper expression of your gender and at what point did you feel you were upholding this ideal? If you've never completely identified with one gender in your life, how can you provide an opportunity in your life for feeling at home in your skin?

* *Meditate upon women's mysteries and men's mysteries.*

Day 314: Developing a Good Disposition

··

Most people like to be around others who have a positive attitude. This can seem fair, when you're developing your spirituality, because energy affects who you become. However, it might seem terribly unfair if you are struggling with a life circumstance anyone would find unpleasant. Nevertheless, it is vital to work on developing a positive disposition. Not only is it generally a more positive life to lead, but it can also make you a far more pleasant person to deal with in a group spiritual context.

If you already have a generally positive disposition, you are blessed. Thank Spirit every day for your positive outlook on life and make a commitment to give thanksgivings whenever you perceive a major blessing. If you are not typicall positive in nature, don't worry too much. Work on replacing any negative habits of mind with positive ones. After these efforts, you need only allow time to do its work. Be gentle with yourself. Remember that just as it takes a long time to build physical muscles, it takes a long time to build spiritual muscles.

* *Work on developing a positive disposition.*

Day 315: Speaking Sincerely or Keeping Silent

Speaking sincerely is an important part of spirituality. Silence is a virtue associated with the element of earth. Nearly every religion emphasizes the importance of honesty. The reason for this is the same reason I rebuke my toddlers whenever they lie. I tell them, "I need to know that you mean what you say and that you say what you mean!" Likewise, if you believe Spirit works when you call, you need to be able to speak your mind so Spirit can act in conformity with your will. On the other hand, it helps to keep the most important of your expressions of Spirit automatically secret, and to only share them when absolutely necessary. This may be more challenging than you think. In our culture we are encouraged to communicate, communicate, communicate. Even to the point where it muddies the original purpose of the conversation.

Today, practice speaking sincerely or keeping silent. Remember a situation in which your strength of mind or Spirit could have been expressed in a way that would have changed the outcome of the situation. Could you have been more truthful? Could you have kept something to yourself? What difference would this have made in your current life?

* Meditate upon the act of speaking sincerely versus keeping silent.

Day 316: Knowledge

Today's exercise is to think about the concept of knowledge. This is the first of four keys that align themselves with the elements. Knowledge is associated with the element of air. Knowledge is intelligence and initiation. It is the gentle breeze that brings the sense of knowing. It is also the hurricane-force winds that blow away everything except the purest expression of truth. Imagine sitting at a desk while taking a test at a college. Your mind goes blank and you begin to panic. Luckily, at the last minute, the answers to the test flood into your head like colorful leaves floating on the top of a river. Knowledge is important because, for most of us, all action springs from knowledge.

Today, meditate upon the power of knowledge. From what in your life do you truly trust your knowledge? Have you ever devoted yourself to serious education in which your knowledge comes from an external source? Conversely, have you ever had to fight somebody on an issue in which your experiential knowledge trumped knowledge procured from an academic source? Today, meditate upon the true source of knowledge in your life.

* Meditate upon the topic of knowledge.

Day 317: Daring

....

The second elemental value I'd like to introduce is the value of daring. This daring virtue is often associated with the element of water. Water embodies the stormy seas that wash upon the shores. This is the essential expression of daring. Imagine a brave surfer who has to cut back his activities based upon the storms outside his windows. When the waves leap high but can be controlled is when this surfer can master the water.

Today, meditate upon the act of being daring. In your workplace, it is quite possible you have to conform to a specific expression of daring. That is okay. But always think of yourself as a representative of humankind. A single rule in a workplace won't hold us back for generations unless some serious danger results. If there is a problem that blocks your sense of logic from evaluating how you interact with daring, confront it now. Most people sense that they are not allowed to evaluate conformity vs. daring. Fight this problem at all costs. Evaluate a daring person in your life. The more freedom you find with your ability to dare, the more freedom you'll find with your connection to Spirit.

* *Meditate upon the topic of daring.*

Day 318: Will
....

The most obvious expression of Spirit may be the ability to will. This ability is often associated with the element of fire, and so it is often an active sense. To will is to push for something to be true. To hope you have the true expression of Spirit among others. Will is an extreme desire ready for action. Will is also an expression of an action, rather than just a snapshot of a moment in time. If you are examining your own will, think how it is based on the success of others. Think about how the failure to will can be as obvious as its success.

Today, meditate upon the topic of will. From what source does your true will spring? What person in your life truly represents a willful person? When have you felt your will was not properly expressed? How can you change your actions now so your will is more accurately expressed? How do you think your will is expressed to others? How does the will of others affect what is happening in the world? Do you perceive this as wrong? What is your will?

* *Meditate upon the topic of your will.*

Day 319: Harming None

A common injunction upon the spiritual person is to harm none. This may seem impossible to the more practical among us. Every time I clap, I kill countless numbers of teeny-tiny organisms. Where does a person draw the line? Obviously, the line is drawn differently for different people. I'm a vegetarian, so I choose to reduce harm in the world by not eating animals. Many people take a stance more pious than mine by claiming they don't even eat milk or honey. And yet, it can be okay to eat meat and reduce harm in the world in other ways.

Today, meditate upon the idea of harming none. For most of us, this will seem like an unobtainable ideal. Every action comes with some kind of consequence. Meditate upon the least harmful actions in your own life. How can you harm as few entities as possible? What sorts of harm are inevitable? What are some ways you can actively reduce harm? For example, volunteering at a shelter for people who have experienced domestic violence is one way to lessen the harm those people experience in the aftermath of the violence.

* *Meditate upon the topic of harming none.*

Day 320: Wisdom
....

What is the true nature of wisdom? No goddess or god is unwise. Such an ignorant representation of divinity would be completely out of character. Nobody would listen to his or her story. Even myths in which deities make mistakes are representations of lessons learned. After all, wisdom is often a hard-won treasure. You cannot become wise without taking some risks. How can you make wise choices in your present life?

Today, meditate upon the kind of wisdom you have obtained thus far in life. Think back to earlier points in your life when you were less wise than you are today. When I was a teenager, I thought I was more mature and wise than other teenagers. Today, this seems laughable to me. I am so much wiser today than I was then, and the difference is obvious to me now. I'm sure as more years pass, I will be wiser still. As you think today of the wisdom you will come to gather, ponder how much you do not yet know. The first step toward wisdom is realizing one's ignorance.

* *Meditate upon the topic of wisdom.*

Day 321: Justice
....

What does it mean to conform to the value of justice? Most of us are not professional judges or jurors on a regular basis. That means we're not usually trying to ignore our often selfish goals for the purpose of evaluating the goals of another. Your sense of justice highly depends upon the values of those around you, especially during childhood. Even infants have a sense of justice. Experimenters have found that when a baby watches a video of two people being served unequal amounts of food, the baby stares longer than when the people are served equally. This, they suppose, is evidence the baby senses something is wrong or unjust. And yet cultural cues shape that baby's sense of justice as he or she grows.

Today meditate upon the topic of justice. Everyone strives for justice, and yet there is injustice in the world due to differing concepts of justice. Think about an example of injustice in the world. This could be an injustice in your workplace or in the political news. What is the source of that injustice? What would have to change in order for justice to be served?

* *Visualise a world in which justice is fulfilled.*

Day 322: Fairness When Giving and Taking

··

In many fables and religious stories, reciprocity is very important. That means everything you put into your spiritual growth you will receive in spiritual blessings. This is why giving offerings to Spirit is such a common practice. You also give and take in your everyday relationships. Strive to balance the give-and-take in your relationships just as you do with Spirit, since Spirit is represented in all things. If you tend to receive a lot from your relationships, it may seem obvious that you have to give back. However, if you tend to be a selfless giver, it may feel hard to take back what you deserve.

Today, make sure you give as much as you receive. This simple act of balancing can help all people concerned to benefit. If there's somebody in your life who gives to you selflessly, find a way to give back to that person. If you tend to be the giver, find a way to ask for assistance. When you receive help or a gift from another person, allow yourself to truly receive gratefully instead of brushing the gift aside.

* *Try to balance the give-and-take in your life.*

Day 323: What Warms Your Heart?

We often talk of something warming the heart, meaning something that affects us in a positive emotional way. When your heart is warmed, you might cry, find yourself at a loss for words, or dance for joy. What does this have to do with Spirit? For many people, spirituality warms the heart. Prayer can invoke the same joyful feeling that comes from looking at a picture of a really cute puppy. If that warm heart and joy aren't present, one can lose motivation or feel disconnected from Spirit.

If you don't yet feel your heart warmed by Spirit, work on that issue. The best way to get started is by flexing your heart-warming muscles. Think of what sets your heart aflutter in your life. Is your significant other a source of warmth in your heart? Recognize your significant other as an expression of Spirit today. Does a particular tear-jerker movie or book warm your heart? Watch the movie again, looking for the hero's journey. Are pictures of cute kittens the only thing that warms your heart these days? Then sign up to foster kittens for a local shelter as a service to Spirit. Find ways to warm your heart on a regular basis, and you'll find that it becomes more sensitive to that feeling.

* Write down what warms your heart.

Day 324: Karma
....

There are two basic definitions of karma. The Western definition is that good things will come back to you and bad things will come back to you, so a wise person should strive to maximize good actions and minimize bad actions. The Eastern definition of karma is different. The classical Eastern definition of karma is that your actions in this world gather karma, but any karma is a bad thing. Even good karma from positive interactions with loved ones ties you to this material world. These ties can be a liability if you're trying to escape the material world and separate from your ego to become closer to Spirit. Some believe karma is a community effort, so everyone has to succeed at connecting with Spirit before true enlightenment can be realized. All for one and one for all.

Today, meditate upon what connects you to the material world. Have certain experiences attached you to your belongings, your home, and your relationships? Do you feel weighed down by these attachments? Does karma affect your connection with Spirit? Do you feel good things come into your life when you perform good acts and that bad actions come back to haunt you?

* Write down your beliefs about karma.

Day 325: Gender Dynamics

Our world may seem to be mighty silly. We place so much importance on simple gender differences. A vagina and a penis are simple fleshly differences. Nevertheless, cultural gender dynamics can affect the roles we play in spiritual communities. In my religion, spiritual teachers take on students of the opposite gender. These gender roles mimic a traditional marriage in which fertility is valued. This doesn't mean people attracted to the same sex or transgendered persons can't practice this particular religion. In other religions, men and women are often limited to specific roles according to gender. This might be frustrating to some who don't want to be limited by gender and can be met with problem-solving by the open-minded.

Today, meditate upon the role you play in the world according to your preferred gender identity. How do you tend to interact with the opposite gender and with people who share your gender? If you practice a specific religion or interact with a spiritual community, is your gender limited to a specific role? If so, why? If you think of gender as a symbolic construct, does this have an important place in your spirituality?

* Meditate upon your gender identity's role in spirituality.

Day 326: Virtues

....

Virtues are characteristics of the soul that foster connection to Spirit. In most cases, virtues are wonderful characteristics to have when interacting in society. Virtues can vary between religions, across cultures, and even person to person. Some virtues I hold dear include compassion, gentleness, kindness, strength, and power. Some virtues aren't as simple as behaviors. For example, I also recognize the virtues of beauty and youth. Even though I value the young people in my life for the virtue of their youth, I recognize that one cannot hold onto physical youth.

Today, write down some virtues you hold dear or you believe can bring one closer to Spirit. Some of these may be virtues you already display. Circle those. Some of them may be virtues you are working on expressing more consistently. Underline those. Ponder how you can become more virtuous. How can you let your virtues shine so that others recognize them? How do those virtues bring you closer to Spirit? Beware of false virtues that may be fed to you from society or the media. If you don't measure up to a virtue, it doesn't mean you are not a virtuous person. It just means that you are better suited to express a different virtue.

* *Write down a list of spiritual virtues.*

Day 327: Spirit Communication
··

Many religions include a belief that those who have died can still communicate with us. This can be a deeply comforting belief, since continuing a relationship with a loved one after death can act as confirmation of an afterlife. Something as simple as a white feather floating on the wind can be seen as a message from a dead loved one that everything is okay. The deceased can also come in dreams or meditation. Some people choose to directly pray to deceased loved ones, speaking aloud as if they were in the same room. Others pray to Spirit as a mediator, asking Spirit to pass the message along to the deceased loved one.

Today, try Spirit communication. Sit down to meditate while thinking of a deceased loved one you trust. Sit in quiet and receptive meditation, writing down any feelings or thoughts that may be pertinent. I suggest you perform this meditation right before bedtime and invite the loved one to visit you in your dreams. If nothing comes to you in meditation, lie down to sleep, making sure to write down any dreams you have, even if they seem to have nothing to do with the deceased loved one. Remember, dreams are highly symbolic.

* *Attempt Spirit communication.*

Day 328: Grief
....

Times of grief are important moments to turn to Spirit. Grief can happen from any sort of loss. A death is the most obvious source of grief, but losing a job, a big move, or a relationship breakup can also be sources of grief. The effects of grief can be cumulative. If you experience more than one of these losses in a three-year period, each one can feel more devastating than if those losses were spaced out. Grief can be a time of doubt and spiritual crisis. It is important to directly address these feelings instead of ignoring them, so you can process your grief.

Today, think about a source of grief in your life or a potential upcoming loss. How can you turn to Spirit in your times of grief? Are there spiritual exercises you can do to let go? How about the ritual using the bowl of water I taught you for letting go of anger? Can it also help you with the emotions associated with loss? How can you use prayer during your grieving time? Are you the sort of person who will want to talk things out with Spirit, or would you prefer to use a flowery memorized prayer at a memorial service as a source of comfort?

* *Plan to use Spirit as a tool when grieving.*

Day 329: Relinquishing Worry

I'm a control freak, so I hate to give up anything, even my worries. I hear stories of people who "let go and let god," and I admire this, but mostly at a distance. It seems scary to give up a problem entirely to Spirit. I want to be the one actively seeking solutions. Consequently, I usually ask Spirit for guidance. However, relinquishing worry can be a way to express faith. Worry is often completely pointless. The problem will persist or go away regardless of whether you worry about it. Letting go of worry can be a helpful way to spiritually clear the way for a solution.

Today, think of an unproductive worry you would like to relinquish. Before you give it up, take a moment to voice the worry. Speak aloud to Spirit about the worry and the worst-case scenario. The worry sometimes sounds silly and loses some of its power when it is spoken aloud. Then, pray to Spirit to take away the worry. Give the worry to Spirit and make a vow to no longer worry about it. When you sense that worry sneaking back into your head, remind yourself you've already given the worry to Spirit and immediately distract yourself with another thought or activity.

* *Choose an unproductive worry and relinquish it to Spirit.*

Day 330: Spiritual Duty and
Responsibility, and How to Ask for More

For the control freak in all of us, asking for more spiritual duties and responsibilities may feel more comfortable than letting go of worry. Take care, however, that you don't take on too much before you're ready. If you dive into more spiritual responsibility before your time, you might feel overwhelmed and quit. However, if you carefully evaluate what sorts of spiritual duties and responsibilities you're ready for, you can grow in your faith.

Today, evaluate what sorts of spiritual duties or responsibilities you'd like to take on in the coming year. For example, you might want to start a new devotional practice, build an outdoor shrine in a garden, or take on a new role in your spiritual community. Think seriously about how you've handled any previous responsibilities of this sort. How realistic is your goal within the timeline you've chosen? Do you want Spirit or somebody else to hold you accountable? How can you hold yourself accountable? What will you do if you fail to achieve your goal? Pray for Spirit to give you this task as a duty.

* Choose a new spiritual responsibility or duty.

Day 331: How Humanism and Non-Believers Fit In

If you've worked this far and still don't believe in the literal existence of any goddesses or gods, that's okay. You can be a non-believer and still practice spirituality or even some religions. You will, however, have to reconcile your spiritual practices and your beliefs. This can be a challenge if you practice with others, or if you wish to follow a specific religion that typically includes a belief in literal divine beings. Even if you firmly count yourself as a believer, think about Spirit today from the point of view of a non-believer so you can be inclusive and accepting of those who struggle with this aspect of faith.

Today, meditate upon Spirit as a symbol. What is a higher power in your life? How can that higher power be worthy of celebration? How is Spirit expressed through the ordinary in ways that should be praised? Imagine two people who believe in Spirit in different ways: One is a non-believer who thinks Spirit is symbolic and the other is a literalist die-hard believer. How can those two people practice spirituality together? How can they get on the same page?

* *Ponder Spirit as symbol and metaphor.*

Day 332: Feeling Confident in Your Faith

When you first picked up this book, it was probably with the hopes you could find more confidence in your faith. We've all met those confident spiritual people. They speak of Spirit with a look of joy in their eyes. They might spontaneously suggest sharing a prayer or talk openly about how Spirit is working in their lives. This sort of confidence is enviable. Well, I'll let you in on a secret. Even the most faithful spiritual leaders have doubts.

Think of your relationship with Spirit as any other relationship with ups and downs. For example, I am married. Some days my relationship with my husband is close and I feel very confident about our marriage. He is the most charming and perfect husband in the world. Other days we argue and act childishly, and I feel like we're setting a terrible example of marriage for our children. At the same time, even in those dark moments, we stay married. Today, make a similar commitment to Spirit. Celebrate those times when you feel a close connection, and vow to remain true to Spirit even when your confidence crumbles.

* *Celebrate confidence and put doubt in proper perspective.*

Day 333: Writing Your Own Statement of Faith

One exercise that can increase your confidence is writing your statement of faith. I already had you write your theory and philosophy. Your philosophy might have a lot of "I think that…" written in it. For your statement of faith, I'd like you to move toward using language like "I believe…" Your statement of faith isn't about how the world works, but how you perceive Spirit working in your life. Like your personal philosophy, your statement of faith may change over time with your experiences. Some experiences will cause you to have deeper faith. Other experiences may cause things you once thought were vital to your faith to fade in importance. This is natural and okay. You can reread your statement of faith over time, especially when you feel you're in spiritual crisis.

Today, write out your statement of faith. Put your beliefs into words. You don't have to write how you know them. Write with confidence, as if these are facts. You can include statements about how you feel your practice with Spirit should deepen. Do you want to include your virtues in your statement of faith? Your values? What else serves your beliefs and strengthens them?

* *Write a personal statement of faith.*

Part Ten

*

Fellowship

Day 334: Prayer Chains

Why do people tend to congregate in fellowships and share worship? Certainly there are many social reasons. Getting together to worship can help people provide one another with accountability while sharing spiritual duties. Today, I'd like to introduce you to a simple spiritual duty that can be shared: a prayer chain. A prayer chain is when more than one person prays about the same thing, usually in sequence, so one person prays right after another to extend the period of time spent in prayer. Very large prayer chains can be arranged so a day or more is spent in prayer. For example, twenty-four people could each take a one-hour shift of prayer to lift the prayer to Spirit for an entire day.

Today, reach out to friends or family to start a prayer chain. Your prayer chain doesn't have to be in the same area. In fact, this is a perfect opportunity to connect people long-distance. If your mom is across the country, you can still work on the same prayer goals. Pick a prayer you can all agree upon. It can be for something as grand as world peace or something as simple as getting a new job. Arrange how long and what time each person should pray. After your prayer chain is executed, talk with one other about your impressions.

* Organize a prayer chain with one or more people.

Day 335: Being Resourceful
···

In order to find fellowship with others, you'll need to be resourceful. If you don't find the perfect group for you right away, keep shopping. Remember when I asked you to think about labeling your faith? This label is the first jumping-off point most people use when finding fellowship. You can search online for local groups or visit local places of worship. If you can't find the people you want, you'll have to be more resourceful. Think outside of the church box.

Try visiting metaphysical bookstores and ask about events or groups that might not advertise. Approach spiritual people you admire and ask which sorts of spiritual memberships they hold. If you still don't find anyone near you to connect with on a spiritual level, you might want to try some long-distance learning. Joining online email lists or other groups can be helpful. And, of course, reading books can be a great starting point. See if there are larger groups located on a national level that might have resources available for you to charter a local group.

* *Look into resources near you for joining*
  or starting a spiritual group.

Day 336: Keeping Others in Your Thoughts and Prayers

"I'll keep you in my thoughts and prayers." What does this common phrase mean? I've already instructed you on how to start and keep a prayer list, but sometimes including others in your thoughts and prayers is not as simple or straightforward as keeping a list. Sometimes you can't ask permission from someone to place him or her on your prayer list. For example, the president of the United States may be in your thoughts and prayers, but he likely didn't ask to be added to your prayer list. And sometimes people refuse to be placed on our prayer list. "Thanks, but no thanks," the person might say, "but think good thoughts for me." What does this mean?

Today, I'll teach you how to keep people in your thoughts and prayers in a general and non-specific way. Instead of going through a prayer list with specific intentions for each person, sit down to meditate and hold that person in your mind. If you do speak a prayer, simply ask for Spirit to give that person energy to do with it what he or she wills, with harm to none and for the highest good of all. Allow yourself to remember that person throughout the day. Perhaps you see a bouquet of flowers at the grocery store that would cheer her up. Perhaps you notice a business card for a service that could solve his problems. Allow the thoughts to lead to actions when appropriate.

* *Keep someone in your thoughts and prayers today.*

Day 337: Best Wishes

....

"Best wishes" is a common closing remark or comment made in response to someone's life news. Spirituality gives you an opportunity to offer your best wishes to someone. This is often also called "sending energy." It differs slightly from prayer because you attempt to send somebody your highest and best wishes, rather than praying for a specific problem to be solved by Spirit. Here are step-by-step instructions for giving somebody your best wishes.

First, sit down to meditate and visualize the person you want to bless. Picture this person happy and with all of his or her needs met. If you're sending best wishes to somebody who is sick, imagine that person well again. As you envision this healthy, happy fellow, allow a feeling of happiness to build in your heart. If you pray, speak your words in the form of a wish. Then, imagine you are releasing that energy through your body and out into the world to work its magic. Fully ground yourself after this exercise. Talk to the person after this exercise, offering practical help if appropriate, and ask if he or she has noticed any differences in life.

* Send somebody your best wishes.

Day 338: Sharing Your Faith with Others

Some religions encourage followers to share the faith with others. Even if you have no such injunction in your spirituality, the urge to share your faith can spontaneously arise. For me, this happens in the same way viewing a beautiful sunset causes me to want to share the experience. "Hey, look over there," I want to say, "isn't that absolutely beautiful?" Likewise, I want others to experience the joy of spirituality I experience. That's why I wrote this book. The trouble with spirituality, however, is that it's not as simple as turning and looking at a sunset. Spirituality requires work, and other people may not desire the same experience enough to bother with the work.

If you do want to share your faith with others, you don't have to knock door to door. Spirit will likely bring people your way who are most receptive to your ideas. Have faith in this process and pray to Spirit for the opportunity to help people by sharing your faith. Then, remain vigilant for opportunities that can come from people openly asking you about your faith. Most of all, let your own personal light shine. Carry yourself in a way that expresses your inner joy and peace. In this way, you can share your faith without pushing it on anyone.

* *Wear your faith as a smile on your face, and shine like a beacon to those who might wish to share it.*

Day 339: Communicating through Art

Earlier I had you create art in order to express the inexpressible. You may have made drawings and paintings, or created a song and played a musical instrument. These expressions of faith are primarily gifts to Spirit, and can be shared as offerings to Spirit alone. However, you can also share these art forms with others. The art doesn't have to be exceptionally beautiful or skillfully done in order to share. Art is supposed to make others feel an emotion. If somebody smiles at your painting or feels the keening sadness in a song, then you have succeeded.

Today, look back through your spiritual journal to find art to share. Perhaps a song, poem, or story you wrote could be shared online or with a friend. Perhaps a painting or a dance could be shared at a local spiritual event. If you don't see anything suitable for sharing, make a new work of art today to share. Think about the feelings associated with Spirit that you may not be able to put into words. Try to express those feelings through your art.

* *Share feelings with another person through art.*

Day 340: Praying with Another Individual

When I work as a chaplain, I am frequently asked for prayer. My fellow chaplains could easily get through a day without people asking them specifically for prayer, but it seems like people are drawn to me to lead prayer. It became a running gag around the hospital that I was a prayer magnet. When I first became a chaplain, I was not used to praying with another person. I had a pretty steep learning curve. I'd like to share some of my strategies here with you in case you find yourself praying with another person.

If you are asked for prayer or if you find yourself offering prayer in a spiritual context, remember that praying with another person is sort of like a dance. Someone typically takes the lead and the other follows. Watch the other person to see if he or she wants to lead. If the other person doesn't take the lead, it is expected you will. You can ask if there's a specific prayer the other person wants to pray. If not, ask what the person wants to pray about. If a prayer on that topic springs to mind, you can use it, or you can hold hands and pray free-form. The other person may choose to speak aloud or may simply stay quiet. You can close your eyes or keep them open according to the preferences of the other person. When you are done, say a closing phrase to indicate you are finished and give the other person's hands a squeeze before releasing them.

* *Offer to pray with another person today.*

Day 341: Praying in Groups

If you join a prayer circle, chances are there will be a standard format you can follow. Use the general rule that if two or more people are doing something, you're probably supposed to do it too. If people are holding hands, closing eyes, or walking in a circle, join in. However, you might find yourself in the position to lead a group prayer someday. So, grab a few friends and practice. Here are some guidelines.

When praying in a group, it is important that everybody is on the same page before the prayer starts. Everyone should agree on the topic of prayer. If one person isn't comfortable with the topic, it might be hard for that person to relate, so get everyone's verbal assent before you get started. If there's a specific prayer that comes to mind, ask if everyone else agrees with that. Songs are excellent for group prayer, because everyone can keep up with the same cadence. This is a good reason to build a repertoire of spiritual songs. When finished with prayer, allow time for people to share their impressions.

* *Practice group prayer with two or more people.*

Day 342: Starting Your Own Group

If you can't find a local group of like-minded people, you may feel inspired to start your own. Decide what sort of group you want. Don't make your focus too broad. If you're desperate for fellowship, you might be willing to get together with anyone who wants to connect with Spirit. However, narrowing the focus of your group can help you gather people who want to continue your group for the long haul.

Decide which sorts of activities you'd like to do with your group. Think about where you will meet. Be resourceful. Look into resources for starting a group near you. You might find existing national groups or curriculum that can help you instruct your new group. There's no sense in reinventing the wheel. Next, find people. It can work well to directly ask friends or family members you feel would be a good fit. Have news of the group spread by word of mouth. Advertise in local spiritual publications, online, and in your nearby metaphysical bookstores.

* Consider starting your own group. Look for resources
  for starting a group. Even if this is not the right time
  in your life to start a group, it can pay to be prepared.

Day 343: Seeking a Teacher

There comes a point in many people's spiritual development in which it seems important to find a guide. When I started looking for a spiritual teacher it was because I had reached that most important stage of wisdom: realizing how little I knew. I wanted to find somebody who had walked the spiritual path before and perhaps gone a little further than me. I felt there was value in serving Spirit the same way that Spirit had been effectively served before. I wanted to know what worked without having to experiment on my own.

Seeking a teacher is challenging because you have to find someone trustworthy. If someone purports to be a teacher, find out who taught them and check in with them. Is this person in good standing? Find current or previous students of this teacher. What thoughts do they have? Most important, ask the teacher whether he or she is accepting students. Don't just find a respectable person and become a hanger-on. If no teacher near you is right, perhaps now is not your time.

* Consider whether you would like to seek a teacher.
  How would you go about finding one?

Day 344: Initiation and Rebirth into a Community: Before, During, and After

Initiation, a conversion ceremony, or a baptism are often the entryways into a faith community. Such a big event can be exciting. As a newcomer, it's important not to take this decision lightly. The good news is that many have traveled this path before, so you can openly ask others about the process. Educate yourself as much as you can, but keep in mind that initiation and rebirth into a community is an experience, so listening or reading about it cannot truly prepare you for something that happens within and to you.

Before initiation, you may still find yourself on the outskirts of the community. Don't rush. Allow yourself to first comfortably settle into your role as an outsider. Ask curious questions. Most of all, realize you may have to ask for initiation, and possibly more than once. During your initiatory journey, stick to the process that works within your faith community. Ask your initiators questions. When it is finished, you may receive more training in your group. Make sure you dive into any new spiritual duties with enthusiasm or ask questions if something makes you hesitant.

* *Where in the initiation are you with respect to faith? Think back to the hero's journey. Is initiation yet to come?*

Day 345: Loyalty

·························

Loyalty is generally considered a spiritual virtue. If you are not loyal to a specific leader, teacher, or congregation, you will find yourself constantly changing alliances. This can stunt your spiritual growth. If you always forge new relationships and abandon old ones, you never have time to develop enough trust to learn important lessons others may share only with trusted and loyal friends. However, loyalty can also be a liability. If there are people in your faith community who are toxic to your spiritual growth, you can find yourself spending all your time arguing with people instead of actually serving Spirit.

Today, meditate on the topic of loyalty. To whom in your life are you loyal? In what area of your life do you find yourself not loyal? For example, I'm very loyal to my family and in my relationship with my husband, but I have often not been loyal to employers, skipping around and job-hopping as it suits me. What are some characteristics of people or groups that encourage your loyalty? What are some red flags you see when you know you're not going to remain loyal to something?

* *Meditate upon the topic of loyalty.*

Day 346: Being Reliable

....

Reliability is an important virtue to have if you're going to be a valuable member of a spiritual community. Unfortunately, spiritual groups often have trouble with reliability. Groups of spiritual people may tend to be flaky. You have a collection of people who might live in their heads and hearts more than in the real world. The group might be close friends, and the informality can cause them to be chronically late. There can also be very real spiritual crises that can cause people to dip in and out of groups as their confidence and faith waver.

Today, work on your personal reliability. If you're chronically late, pray for punctuality, set your alarm earlier, and vow to give yourself extra time. If you rarely show up to meetings, commit to be more reliable and set up a reward system to treat yourself if you consistently go to meetings. Look for the weak spots in your life and tighten them up. That way, you can put your best foot forward in a spiritual group.

* *Make yourself more reliable in an area*
  of life in which reliability is a struggle.

Day 347: Drama and Trolls

Any time you get a group of humans together, there's going to be drama. This can be harshly disillusioning when joining a spiritual group. Here is a group of people who are supposedly directly working on themselves with Spirit, and low and behold they turn out to have the same petty squabbles and social failings as any other group of people. Why bother? The good news is that spiritual groups can and do work through drama and make Spirit a priority, even if there are plenty of human issues at work.

Today, analyze a spiritual group or another group in your life and look for drama and trolls. Trolls are troublemakers and join groups in order to stir the pot. A group with good leadership will be able to withstand trolls, as the leaders will simply kick the trolls out or set appropriate boundaries to stop their influence. If trolls and drama are rampant at every meeting, however, this is a sign of poor leadership. Approach the leadership privately to discuss the problem, or find a group that has better leadership.

* Be vigilant for trolls, and for goodness sake don't feed them.

Day 348: Generosity

Generosity is a spiritual virtue that can take many forms. You can be generous with your money, your time, or your effort. Generosity is vital to spirituality for many reasons. When you work in a community, each person needs to be generous in order for the group to function as a whole. When working with Spirit, you have to be generous with your time and effort in order to receive blessings. And, of course, giving to charity or volunteering can be a generous expression of spirituality.

Today, meditate upon the topic of generosity. Who is a generous person in your life you would like to emulate? Do you believe generosity is repaid by Spirit? For example, is good karma returned as positive blessings in this lifetime? What are some ways you can build generosity into your life? For example, donate to charity every holiday season, or commit to doing something special on the birthdays of your loved ones. Generosity is connected with acts of service, and acts of service are widely recognized as spiritual. Mastering generosity can be a discipline that is both joyful and fulfilling.

* *Meditate on the true nature of generosity.*

Day 349: Gracefully Surrendering Pride
....

Pride can seem like a paradox in spiritual literature and in the opinions of the spiritually minded. It is good to have confidence and openly recognize your gifts and thank Spirit. And yet, pride is discouraged. Pride is an umbrella term for a feeling that can have positive or negative ethical implications. Specifically, when spiritually interacting with other people, pride can be a barrier to worship. A person's personal pride can cause them to talk long and loud about a topic that is unrelated to the spiritual aims of the group. Worst of all, a leader who is too prideful to step down from his or her position of power when appropriate can completely derail a spiritual group.

One day, we will all have to surrender our pride for the greater good of others. Think about the simple act of quitting driving when you become too elderly to properly operate a vehicle. Are you the sort of person who would give up that power without a fight? If not, you might find yourself in other positions of power and unwilling to step down when the time is right. Today, meditate upon the positions of power you hold in your life and how your pride and ego are associated with those roles.

* *Meditate upon the role pride plays in your life.*

Day 350: The Three Gates of Speech

From a common Sufi prayer: "Let no words pass through my lips today until they first pass through these three gates of speech: Is it true? Is it necessary? Is it kind?" I pray this prayer every morning, since I tend to be a blunt person. Note this sort of speech filtering is different from simply avoiding specific topics of conversation. You must be mindful of the manner in which your message is delivered to ensure kindness. Also watch the timing of your message, for the need or necessity must be there first.

Try praying the prayer of the three gates of speech today. Then, observe yourself for successes and mistakes. When and with whom do you feel most successful controlling your speech? If you slip up, can you pinpoint the reason? Perhaps you were feeling grouchy or hungry or distracted, or perhaps the person to whom you were speaking said something provocative. If you find this practice connects you with Spirit, try the prayer again tomorrow and see if you improve. It's a learned skill.

* Pray the prayer of the three gates of
  speech and observe how it affects you.

Day 351: Live and Let Live

Tolerance is another common spiritual virtue, but this one differs in expression from culture to culture. Some people take the idea of "live and let live" to extremes, either emotionally or literally. Tolerance can be linked with the idea of harming none, and can cause people to endure large amounts of harm in order to hold fast to their spiritual ideals. Have you ever endured harm out of love for another person? A gentler hold on the idea of "live and let live" is that one should simply pick one's battles. If somebody espouses a view you don't like or lives a lifestyle you would not choose, continue to focus on your life rather than correcting theirs.

Today, meditate upon the idea of tolerance. Do you consider yourself a tolerant person? Do you believe tolerance is a virtue, a liability, or both? What are the limits of your tolerance of the behavior of loved ones? Is your tolerance level different for strangers? If Spirit is everywhere, does that mean strangers should be tolerated like loved ones? If you want to increase your level of tolerance, where should you start? How can you set boundaries in your life to increase your tolerance of others' behavior?

* Meditate upon the topic of tolerance.

Day 352: Speaking and Listening

So much spiritual knowledge is not written in books. Instead, it is lore passed down as wisdom from person to person. The tricky thing is sometimes this wisdom comes out of the mouths of babes or from complete strangers or friends, rather than from a wise guru or spiritual leader. Thus, you must always be listening. The voice of Spirit can come from anyone. Today's exercise is one of giving and taking but also of listening.

Today, try to equally speak and listen in conversation. If you find yourself talking too much, stop and listen to the other person. Pay attention, also, to the intensity of the conversation. It's easy to have a one-sided conversation in which you've tuned out because your thoughts are on something else, or on the next thing you want to say. If you find you're the one giving the conversation less intensity, consciously put aside distractions and tune in. You may find that listening more than speaking brings you a greater feeling of connection with Spirit. But if you find you're listening too much without getting a word in, share your point of view. Conversation equality is the goal to strive for on most days.

* *Try to equally speak and listen in conversations today.*

Day 353: Greedy Others
·····································

Spiritual people often choose a path of generosity and service. As a result, it is easy for such people to be taken advantage of by others. Greed exists in the world even if there is plenty of abundance to go around. There is no sense feeding the greed of others, even if those other people are people you love very much. You are an important person in the eyes of Spirit, and you must have time to serve others but also yourself.

Today, meditate upon the issue of greed when it appears. When do you evaluate the motives or needs behind the requests of others? Is this necessary unless it infringes unduly upon your own life? In some cases, you may need to deal with greedy people. For example, I'm a parent, and my young children are very needy. I have to walk a fine line between indulging all their desires and working to develop their independence and sense of empathy for others. How can you draw boundaries with the greedy people in your life? Can those boundaries shift so you need to listen less and less to the voice of greed?

* Meditate upon the place of greed in your life.

Day 354: Choosing Your Friends Wisely

Spiritual people who develop tolerance often run into the problem of spending time with friends who are the antithesis of their spiritual goals. The friends you choose matter. If you spend time with somebody who is constantly complaining and lamenting life, you might find your own thoughts drawn to that kind of negativity. If you spend time around friends who deride your values and your faith, you can lose your motivation to keep trying. This doesn't mean you can't be friends with people who don't believe and think exactly as you do. Think of your friendship circles as rooms in a house. If you spend all your time in one room of the house, the environment will affect you accordingly. But, if you allow yourself to wander from room to room and even take a break outside, you can mediate the effects.

Today, think about the friendships you keep. Take time to appreciate the friends who have strengths that inspire you. Take note of any friends who bring you down. Are there boundaries you can set with those friends? Is there support you can offer to those friends to encourage them to change, or do they not wish to change? If they don't want to change, you may have to set some limits.

* *Evaluate the friendships you keep.*

Day 355: Joyful Greeting and Parting

Worship services across all religions have joyful greeting and parting ceremonies. When people of faith get together, there is often laughing and singing and smiles shared all around. When parting ways, people might do so with a physical gesture like a hug or handshake, and the worship service might end with a song or dance or other joyful procession back out into the world. After all, the people leaving now carry Spirit inside of them wherever they go.

Today, evaluate the way you greet other people in your life and the way you say your goodbyes. Are you likely to plop down on your friend's couch and begin complaining without first joyfully greeting your friend? When your significant other comes home, do you rattle off a honey-do list before first expressing your love and joy? How can you give time and space in your relationships for a friendly greeting? Also, think about how you part ways with people you care about. Imagine each time might be the last you ever see that person. What words would you like expressed?

 * *Evaluate your greetings and partings in relationships.*
   Is there room for improvement?

Day 356: True Love

....

Love is the most pure expression of Spirit. The world's religions point out many different forms of love in their scriptures and stories. There is the love between two people who choose to spend their lives together as sexual partners, there's a love between parent and child, and there is a love of duty and love for one's nation. The ways to express love are truly limitless. If you find love lacking in your life, you may find yourself feeling disconnected from Spirit. Luckily, there are myriad ways to find love. You don't need a boyfriend or girlfriend. Get a pet kitten or share a fun night with friends to help renew your sense of love.

Today, reflect on all the sources of love in your life. Who tops your list of loved ones? How many different forms of love can you count in that list? How do you feel when you express love for one of those people? Can you manifest that heart-warming feeling by just thinking of one of those people? How can you invite more loved ones into your life? Is there somebody you should call today so you can express your love?

* *Reflect on the many sources of love in your life.*

Day 357: Peace

....

Peace is another deep expression of Spirit in many faith traditions. Some people believe one of the deepest expressions of Spirit is true peace, whether that means peace between people or simply inner peace. Today, think about the types of peace you value. Are you an idealist who wants to pray daily for world peace? Or are you a pragmatic person who wants to be able to find a deep source of internal peace when somebody says or does something that annoys you so you won't behave angrily?

Today's meditation will be about peace, so make sure you remove any distractions that could ruin your mood. Sit down in meditation and focus on your inner self. Imagine there is an inner source of stillness and peace inside you. Visualize what that might look like. If you sense other feelings creeping in, think "I choose peace" and turn your mind back to your meditation. Imagine sharing that sense of peace with others. Think of giving your loved ones peace during every interaction. Finally, visualize peace radiating away from you throughout the world, allowing anyone who wants that energy to accept it.

* *Meditate on peace.*

Day 358: Leadership

Many people are called to spiritual leadership, but spiritual leadership can take many forms. Some people choose to become clergy of a specific religion. Others choose to lead small prayer or discussion groups. Every parent becomes a spiritual leader by default, because his or her children will ask questions about Spirit and will look to that parent as an example of how one should interact with Spirit. As you become more spiritual, you might find that friends or even strangers approach you with spiritual topics or questions.

Today, ponder the role of spiritual leadership. Are you a natural leader, or is leadership something you usually avoid? Assuming some form of spiritual leadership is inevitable, how can you better prepare yourself to be a spiritual leader? Who are leaders you would like to emulate? How did they acquire the attributes that make them great leaders? Take active steps today to improve yourself. Perhaps you can research some classes or books that might improve your leadership skills. The best leaders are sometimes those thrust into the role by circumstance, so there's no time like the present to begin preparation.

* *Ponder the role of spiritual leadership in your life.*

Day 359: Trustworthiness

Earlier in this book I had you ponder the relationship between love and trust to decide how you can become more trustworthy. Today, think about this again from the lens of spiritual communities you might be join. Reliability certainly plays a role, as does a level of proper behavior as dictated by community standards. You also need to think about the trustworthiness of others in your spiritual community. I believe trustworthy leaders and peers are vital for fellowship. If you cannot trust your spiritual teachers, then you cannot properly learn. If you cannot trust your fellows, then you cannot openly share your most personal and private prayers.

Today, think about the trustworthiness of spiritual people in your life. If you have been exploring spiritual communities, how do you know their members are trustworthy? If you want to find a spiritual teacher, how can you know that he or she is trustworthy? Do you find yourself easily trusting people in your life, or do you hold your trust back? If you have a hard time trusting others, how can you actively develop your ability to trust?

* *Meditate upon the trustworthiness of spiritual people in your life.*

Day 360: Bargaining and Money

Another way of looking at the give-and-take between people is bargaining. One person offers something and another person either takes the offer or makes a counteroffer that is more in his or her favor. Some religions actively encourage bargaining, while others do not. In my religious tradition, it is forbidden to bargain over property that is meant to be used for spiritual purposes. Instead, one must pay full price. In my religion, it is also forbidden to charge for bringing somebody into the religion. The reasons behind these rules are so that the motivations behind spiritual aims are not corrupted.

Historically, there have certainly been many stories of money and corruption associated with religion and spiritual people. Today, meditate upon the relationship between money and Spirit in your life. Do you give money to any sort of religious establishment or spiritual person? Do you accept money for any kind of spiritual act? Do you believe money inherently corrupts, or can good, spiritual people be honored for their time with appropriate monetary gifts? Do you think of money as a necessary evil, or as an energy or tool that can be positively used?

* *Meditate upon the place of money within spirituality.*

Day 361: What Are Your Intentions?

"What are your intentions?" It is usually a question asked by a father to a boy who is courting his daughter. This phrase is one you should ask yourself whenever you forge a new relationship with a spiritual group or teacher. In some communities, a relationship with a spiritual teacher is like a marriage. You can't undo a conversion, a baptism, or an initiation any more than you can dissolve a marriage to the point where it never existed. The experience you share in a spiritual context can last over a lifetime.

Today, think about your intentions, and write down a statement of intention. If you're a part of a spiritual community, write down what you would like to gain from the relationship with others. Are you hoping to rise to a place of spiritual leadership, or are you simply seeking fellowship? Even if you're not yet a member of a spiritual community, write down what you intend to gain from reading books like this. What do you hope to know, to understand, and to be able to do?

* *Write down a statement of intention. Share this statement with any spiritual teacher in your life.*

Day 362: Supporting a Leader

....

In my spiritual circles, we don't have a huge problem with corrupted leaders, but we do have a huge problem with leadership burnout. Spiritual teachers and leaders give of themselves so freely and it can sometimes seem like a thankless job. Such leaders spend their time running worship events, teaching workshops and classes, and even waking up to take a phone call from a distraught student in the middle of the night. If a leader doesn't practice a lot of self-care, he or she will eventually quit just to get peace and quiet.

Today, think of the spiritual leaders, teachers, or mentors in your own life. This could be an inspirational figure, your mother, a volunteer at your place of worship, or a good friend. How can you be more appreciative and respectful of this leader? For example, is there any way you can help get events rolling on time and cleaned up afterward so the leader isn't starting early and staying late? Are there ways you can help keep personal business out of your spiritual work so the leader isn't distracted by drama and petty squabbles? Is there a gift of appreciation you can give?

* Brainstorm ways to support a spiritual mentor in your life.

Day 363: Resolving Conflict
....

Conflict is inevitable, even in groups of spiritual people. In fact, conflict should be especially expected in groups of spiritual people, because conflict is how some people learn. Not to mention, spiritual groups deal with heavy stuff. Welcome conflict and approach it with a positive attitude and an open mind. If you're dealing with friends, keep in mind that you all love each other and want to stick together. Avoid ultimatums or walking away from everything and work on a resolution to the conflict.

Try the following steps when solving your next conflict. First, join together in prayer to Spirit. Consider asking for the truth to be revealed and for the conflict to be resolved. Next, share all the facts about the situation at hand. The way someone feels can be a fact, but it should be shared in the form of "I feel _____ when _____ because I need _____" to avoid accusations. Allow everyone to contribute a possible solution, and let go of ownership of each solution as it is presented. Finally, everyone should try to reach a consensus on a solution. If this is hard, try getting everyone to agree to try one solution for a set period of time and to re-evaluate later.

* *Try a spiritual approach to conflict resolution.*

Day 364: Parting Ways

There comes a time when people must part ways with even the most beloved spiritual communities. Perhaps the parting is peaceful, and the reason you're leaving is because you're moving across the country or because you're starting a new group. Perhaps the reason is born out of conflict, and you are parting ways because of a personality clash or ideological differences. Whatever the reason, it is important to respectfully part ways with spiritual groups, especially if you're newly exploring groups as a spiritual tourist. It is not fair to have a group of people invest their spiritual energy into you only to suddenly disappear. Here are some guidelines I would advise spiritual seekers to follow.

Firstly, if you're a spiritual tourist or are unsure about whether the community is right for you when you join, say so. Be open about any confusion or unease, and let them know if you're trying things out for a day or a month. If you do encounter any conflicts, approach the spiritual leadership and give them a chance to help with conflict resolution or even refer you to another group. When you leave, come to one last meeting to respectfully say your goodbyes.

* *Commit to being honest about your intentions
  and respectfully parting ways when necessary.*

Day 365: Including Everyone
....

As you go out in this wide world with your 365 days of connecting with Spirit under your belt, you are going to run into an awful lot of wonderful people, many of whom will be very different from you. There is a place for every good spiritual person, regardless of any theological differences. I believe you will now be an ambassador for Spirit in any communities you enter, so I ask that you look for the strengths in everyone you meet.

Today, think of something likable about every person you come into contact with. Look for strengths even in attributes that seem to be grating. If somebody is less able than you, look for the things that person can do. If that person has a personality that doesn't quite mesh with your own, think about a friend who might get along with that person very well. You may find some people are best met with tolerance, while other people are best met with resourcefulness. Today, see Spirit in everyone. Realize the Spirit you see in each person is also the Spirit that resides within you.

* *Go forth and see Spirit in everyone you meet.*
  Meet everyone halfway.

Bibliography

Albertsson, Alaric. *To Walk a Pagan Path: Practical Spirituality for Every Day.* Woodbury, MN: Llewellyn Worldwide, 2013.

Alvarez, Melissa. *365 Ways to Raise Your Frequency: Simple Tools to Increase Your Spiritual Energy for Balance, Purpose, and Joy.* Woodbury, MN: Llewellyn Worldwide, 2012.

Batterson, Mark. *The Circle Maker: Praying Circles Around Your Biggest Dreams and Greatest Fears.* Grand Rapids, MI: Zondervan, 2011.

Blake, Deborah. *Everyday Witch Book of Rituals: All You Need for a Magickal Year.* Woodbury, MN: Llewellyn Worldwide, 2012.

Chopra, Deepak. *The Book of Secrets: Unlocking the Hidden Dimensions of Your Life.* New York: Three Rivers Press, 2004.

Danaan, Clea. *Living Earth Devotional: 365 Green Practices for Sacred Connections.* Woodbury, MN: Llewellyn Worldwide, 2013.

Fowler, James W. *Stages of Faith: The Psychology of Human Development and the Quest for Meaning.* New York: HarperCollins, 1995.

Luhrmann, T. M. *When God Talks Back: Understanding the American Evangelical Relationship with God.* New York: Knopf, 2012.

Roberts, Elizabeth, and Elias Amidon. *Earth Prayers from Around the World: 365 Prayers, Poems, and Invocations for Honoring the Earth.* New York: HarperCollins, 1991.

Roderick, Timothy. *Wicca: A Year and a Day: 366 Days of Spiritual Practice in the Craft of the Wise.* Woodbury, MN: Llewellyn Worldwide, 2005.

To Write to the Author

If you wish to contact the author or would like more information about this book, please write to the author in care of Llewellyn Worldwide Ltd. and we will forward your request. Both the author and publisher appreciate hearing from you and learning of your enjoyment of this book and how it has helped you. Llewellyn Worldwide Ltd. cannot guarantee that every letter written to the author can be answered, but all will be forwarded. Please write to:

Alexandra Chauran
℅ Llewellyn Worldwide
2143 Wooddale Drive
Woodbury, MN 55125-2989

Please enclose a self-addressed stamped envelope for reply, or $1.00 to cover costs. If outside the USA, enclose an international postal reply coupon.

Many of Llewellyn's authors have websites with additional information and resources. For more information, please visit our website at http://www.llewellyn.com.

GET MORE AT LLEWELLYN.COM

Visit us online to browse hundreds of our books and decks, plus sign up to receive our e-newsletters and exclusive online offers.

- Free tarot readings • Spell-a-Day • Moon phases
- Recipes, spells, and tips • Blogs • Encyclopedia
- Author interviews, articles, and upcoming events

GET SOCIAL WITH LLEWELLYN

 **Find us on Facebook**

www.Facebook.com/LlewellynBooks

Follow us on

www.Twitter.com/Llewellynbooks

GET BOOKS AT LLEWELLYN

LLEWELLYN ORDERING INFORMATION

Order online: Visit our website at www.llewellyn.com to select your books and place an order on our secure server.

Order by phone:
- Call toll free within the U.S. at 1-877-NEW-WRLD (1-877-639-9753)
- Call toll free within Canada at 1-866-NEW-WRLD (1-866-639-9753)
- We accept VISA, MasterCard, and American Express

Order by mail:
Send the full price of your order (MN residents add 6.875% sales tax) in U.S. funds, plus postage and handling to: Llewellyn Worldwide, 2143 Wooddale Drive, Woodbury, MN 55125-2989

POSTAGE AND HANDLING:

STANDARD: (U.S. & Canada)
(Please allow 12 business days)
$25.00 and under, add $4.00.
$25.01 and over, FREE SHIPPING.

INTERNATIONAL ORDERS (airmail only):
$16.00 for one book, plus $3.00 for each additional book.

Visit us online for more shipping options. Prices subject to change.

FREE CATALOG!

To order, call
1-877-
NEW-WRLD
ext. 8236
or visit our
website

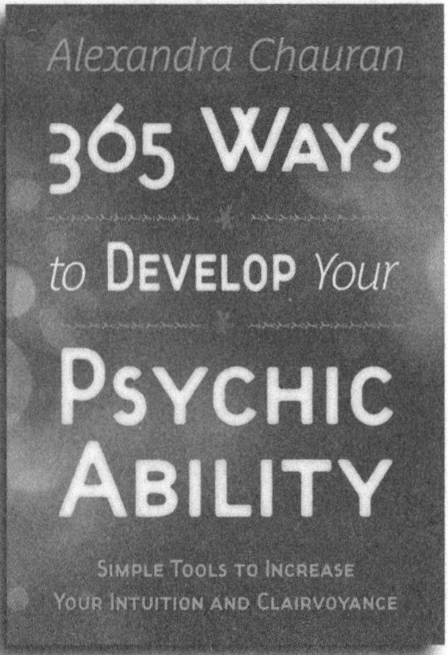
Alexandra Chauran
365 Ways
to Develop Your
Psychic Ability
Simple Tools to Increase
Your Intuition and Clairvoyance

365 Ways to Develop Your Psychic Ability
Simple Tools to Increase Your
Intuition and Clairvoynace
ALEXANDRA CHAURAN

Unlock and strengthen your innate psychic potential with 365 fast, effective ways to develop your abilities. Beginning with simple observation skills and moving forward to trance and divination techniques, this book's step-by-step practices guide you to psychic mastery.

Formatted to fit your personal pace and learning style, *365 Ways to Develop Your Psychic Ability* shows you how to build your psychic muscles day by day. Learn meditation, trance techniques, divination, and how to perform readings. Discover extensive exercises on scrying, clairvoyance, intuition, empathy, and more. Using quick and accessible methods that build upon one another, this comprehensive book helps you become a proficient psychic.

978-0-7387-3930-4, 360 pp., 5 x 7   **$16.99**

Richard Webster
365
Ways to
Attract
Good
Luck
Simple Steps to Take Control
of Chance and Improve
Your Fortune

365 Ways to Attract Good Luck
Simple Steps to Take Control of
Chance and Improve Your Future
RICHARD WEBSTER

What is good luck and how can you attract it into your life? Best-selling author Richard Webster demystifies this age-old concept and shares 365 easy ideas anyone can use to increase their good fortune in every area of life.

From acting on your hunches to using lucky charms, from carrying a badger's tooth to random acts of kindness, the techniques presented in this entertaining and informative book are sure to tip the odds in your favor. With tried-and-true advice, unexpected tips, and everything you need to know about lucky days, numbers, months, and more, this easy-to-use guide is brimming with wise counsel for increasing your good luc

978-0-7387-3893-2, 240 pp., 5 x 7   **$16.99**

Melissa Alvarez

365 Ways

to Raise *Your*

Frequency

Simple Tools to Increase
Your Spiritual Energy
for Balance, Purpose, and Joy